To Para —

I hope you enjoy the
book and wish you the
best of luck!

Michael You

Sports in the Aftermath of Tragedy

From Kennedy to Katrina

Michael Gavin

THE SCARECROW PRESS, INC.
Lanham • Toronto • Plymouth, UK
2013

Published by Scarecrow Press, Inc.
A wholly owned subsidiary of The Rowman & Littlefield Publishing Group, Inc.
4501 Forbes Boulevard, Suite 200, Lanham, Maryland 20706
http://www.scarecrowpress.com

Estover Road, Plymouth PL6 7PY, United Kingdom

British Library Cataloguing in Publication Information Available

Library of Congress Cataloging-in-Publication Data

Gavin, Michael, 1976-
Sports in the aftermath of tragedy : from Kennedy to Katrina / Michael Gavin. p. cm
Includes bibliographical references and index.
ISBN 978-0-8108-8700-8 (cloth : alk. paper) -- ISBN 978-0-8108-8701-5 (ebook) 1. Sports--Social aspects--United States. 2. Disasters--United States. 3. Crises--United States. I. Title.
GV706.5.G396 2013
306.4'83--dc23
2012029315

™ The paper used in this publication meets the minimum requirements of American National Standard for Information Sciences Permanence of Paper for Printed Library Materials, ANSI/NISO Z39.48-1992.

Printed in the United States of America

Contents

Introduction

Narrating Tragedy: From Kennedy to Katrina, from Sports to National Identities

With smoke still billowing from the now-destroyed Twin Towers, Alan "Bud" Selig postponed the Major League Baseball season indefinitely. Throughout the nation's newspapers and television stations, mainstream news commentators suggested the postponement and resumption of Major League Baseball's season was particularly important in how Americans would remember the 9/11 tragedy. Commentators lauded Selig's handling of the major league's schedule by contrasting it with their memory of National Football Commissioner Pete Rozelle's decision to continue the 1963 NFL season after President John F. Kennedy's assassination.

In 1963, with President Kennedy laying dead in Dallas, Texas, Rozelle phoned White House press secretary Pierre Salinger in Honolulu, Hawaii. After receiving "what amounted to the dead president's permission to play" from Salinger, Rozelle announced the games would take place as scheduled, saying, "Football was Mr. Kennedy's game."[1] Although the NFL continued its planned schedule, the games themselves did not run on the nation's television screens that Sunday. Instead, the President's funeral was aired on all three networks. The only people to witness the games, the athletes, and the tributes to Kennedy in the stadiums were those in attendance. Although only a fraction of American citizens saw the games, Red Smith of the *New York Herald Tribune* and Arthur Daley of the *New York Times* were among many sports columnists from major American cities who vilified Rozelle for shaming "the nation" by "h[anging] up [the NFL's] business as usual sign."[2] When that year's Army-Navy game took place, on, of all days, December 7—Pearl Harbor Day—Daley suggested that the nation would soon "return to normalcy," and Smith argued that "quiet resumption of normal activity" would occur through continuation of college football.[3] In the context of the Cold War, these columnists constructed sport and its association with the military complex as capable of returning the nation to normalcy after Kennedy's assassination.

Similarly, many columnists' work in the immediate aftermath of the terrorist attacks of September 11, 2001, elevated the New York Yankees

1

(as well as other teams in the New York area) to national significance, calling them "team America" or "America's team."[4] Later in the season, when the Yankees made a mythical run to the World Series, many columnists suggested the team "symbolized the perseverance of the . . . country in the wake of the worst terrorist attacks in the nation's history."[5] Collectively, the sports columns of both the terrorist attacks and Kennedy's assassination argued that sport pays a service to national identity in the context of tragedy—one that stabilized, even solidified, a tough and vigorous defense against and/or in response to an enemy abroad.[6]

Just four years later, as water was still settling in the French Quarter after Hurricane Katrina, many Americans watched their fellow citizens in New Orleans raging at the late response of the George W. Bush administration. Images of black citizens huddled on rooftops and in a filthy Superdome endure. Although the NFL season was not postponed, some columnists, such as Jon Saraceno of *USA Today*, suggested that it should have been, and again referred to the Rozelle decision after Kennedy's assassination.[7] Many columnists suggested the Saints team was "capable of healing a reeling nation," and many others referred to the Saints as "America's team," again pinning a national identity onto a sports team from a tragedy-stricken area.[8] In addition, many columnists wrote of the New Orleans Saints in a fashion reminiscent of how their counterparts had written of the New York Yankees in 2001. The Saints' first home game was played, coincidentally, on September 11, invoking memories of the terrorist attacks four years earlier. And lest we forget, too, the New Orleans Saints, displaced from the water-and-wind-damaged Superdome, played all their 2005 "home" games in opponents' stadiums. As a result, they played their first "home" game against the New York Giants at Giants Stadium, invoking memories of 9/11 and rhetoric of their being "America's team."[9] To make sense of the hurricane and the images of black bodies writhing in hunger, columnists drew connections between the coincidental date of 9/11 for the Saint's first game of the 2005 season, and their first "home game" being played in the Meadowlands Stadium, home of the New York Giants; between the terrorists that demolished the World Trade Center and the water that flooded New Orleans streets; and, yes, the teams representing those two cities. A year later, the Saints returned to the Superdome. Many columnists deemed the first game in the Superdome after Katrina as proof of New Orleans' return to "normalcy."[10] Likewise, as the Saints made their surprising run to the NFC championship game in 2007, columnists suggested the Saints provided New Orleans a sense of normalcy and hope. And in February 2010, after the Saints won their first Super Bowl, many columnists argued the region had healed.[11] In the process, all of these columnists, for their audiences, tied sporting events to national tragedy in memories of what it meant to be American.

In the case of Katrina, however, many columnists resisted the tendency to construct an America that was strong and vigorous. William Rhoden of the *New York Times* wrote, for instance, that "what Katrina illustrated, quite graphically, [wa]s that the economic problems confronting communities from which many professional athletes come are too large for one foundation to solve."[12] Rhoden and columnists like him argued that the poverty and structural racism that was on display during and after Hurricane Katrina was covered up by traditional rhetoric used by peer columnists to tell the stories of sporting events following national tragedy. Likewise, with the fratricide of American hero, soldier, and former Arizona Cardinals safety Pat Tillman, many columnists revised their stories about American strength in the context of the War on Terror. They even argued that the stories about the New York Yankees representing a national response to terror implicitly supported a problematic war.[13] In short, then, sports columnists continuously commented on sport's relationship to tragedy in order to comment on what it meant to be "American" in specific moments in time.

The connection between sporting memories and definitions of national identity are far from tenuous. My own experiences watching the 2001 major league baseball postseason in which the New York Yankees made an emotional run to the World Series are bound up with memory of September 11 and nostalgia about baseball that would be easier to leave uncomplicated. Likewise, the euphoria I felt when the Saints won their first home game of 2006, their first game in the refurbished Superdome, is one that I wish I could couple with an assertion of the refurbished state of New Orleans. Despite such desires for simplistic and sanitized memories, the columns that constructed these sporting events as meaningful to the nation and cultural memories of tragedy, potentially lead to what I call a mythological version of America, one that is hardly benign.

For how we remember significant moments in history is partially how we imagine the country itself. In *Tangled Memories*, Marita Sturken underscored that specific moments, such as a presidential assassination, can be traumatic for an entire culture, and that these moments, because they are remembered by a wide range of individuals within a culture, become defining of the culture itself. She argued that media assist in producing the stories by which these moments are remembered, and that how they are remembered is as important as that they are remembered. Likewise, Marianne Hirsch and Valerie Smith argued that cultural memories allow individuals and groups to recall a shared past on the basis of common or contested norms and stories.[14] Columnists writing in the context of tragedy provided for readers the materials to establish their own cultural memories of national tragedy and so national identity.

This is why sport played no small part in the way significant moments for the nation are remembered. What sports fan or baby boomer does not recall Al Michaels's famous call of, "Do you believe in miracles?" that coupled the 1980 USA Olympic hockey team's win over the Soviet Union in the context of the Cold War and the Iranian hostage crisis of 1979–1980?[15] Likewise, many remember sporting events and athletes' feats the same way we remember national tragedies like the Kennedy assassination: We remember through our own and others' bodies. That is, we remember by locating our own bodies in a particular place and time, and through bodies that come to represent the tragedy itself—we all remember where we were when we first heard of the September 11, 2001, terror attacks, for instance.[16] But consider Walter Shapiro's column in *USA Today* about the 2001 New York Yankees' run to the World Series, the thesis of which connected the Yankees with national healing from terror: "[N]obody would forget where they were when they heard of Scott Brosius' home run."[17] Still, it is not just athletes' bodies that sports columnists and mainstream audiences often connect to sport and cultural memory of national tragedy. Many sports columnists wrote of, and many American citizens yet remember, President George W. Bush's ceremonial first pitch of game three of the 2001 World Series as a significant event in cultural history. Representing tragedy through athletes and national officials, though, often explicitly frames a sporting event in a mythological narrative regarding national identity. In terms of sporting events in the context of national tragedy, the athletes that columnists represented as telling of the tragedy were some of the very materials readers used to frame their memories of sport and the tragedies related to them. However, as columnists emphasize politicians' appearances at games, or athletes' feats as reflective of a national character, the narratives often cater to mainstream audiences who have little reason, as result of race or class privilege, to challenge the mythological national identity being established.

In *Making the American Team*, Mark Dyreson illustrated that beginning in the mid-1800s, elites used sport as a mechanism to discuss and represent the virtues of democracy, even if that democracy was not manifest in reality. The rituals associated with the patriotism, such as the national anthems, presidential first pitches, or Navy flyovers at games, continue to represent and encourage a national identity in which military strength or an ephemeral kind of patriotism is a central construct.[18] But such representations of national identity according to S. W. Pope tout "the ideals of patriotism and democratic participation . . . despite the pervasive, often discriminatory class, race, ethnic, [sexual], and gender" discriminations existent in sport and the nation-state.[19]

More bluntly, columnists writing of tragedy and sport often emphasized rituals associated with national strength or democracy to deliver meaning to the tragedy in question. Such emphasis substituted for representation of bodies or structures that would reveal the failures of democracy and subsequently confront the power of those historically privileged in America. As such, many columnists produced cultural memories for the nation that avoided the existence of oppression the tragedy in question may otherwise have exposed. Hence, the identity historically privileged in sport media was reasserted through many of these stories of tragedy as they emphasized rituals at games and the virtues of democracy while avoiding the realities of, for instance, racial oppression that led to or were exposed through tragedy. Specifically, the identity held up as reflective of *the* nation was rhetorically constructed through such emphasis in an overwhelming majority of sports columns written in the context of the John F. Kennedy, Martin Luther King Jr., and Robert Kennedy assassinations; and Magic Johnson's announcement that he contracted HIV.

However, in many tragedies since 1992 the versions of national identity constructed by mainstream sports columnists were not as uniform as those established before that year. While many columnists of and beyond the 1990s continued to create a national identity of military strength, democracy, and equality, a significant number of columnists writing in the new century challenged such mythological constructions of "Americanness," and in the process drew attention to inequality. Columnists who challenged mythological national identities were implicitly, if not overtly, also more inclusive of minority identities than their counterparts, and/or critical of the nation-state. As such, by the mid-1990s, sports columns written in the context of national tragedy were sites where significant disputes regarding what it means to be "American" occurred. Moreover, such sports columns potentially served to redefine mainstream audiences' versions of "Americannes" and how to conceive of tragedy—a single event, or systemic oppression, for instance.

WHITE NATIONAL IDENTITY AND SPORTS PAGES: A HISTORY

In the mid-1800s, newspapers separated different types of news from one another. In the 1870s, newspapers created separate sports sections, whereas previously they scattered sports news throughout the paper. This reorganization of the newspaper led to the false notion that sport, politics, and nationalism are separate from one another.[20] At nearly the same time that the sports section secured a special space within newspapers, the baseball fields and the heavyweight boxing title were, either through athletes' imposed regulations or through official league rules, reserved only for white males. White athletes and the contests between them thus dominated sports writing, and the imaginations of those reading it. Readers' enjoyment of sport derived from viewing white, heterosexual males, and implicitly believing these athletes were both "normal" and representative of the nation.

In other media during the late 1800s and early 1900s, what Martha Jane Nadell called the "graphic revolution" took place.[21] The baseball field was resegregated at the same time figures like Aunt Jemima were portrayed in advertisements and on grocery shelves throughout the country. Similarly, Jim Jeffries, heavyweight boxing champion from 1899–1905, refused to fight black opponents, so the stories of heavy-weight boxing's championship were dominated by white males.[22] The proliferation of media during this era, coupled with these examples of segregation and stereotypes, indicates that sport media was part of a wider movement in America in which the white, male, and heterosexual was normalized and privileged on a larger scale than ever before.

Given that sport sections were one of the major means of selling papers and that the typical athlete was represented in these sport sections through both words and photographs, it is hardly a far leap to conclude that sports pages, despite being removed from the political sections of newspapers, were playing a political role in organizing a dominant national identity and memory.

In "Hegemony, Relations of Force, Historical Bloc," Antonio Gramsci argued that who controls the knowledge about identities and the mechanisms of power is in fact the group in power. He argued that the subordinate "buy" into the dominant class's power, because that power is presented and accepted as common sense. In this way, knowledge and power work together while presenting themselves as benign and the "normal condition of things."[23] In this way, the "normal" condition of sports was rife with power.

RHETORIC OF TRAGEDY

Because national history and identity are often associated with memory of tragic moments, these columnists who wrote of sport in the context of national tragedy also established memories for reading audiences. Sigmund Freud argued that memory is characterized by forgetting and that, as a result, what is remembered can be studied for what is repressed/forgotten. However, in the case of columnists who create memories of national identity, what is often repressed/forgotten plays a significant political role. (That is, when columnists suggested games paid a service to the nation, they often denied ongoing oppressions or problems in the country in favor of constructing the mythological national identity. In doing so, they often ended their own stories of tragedy cleanly with the team's win or ceremony at a game serving as the story's climax.)

Collectively, columnists employed a number of rhetorical strategies in writing of games that followed tragedy that can be explained through simple trauma and Freudian theory. Given that these tragedies are often characterized as traumatic experiences for the nation at large this application of trauma theory to understand sports columnists' rhetoric is hardly a far stretch.

Freud's most salient example of language development concerning trauma was that of the forte-da game. In *Beyond the Pleasure Principle*, Freud used the example of an eighteen-month-old child, who, upon witnessing his mother's exit from a room, tossed a wooden toy and uttered the word "forte." Upon retrieving the toy, the child would exclaim, happily, "da." Through this example Freud theorized that children attempt to master traumatic experiences (the mother's leaving) through creating pleasurable ones (the retrieval of the toy) through language. Freud wrote of the child, "That the unpleasurable nature of an experience does not always unsuit it for play."[24]

This example transfers nicely to the role of columns about sporting events in moments of cultural and national tragedy. Through the 1960s, columnists generally avoided substantive writing of the traumatic in favor of the game through an act of substitution. Just as the child substituted play for his mother, columnists often substituted the space of tragedy and trauma for the space of play. In setting the story of the tragedy in a game, a stadium, columnists transformed trauma and tragedy into something pleasurable. Stadia, full of people that did not experience the actual trauma, were often said to be representatives of the tragedy. Hence, the first convention of the rhetoric of tragedy is the substitution of places. The substitution fits the story of national tragedy into a place where mainstream audiences' attention is on a game, not on tragedy or trauma.

This substitution, however, is the foundation of second, third, and fourth conventions. In *Patriotic Games*, S. W. Pope wrote that sport's mythology often served the purpose of sealing fans' imaginations from the political realities of the nation despite the fact that sport played a significant role in establishing those realities.[25] Writing specifically of baseball, he suggested that sports writers were among the many who "shaped the meanings" of sport "to coincide with their own" white middle-class value systems.[26] Narratives that create national mythologies through sport, however, are possible only by the avoidance or repression of moments and political memories that would reveal the nation as oppressive or unjust. This is the second convention of the discourse of tragedy—that of presenting the nation as innocent, socially just, or strong after tragedy. This convention occurred when sports columnists continually proclaimed the national identity to have returned to stability, normalcy, through the games. Sports columnists often used phrases like "sport allowed a healing" or "a return to normalcy" to describe the significance of sporting events after tragedy. These phrases, however, often can be seen as an act by which the dominant class reasserts its power. In the case of sport, a return to normalcy is often returning sport to the place of what has been considered apolitical, the place of espousing a mythological national identity. In this way, the very notion of sport, America, tragedy, and normalcy can be viewed as serving those who already were in power prior to the tragic moment, or privileged by race, class, gender, or sexuality.[27]

For example, many sports fans remember the late Whitney Houston's rendition of the "Star Spangled Banner" at Super Bowl XXV as providing a catharsis for those weary of the nation's most recent military engagement, Operation Desert Storm. Of the game, Bob Morris wrote the Super Bowl not only provided a break from the awful news about war, but also that "Tampa Stadium wasn't the setting for a football game as much as it was a giant pep rally for America and, like it or not, our decision to go to war against Iraq."[28] Ironically, this rhetoric denied the same global implications of war and the political realities present in Iraq that, a little more than a decade later, would be revisited through the Iraq War. Columnists who used rhetoric that testified to American ideals rather drew attention to the oppression in Iraq, were, ironically, in the process of creating cultural memories of a nation of vigor and strength while also denying the intersection of oil, power, oppression, and corrupt politics existent in Iraq. Denying these realities obscured American citizens' understanding of the nuanced cultures in the Middle East and ultimately perpetuated the sort of misunderstanding that would, a decade later, make the conflation of Iraq and Afghanistan simple to achieve by the George W. Bush administration as they carried out the War on Terror; a war that was also touched by sports and tragedy.

The third convention was revealed when columnists favored athletes' feats or political ceremonies at these games as meaningful to national character. This convention focused on the internal bodies of athletes or politicians' and/or service peoples' presence at games to speak to a national character. We saw such rhetoric in columnists' memories of American hero, Arizona Cardinals safety-turned-soldier, Pat Tillman. After his death in the Iraq War, some columnists focused on Tillman's unique soul and heart to suggest that he was "what was best about America.[29] In *Body Language* Gerald Early wrote that "[unlike politics sports] do not etherealize the body but make it even more concrete. . . ."[30] But in the context of national tragedy, columnists often focused on the internal—the heart, the soul, the character of the athlete, and his/ or her subsequent ability to reflect the nation's character, will, and/or soul. This turn to the internal character of the athlete as reflective of national character instead of material descriptions of those injured or oppressed was an example of what Bill Nichols called "disembodied knowledge."[31] He argued that disembodied knowledge speaks of politics without minority people and allows for rhetoric of democracy and citizenship to manifest despite oppression's existence in the country or beyond. Lauren Berlant suggested that this rhetoric privileges the white male because the minority realities are avoided in discussions of national character. In short, columnists' stories of the internal body lent themselves to a focus on the spirit of individual athletes and aligned them with the spirit of *the* nation;

an innocent nation where oppression is overwhelmingly absent, and the dangers of unthinking patriotism are altogether ignored. Hence, the focus on politicians' or military presence at games was a limitation on the sort of national identity that would be constructed through stories of tragedy and sport. Such was the case in columns about Tillman's internal character.

The fourth and final convention of the discourse of tragedy was found in the use of past tragedies to make sense of contemporary ones. Columnists often referred to the same few national tragedies to make sense of those just witnessed. This in itself was a form of setting the stories of tragedy in a narrow storyline, which George Lipsitz has argued, recreates old knowledge.[32] For instance, when columnists continuously referred to President Kennedy's assassination to make sense of new tragedies, the meaning of that new tragedy was shaded by columnists' memories of the national identity established in 1963.

In sum, these rhetorical conventions of healing, redemption, and overcoming limit how we remember tragedies and so how we define our version of country. Sturken argued that cultural healing from trauma is possible through popular culture's retelling of tragedy: "Indeed, memory often takes the form not of recollection but of cultural reenactment that serves important needs for catharsis and healing."[33] This healing and redemption may actually encourage attention to tragedy's story closing and avoidance of the political and social realities potentially exposed through tragedy. That is, columnists often suggested sport "healed" the wounds of the "nation"; provided a "diversion" from tragedy; "united" the country; or spoke to ideals of American freedom, strength, or diversity. While the columns using such rhetoric often acknowledged the significance of the tragedy in question, they also avoided substantive discussion of the oppressions that the tragedy may otherwise have exposed. Rhetoric of healing and diversion, unification and freedom often avoided disrupting white, middle-class, heterosexual values. For this reason, the very notion of "nation," "national memory," and "tragedy" were also racialized by sports columns using such rhetoric. Closure of the tragedy asserted the mythological nation's innocence by etherealizing columnists' definition of "American," rather than using more concrete descriptions of the racism, poverty, and sexism that seemed fundamental to tragedy's story and the concept of "normalcy" in America. The effect of using any or all of these conventions, rather than resisting their use, was a reassertion of the power that existed prior to the tragedy.

SPORTS PAGES AND THE POLITICAL NEWS

In making these claims to professionals in the field of sport journalism and academia, as well as to sports fans in general, I have often been confronted with an argument that touting patriotism in the context of national tragedy does not necessarily equate to racial privilege or problematic constructions of national identity. I certainly understand this argument. However, I would also argue that touting national ideals like national strength in the context of assassinations of political figures associated with racial movements limits the substance of sport writing, a profession that relies on a readership of perhaps a more widely diverse group of people than most others. Similarly, there is a certain desire to save the reputation of columnists in claiming that their championing of American ideals in the context of tragedy was part of the conventional way in which writers approached these events. This, however, is my point. The traditional way of writing about these events is what mainstream readers desire. This conventional way of writing tells us something about ourselves and what we like to think of our country, even when evidence of oppression and inconsistencies in the nation is overtly obvious to us.

To expand, in *Sensational Designs* Jane Tompkins wrote that "stories should . . . be studied . . . because they offer powerful examples of what a culture thinks about itself, articulating and proposing solutions for the problems that shape a particular historical moment . . ."[34] In *Defining Americans,* Mary Stuckey argued that the presidency is the single site at which Americans look to debate definitions of national identity. She argued, too, that presidents historically have shaped their visions of nation so that people will see themselves as part of that nation.[35] Clearly, after moments of national tragedy citizens look to the presidency for direction on how to react. I would argue, too, that especially after moments of national tragedy, the presidency holds a significant role. Whereas in other moments, individuals may debate the efficacy of a specific president, in moments after tragedy, a majority of Americans look to the American president for guidance. As such, these tragic moments provide the presidency and sporting events with the potential to define for culture understating and memories of the moment.

In *Racial Formations in the United States,* Michael Omi and Howard Winant argued that racial constructs are forged through a "sociohistorical process" and that one of those processes is through presidential rhetoric.[36] Hence, the presidential rhetoric immediately after tragedy allows a contextualization of the racial and national debates of race in which the sports columnists were engaged. It also allows insight into the dominant culture's view of its own make-up.[37] It is with this in mind that I argue sports media provides scholars and intellectuals outside of academia an opportunity to consider the current news media with a different frame of reference. In fact, I began this study of sport and national identity as a result of a sincere concern with a cultural shift in media and academics that potentially leaves problematic representations of the nation unchallenged.

In *Cultural Moves*, Herman Gray argued that diverse representation of identities and ideas in mainstream media (and I add academia and sports writing) means very little if people refuse to consume and/or create images or stories about people other than themselves.[38] Gray suggested that the proliferation of niche markets potentially leads to a further isolation of different ideas and political standpoints from one another. Hence, my concern is that much of the media confronting mythological national identity and scholarship that seeks activism preaches to the choir.

In this era of niche marketing, sport media may have the capacity to perform a sort of political work because it reaches audiences that may otherwise be isolated from one another. That is, a Fox News audience and an MSNBC audience may consume stories on the same event from such diverging angles that there is no common ground with which to engage a debate. However, those same audiences may consume stories about sport and nation that seem apolitical but provide an entry way into discussions of national identity. I am not necessarily writing of numbers here, but standpoints reached.

In my mind, one of the most salient examples of sport media providing individuals with opposing views the potential to talk about controversial, political notions of "Americanness" occurred in a Monday Night Football commercial. On November 15, 2004, Monday Night Football opened with a commercial promoting the new and risqué ABC television show "Desperate Housewives." The commercial, set in the Philadelphia Eagles' pregame locker room, showcased a post-shower Nicolette Sheridan dressed only in a towel. In a sultry voice, Sheridan pleaded with Eagles wide receiver Terrell Owens to stay with her in the empty facility. Owens, in a wooden acting debut, at first politely rejected the offer. Seeing that Owens was committed to playing the game, Sheridan dropped her towel and Owens quickly changed his mind, insinuating that he would rather have sexual relations with Sheridan than play in the much-anticipated contest.

What followed the next morning was a barrage of talk show pundits and newspaper columnists critiquing the commercial in terms of its "suitability for children" and its "moral values." The advertisement, too, aired only two weeks following the 2004 presidential campaign, a presidential race that was characterized by venomous rhetoric and that divided the nation politically. During this campaign, although there was significant discussion about equality, very little robust discussion about race, class, gender, or sexual identity was held between candidates of opposing parties. Still, Karl Rove, George W. Bush's campaign strategist, made "moral values" the central construct of his campaign. "Moral values," though, was a phrase that motivated voters despite its rather vacuous meaning; a phrase that split the country politically without any real consensus of what it meant. After the Monday Night Football commercial, however, sport talk shows served as forums for the politically divided nation to discuss the identity issues that had been voted upon just two weeks earlier in terms of what "moral values" meant. *Sports Illustrated's* Peter King wrote, "I think ABC Sports should be absolutely, positively ashamed of itself!—that's a really nice example Owens—who talks of being such a God-respecting, religious man—is setting, letting a naked woman jump into his arms on national TV."[39] To some, that is, the image of Owens with Sheridan violated their notion or morality. For some it did not. However, I would argue that debating the image of a black man and a white women engaged in a potentially sexual relationship in terms of its morality was much more possible when the debate was set in the context of the seemingly safe sphere of sports.

For instance, on the radio talk show *Mike and Mike in Morning,* Mike Greenberg and Mike Golic refused to consider that the commercial informed, resisted, and/or reinforced racial stereotypes. This is a stance often taken by these gentlemen, entertainers who I enjoy each day on the way to work. Yet they respected a difference of opinion asserted by Tony Dungy, head coach of the Indianapolis Colts. Greenberg asked Dungy, "The racial side of this . . . had this player been Brett Favre or whomever, would you have had less of a problem with it?" Dungy's response was, "I would have had a problem with it, but I guess it hit me because I am African American. And I just think we play into the stereotype."[40] Kandice Chuh wrote that the construct of the idealized white woman was the embodiment of the national spirit, which lead to anitmiscegenation laws, and that established clear lines between white and other races' spaces:[41] Terrell Owens, a black male willing to have sex instead of play in a game for which he was responsible, reinforced the negative stereotype of the irresponsible athlete. He also reinforced the stereotype of the oversexed black male ready to "ruin" the white lady, the very nightmare of the white male, which underpinned much racism of the 19th and 20th centuries. Dungy's outrage at the commercial was based on his knowledge of all three stereotypes. Dungy said, "[Terrell Owens] should be thinking about the fact that maybe this would end in a rape trial. Let's be honest. Let's not say this is a spoof that didn't hurt anybody."[42] The negative reaction toward the ad, overwhelmingly from whites, suggested that much of American culture, knowingly or unknowingly, yet suffers from a psychological hangover from Jim Crow days. To be clear, whereas the tendency of politicians not to discuss race is intentional, the debate about this ad was centered on race.

It seems, in short, that sport provides a safe space for culture to discuss political issues that politicians are weary to engage in. Further, sporting events garner a wider audience in terms of standpoints reached than do niche-marketed cable news networks. And sporting events that immediately follow national tragedy often garner an even broader audience that can potentially engage in the debate about national identity surrounding the sporting event itself. Take, for instance, the fact that the

2001 World Series was, at the time, the most watched World Series in history. Similarly, the Saints first "home games" of both 2005 and 2006 registered to be among the most watched regular season NFL games of each year. Likewise, Super Bowl XLIV, which featured the New Orleans Saints, was the most-watched television program in history. [43] These games that followed tragedy were watched by a bigger portion of the nation-state than those games unassociated with tragedy. In a time of tragedy, and in an era characterized by niche marketing, these stories that columnists told about sport and nation, then, did have a hold over the imaginations of readers—and their audience extended beyond that which would normally be considered a "sporting audience." These stories, too, were constructing for many members of the audience definitions of "Americanness" in moments that would be remembered as uniquely "American." What is interesting about these stories is they often served one of two purposes. One was to establish a definition of "American" that would also marginalize many of those reading the columns. The other was to expand the definition of "Americanness" by drawing attention to the fact that prior definitions were often too narrow. The moments, to me, provide those of us interested in social justice a real opportunity to re-theorize what should count as a theme worthy of study.

In *American Studies in a Moment of Danger*, George Lipsitz argued that we need to strike a balance between being politically active and translating our work beyond the walls of academia if we are going to challenge normative approaches to race and national identity.[44] Ultimately, I see the moment's urgency, catalyzed by niche marketing, as full of potential for intellectuals and providing sports scholars the capacity to reach beyond the academy's walls with their work.

In sport media more voices critical of national mythologies are present now than were in the 1960s, and this is certainly a sign of American mainstream media and audiences shifting their points of view regarding identity. This shift to a sport media with more voices critical of national mythologies may be a result of more minority voices being given space in the sports pages; a marketing strategy of sports publications and sections to reach a range of political tastes despite the niche-marketed news sphere; a change in perceptions of national identity among some people in mainstream sport media culture since the 1960s.[45] There also is an argument to be made that a younger generation of sports columnists has an increased awareness of the necessity of constructing a more diverse national identity than one that simply privileges the white male. To be sure, the further away we move from the 1960s, the more inclusive many of the voices comprising mainstream sports columnists are. However, there are yet many mainstream sports columnists that adopt similar if not the same version of national identity that their counterparts in the 1960s did. Clearly, also, many columnists today, having lived the early part of

their lives during or after the civil rights movement, have confronted
problematic versions of national identity. But the benefit of being born
during or after the 1960s does not equate to adoption of an inclusive
point of view with regard to national identity and/or race. For instance,
the majority of columnists writing about the New Orleans Saint's ability
to "heal the nation" after Hurricane Katrina were products of the baby
boomer generation. In contrast, Robert Lipsyte of the *New York Times* has
been writing columns that confront national mythology since the mid-
1960s. Hence, while with a new generation of sports columnists came a
sports page consisting of voices more inclusive than those in the 1960s, it
did not rid the sports pages of mythologies. More clearly, with a new
generation of editors, publishers, and news organizations' executives
came a renewed possibility for columnists who confronted mythological
national identities to secure jobs in mainstream newspapers and maga-
zines. But to claim that such columnists did not exist prior to this generation or that minorities always confront mythologies of racist, sexist approaches to nation would be an oversimplification. It is more precise to
say that by 2001, space was given to a variety of standpoints in mainstream sport media, while throughout the 1960s, that same space was
given almost exclusively to those privileging mythological constructs of
national identity. Likewise, it is in my opinion, precise to say that sports
pages have within them much more politically diverse columns and
readership than many of our cable news stations do, and as a result, they
deserve further study.

In the end, I hope this interdisciplinary project sheds light on a space
in mainstream media that plays a significant role in how power and
privilege work and that is also rife with potential to reach out to an
audience that is more politically diverse than many of our current cable
news stations and classrooms.

NOTES

1. See Charles P. Peirce, "Black Sunday: Forty Years Ago this Weekend, as America Grieved for President John F. Kennedy, Stunned NFL Players Were Told to Take the
Field," *Sports Illustrated,* 24 November, 2003, 58.

2. Red Smith, "De Gustibus," *New York Herald,* 28 November, 1963, sec. 4. Also see
Arthur Daley, "A Strange Afternoon," *New York Times,* 25 November 1963, sec. L; Jack
Mann, "Reaction at Aqueduct—Tears, Shock, Disbelief," *New York Herald,* 24 Novem-
ber 1963, sec. 4. All quoted below.

3. Daley, "A Strange Afternoon"; Smith, "De Gustibus"; Jack Mann, "Big D," *New
York Herald Tribune,* 2 December, 1963, sec. 4; Red Smith "Five for Navy."

4. See Hal Bodley, "Selig Facing Difficult Decision on Resuming Games," *USA
Today* September 13, 2001, sec. C; Edward Wong, "Runs, Hits, and Healing at Stadium," *New York Times,* September 26 2001, sec. 1.

5. Josh Dubow, "Booing New York Means Baseball's Back to Normal," 15 March
2002,http://www.lexisnexis.com. See also Steve Wilstein, "Patriotism and Protest at
Yankee Stadium," The Associated Press, 22 July 2004: http://www.lexisnexis.com;

Roger Angell, "Can You Believe It?" *The New Yorker*, 26 November 2001; William Rhoden, "This Time, a Deeper Appreciation," *New York Times*, 24 October 2001, sec. S

6. See Mike Dodd, "The World of Sports Is on Hold," *USA Today*, 12 September 2001, sec. C.

7. Jon Saraceno, "NFL Should Have Delayed Its Openers," *USA Today*, 9 September 2005, sec. C.

8. See Michael Silver, "The Saints Come Through," *Sports Illustrated*, 19 September 2005; Harvey Aaraton, "Just Sports Business as Usual if the Saints Go Marching Out," *New York Times*, 20 September 2005, sec. D; Michael Wilbon, "It's Not a Rivalry if the Other Team Never Wins," *Washington Post*, 19 September, 2001 sec. D; Dave Anderson, "The Saints Are Now America's Team," *New York Times*, 15 September 2005 sec. D.

9. Although the game took place in New Jersey, columnists, as I show in chapter 5, emphasized the Giants' association with New York in writing of the Saints' role in their stories of Katrina.

10. Nancy Armour, "As New Orleans Rebuilds, Saints' Return Another Step Toward Normalcy," *Associated Press*, 11August 2006, http://www.lexisnexis.com; Israel Gutierrez, "For One Night, New Orleans can be 'Normal,'" *Miami Herald*, 20 September 2006. http://www.lexisnexis.com; Judy Battista, "Evening of Good Will Turns Giants' Way," *New York Times*, 20 September 2005, http://www.proquest.com.

11. Lisa Olson, "A Story of Hope, but There's Much More to Do," *New York Daily News*, 21 January 2007.

12. William Rhoden, "Amid Ruins of Home, Sorrow and Solidarity," *New York Times*, 18 September 2005. See also Tim Layden, "Marching In," *Sports Illustrated*, 22 January 2007; Rick Reilly, "Sports to the Rescue," *Sports Illustrated*, 6 September 2005.

13. See Steve Coll, "Barrage of Bullets Drowned Our Cries of Comrades," *Washington Post*,1 May 2005, sec. A,; Frank Rich, "It's All Newsweek's Fault," *New York Times*, 22 May 2005: 4.13; Dave Zirin,"Pat Tillman, Our Hero,"*U.S. News & World Report*, 10 May 2004.http://www.proquest.com; Dave Zirin, "Pat Tillman, Our Hero,"*U,S, News & World Report*,10 May 2004, p 72; Frank Rich, "It's All Newsweek's Fault," *New York Times*, 22 May 2005, sec. 4, p 13; Gary Smith, "Remember His Name," *Sports Illustrated*, 5 September 2006,88–101; Terry McDonnell, "Brothers," *Sports Illustrated*, 5 September 2006.

14. Marianne Hirsch and Valerie Smith, "Feminism and Cultural Memory: An Introduction," *Signs*, 28 no. 5 (2002).

15. See *Sports Illustrated 50* (New York: Sports Illustrated, 2004), 112. This is a memory project that purports to highlight the most significant moments in sport history and shows the 1980 USA hockey team celebrating the win. See also *Do You Believe in Miracles*, HBO films, 2005. In this film, sports columnists, commentators, and participants remember the USA Olympic hockey team's win as having "lifted the nation" in a time of economic instability and the Cold War.

16. Marita Sturken, *Tangled Memories*, (Los Angeles: University of California Press, 1997), 218.

17. Walter Shapiro, "Baseball Strike Talk Cheapens Post-Sept, 11 Patriotism," *USA Today*, 28 August 2002, sec. A.

18. Mark Dyreson, *Making the American Team* (Chicago: University of Illinois Press, 1998).

19. S. W. Pope, *Patriotic Games* (New York: Oxford University Press, 1997), 118.

20. See Charles Fountain, *Life and Times of Grantland Rice* (New York: Oxford University Press, 1993).

21. In *Enter the New Negroes, Images of Race in American Culture*, Nadell's premise was that this revolution of "visual images, present in advertisements, postcards, magazine and novel illustrations, sheet music, posters, and lithographs, w[as] paramount in codifying ideas of race Martha Jane Nadell, *Enter the New Negroes* (Cambridge, Harvard University Press, 2004). 17.

22. Likewise, from 1882–1908, a black male did not enter the ring to fight for the title as a result of the champions' imposed rules.

23. Antonio Gramsci, "Hegemony, Relations of Force, Historical Bloc," *Prison Writings*, http://www.marxists.org/archive/gramsci/editions/reader/index.htm (10 Sept. 2003).

24. Sigmund Freud, *Beyond the Pleasure Principle* (trans., James Strachey, New York: W. W. Norton, 1989), 13.

25. S. W. Pope, *Patriotic Games*, 82.

26. S. W. Pope., *Patriotic Games*, 79.

27. Lauren Berlant, *The Queen of America Goes to Washington City* (Durham, NC: Duke University Press, 1997), 36.

28. Bob Morris. "America Gets Needed Break at Superbowl." *Orlando Sentinel*. 8 Jan 1991: B1.

29. Lauren Berlant, *The Queen of America Goes to Washington City*, 36.

30. GeraldEarly, *Body Language* (Saint Paul: Gray Wolf Press, 1998), vii, xi.

31. In "Getting to Know You: Knowledge, Power, and the Body," Bill Nichols suggested that the ephemeral issues of politics, race, gender, and power are not so well discussed as they are represented through the body. Discussion of these issues results in what he called disembodied knowledge. In contrast, "Images are always of concrete, material things recorded at specific moments in time, but these images can be made to point toward more general truths or issues. . . . Representation operates neither univocally nor transparently, but it continues to function as a mediation between one person's reality and that of another." Bill Nichols, "Getting to Know You," *Theorizing Documentary*, ed. Michael Renov (Routledge: New York), 176. Also see Lauren Berlant, *The Queen of America Goes to Washington City* (Durham, NC: Duke University Press, 1997), 238.

32. George Lipsitz, *American Studies in a Moment of Danger* (Minneapolis: University of Minnesota Press, 2001), 191–96.

33. George Lipsitz, *American Studies in a Moment of Danger*, 17.

34. Mary Stuckey, *Defining Americans* (Lawrence, KS: University Press of Kansas, 2004), 2.

35. Mary Stuckey, *Defining Americans*, (Lawrence, KS: University Press of Kansas, 2004), 2.

36. Michael Omi and Howard Winant, *Racial Formation in the United States* (New York: Routledge, 2002), 54.

37. The presidential rhetoric, coupled with the columns about tragedy, also allows my analysis to link the microlevel—individual columnists' writing/imaginations—to macrolevel concerns—like myth, dominant national identity/imagined communities. Specifically, the book uses the terms myth, construct, and imagination in ways that are often implicitly intertwined. Columnists constructed their own versions of national identity and were in the process of doing so for readers. The theoretical terminology that connects media culture, in this case sports columns, to national identity, summarized above, is "imagined communities." However, the imagined communities of which columnists were a part when they wrote, and that they subsequently supported and/or resisted in writing of tragedy, were partially constructed by the dominant imagined community/national identity of the period. Likewise, as columnists wrote that sport served a nation in the context of tragedy, they implicitly if not overtly were informed by the historic, mythic sort of national identity. S. W. Pope writes in terms of sport's nostalgia and nationalism. In this way, columnists' imaginations were dialectically intertwined with the imagined community/dominant nation, itself having a historic attachment to a mythology sport served. Hence, these terms, while not interchangeable, were part of a matrix by which, I argue, sports columns revealed and constructed versions of national identity in the context of tragedy. Moreover, the individual columnists' imaginations were part of a media constructing and constructed by imagined communities mainstream media itself constructed prior to their writing.

38. Herman Gray, *Cultural Moves* (Los Angeles: University of California Press, 2005).
39. Qtd. Peason.
40. Dungy, Tony. Interview. *Mike and Mike in the Morning.* ESPN. ESPN radio, 18 Nov. 2004.
41. Chuh, Kandice. *Imagine Otherwise* (Durham, NC: Duke University Press, 2003).
42. Dungy, Tony.
43. All statistics gathered from Nielsen ratings, 2001, 2005, and 2006.
44. George Lipsitz, *American Studies in a Moment of Danger*, 1–23.
45. Nielsen gathered data on contemporary television, newspaper, and Internet use 2003–2004. That data illustrated that sport media captures a more diverse audience in terms of race, class, and gender than the most popular "mainstream" news organizations and may, as a result, be a site where the potential to change dominant or white conceptions of national identity could manifest. *Sports Illustrated* had a readership of more than 20 million and its audience is two-thirds white. While this was an overly white readership, consider that the viewership of news stations like CNN, FOX, and MSNBC all have at least a 90 percent white viewership. And 16.9 percent of ESPN's *SportsCenter's* audience, as opposed to 8.2 percent of the audience of CNN, was black. ESPN's garnering of women watchers (20 percent) was increasing at rates more significant than other programs. Moreover, 40 percent more viewers interested in stories concerning national issues went to cable, not network, news television, according to a *Washington Post* market segmentation study carried out 2004–2005. But cable news stations, according to Bill Alpert, were ideologically divided by political standpoint (FOX is for conservatives Alpert wrote, and CNN for liberals). All of this data suggests that, beyond the fact that cable news channels were gathering ideologically homogeneous audiences, they were also not reaching audiences that were representative of the nation-state. Likewise, these news outlets were constructing knowledge of the nation more now than ever; this knowledge is dialectically produced with consumer taste. Thus, unchallenged, hegemonic notions of national identities are provided through cable news.

ONE

War Games

On January 20, 1961, President John Fitzgerald Kennedy stood in the frigid Washington, D.C. air and delivered an inaugural address, the content of which revealed the national character he would seek to establish through his administration. Wearing neither a hat nor coat, he constructed his nation as vigorous, virile, and willing to exercise military force against the spread of Communism.[1] He said, "Let every nation know, whether it wishes us well or ill, that we shall pay any price, bear any burden, meet any hardship, support any friend, oppose any foe to assure the survival and the success of liberty."[2]

Kennedy's assertions of national strength in the name of liberty came in the context of the Cold War, where the notion of American stability and strength was continually challenged by the Soviet Union. Kennedy, throughout his presidency, crafted an image and message of national and military strength in response to Gallup polls that suggested American voters would welcome both in the context of the Cold War.[3]

In a commonly used stump speech during his presidential campaign, Kennedy promised to "mold our strength and become first again . . . [He] want[ed] the people of the world to wonder not what Mr. Khrushchev [wa]s doing [but] what the United States [wa]s doing."[4] Likewise, in *High Noon in the Cold War*, Max Frankel illustrated that Kennedy's rhetoric and image of strength were both crafted with the intention of ceasing the Soviet Union's spread to Cuba and Berlin.[5] Finally, Shawn Parry-Giles argued that national politicians and mainstream American media had, throughout the 1950s and early 1960s, normalized Cold War rhetoric, which asserted American might and implied military strength.[6]

Often during his presidential campaign, Kennedy extended his Cold War rhetoric by connecting military might with moral superiority. Kennedy argued that the belief in and exertion of American strength was moral because of a single American trait that separated his country from Communist countries: its democracy. So moral was Kennedy's America and its democracy, in fact, that he claimed "God's work" was America's.[7] Hence, Kennedy's construction of a strong, virile, and moral American identity was implicitly an argument about America's place in the global community and how America stacked up against Communism.

However, two years after his inauguration, on August 28, 1963, the nation's morality was confronted when 250,000 people from all over the nation traveled to Washington, D.C., to participate in the March on Washington. The purpose of the march was to protest the unfair and unequal treatment of racial minorities and women. In newspapers across the country, reporters quoted President John F. Kennedy's words that the march "'advanced the cause of 20 million Negroes' and all mankind."[8] Laurence Burd wrote that A. Philip Randolph and nine other leaders of the march "met in the White House cabinet room with the President." There Kennedy noted that the march signified a growth in public awareness about civil rights, but that despite progress, "'we have a very long way to travel.'"[9] Along with Burd's article, a photograph of Kennedy and Vice President Lyndon Johnson with the ten African American leaders ran on the top of the page. The very need for a civil rights movement, though, belied the moral national identity that Kennedy had constructed. The mythological identity of national might and morality was one that also repressed any acknowledgment of the structural and systemic oppression characteristic of the nation's Jim Crow laws.

Three months after the March on Washington, Kennedy lay dead in the same building in which he shook hands with the race leaders. Renowned sports columnist Red Smith argued that the assassination required "a day of mourning" for the "nation."[10] Sid Ziff of the *Los Angeles Times* suggested the cancellation of regularly scheduled programming by radio and television be executed "to impress upon the people, over and over again, the sense of tragedy."[11]

(WHITE) NATIONAL BODIES

Two days after the assassination, an Associated Press column referring to Kennedy's advocacy of physical fitness underscored that the fallen president "emphasized the importance of building the body as well as the mind."[12] *New York Times* sports columnist Daley wrote that Kennedy "was vitally interested in every phase of athletics."[13] As evidence to support this claim he cited Kennedy's attendance at boxing matches and Hall of Fame dinners, and his wealth of sporting knowledge. Omitted from the elements comprising Daley's version of sport, interestingly, was its racial make-up, despite the fact that Kennedy had worked to desegregate professional and collegiate sport.[14] In short, Daley avoided racial policy in constructing his memory of Kennedy. Another AP column implicitly constructed a mythological national identity by representing only white males in referring to athletes' association with national identity and the military:

> President Kennedy did not merely stress the importance of physical well-being. . . . He also created a Youth Council on Fitness under the supervision of Oklahoma's football coach Bud Wilkinson. The program was encouraged throughout all primary public schools throughout the country. . . . He appointed Gen. Douglas MacArthur the final-say in the dispute [between the Amateur Athletic Union and the U.S. Olympic Program.] He had surrounded himself with football men, feeling they were rounded citizens best trained to meet today's problems.[15]

Although African Americans were participating in sport throughout the country, white males were constructed as the citizens most capable of addressing this nation's problems. Hence, the face of sport and the nation served through it was white and male. Further, sport paid a service to a national identity of military strength as General MacArthur was aligned with Kennedy's association with athletics. These columnists thereby situated Kennedy in their imagined nations by emphasizing the militaristic aspect of his administration while repressing the racial—much like Kennedy's rhetoric regarding the Cold War did. And this mythological nation's problems were related to physical fitness and training youth for the Olympics, not the social and racial oppressions that Kennedy's policies within and beyond sport addressed. The default rhetoric of sports columns was to create a mythological national identity that focused on the military and avoided the reality of racial oppression. This was true despite the racial aspect being a major part of Kennedy's administration: men of color were part of the sports complex about which these columnists wrote, and Kennedy worked to desegregate sport.

Advocacy of physical fitness and in espousing military might had a history in the presidency, though. W. W. Abbott introduced President Washington's personal papers by noting the president's athleticism and referencing his prowess in war.[16] Similarly, earlier and throughout his presidency, Theodore Roosevelt put emphasis on sport's ability to ready the nation-state's young men for war. In *Manliness and Civilization* Gail Bedermen chronicled Teddy Roosevelt's rhetoric and noted that the emphasis of physical prowess and sport during his administration was part of a greater project to conflate race, masculinity, and sexuality. She further wrote that the rhetoric was not the most powerful means through which this conflation occurred. Rather, "middle-class constructions of male power would become firmly based on the violence and sexuality of this journalistic version of primitive masculinity."[17] This masculinity was emphasized in the rhetoric of the news pages that touted nationalism and eventually led the nation to the Spanish American War. S. W. Pope wrote that "the American sporting tradition was profoundly transformed by the military's widespread incorporation of sports into the war effort."[18] He continued to suggest that "riding patriotic fervor, many physical educators linked mass athletic activity with the democratic ideal" and citizenship.[19]

In the same vein, as sports columnists projected Kennedy's presence in sport stadiums and focused on his advocacy of physical fitness they were, in effect, involved in a construction of national identity that would support and be informed by the military complex.[20] This focus on the military complex and the repression of racial discussion continued throughout the month after Kennedy's assassination. Columnists wrote of fans' attendance at the 1963 Army–Navy game to establish the make-up of their own mythological nations. Smith led his column: "Silent in the sunshine, 100,000 citizens stood."[21] Jesse Abramson of the *New York Times* wrote that a "cross section of the public" attended the Army–Navy game, but he identified only white national officials by name.[22] Leonard Koppett of the *New York Times* reduced Kennedy's position from national official to fan and thereby made Kennedy's actions reflect those of "the people." He wrote that "at the many events [Kennedy] had attended, he seemed to respond as a fan, rather than as a public figure making ceremonial appearances."[23] These columns all constructed "the public," or the nation's "citizens," as represented at the game, but only mentioned white males as present in the stands. These columnists established fans of the military's sporting teams as citizens. While it is certain that women and minorities attended the game, these columnists did not mention them in their construction of "the public."

Moreover, Navy's varsity team consisted of only white males until 1964, and Army's consisted of only white males until 1966. The game considered to reflect national citizenship comprised of only white males.[24] The nations that Smith, Abramson, and Koppett constructed were full of white athletes and politicians, despite the fact that Kennedy's administration played a significant role in integrating the NFL, even threatening the Washington Redskins with court action if the organization refused to sign black players; and despite the fact that sport was full of black males interested in civil rights.

As a result, when the columnists focused on the all-white Army–Navy games to remember Kennedy and his relationship to sport, they were not only avoiding topics that would confront the mythological, white national identity of so-called moral strength, but they were also asserting it. Black citizens were altogether marginalized from the field of play columnists used to construct their nations even though Kennedy worked to allow some of these athletes on the field of play. Hence, columnists' who wrote of national identity and the Army–Navy games emphasized physical fitness and privileged whiteness simply by marginalizing race from their nations; just as the political rhetoric of national morality did. Moreover, columnists' rhetoric suggested that sport paid a service to the nation and memory of Kennedy, but constructed both in terms that sealed out the reality of racial strife beyond the stadium walls.

For instance, Smith wrote of the Pentagon's decision to allow the 1963 Army–Navy game to be played in the wake of tragedy and suggested the game was of primary importance in establishing how Kennedy would be remembered.

> No doubt there are less important questions, though none come to mind at the moment. Decent sport which the President admired and encouraged, does not dishonor his memory now. Indeed, the game with all its pageantry could create an opportunity for the young men of West Point and Annapolis to pay public tribute to the Commander in Chief.[25]

The athletes Smith imbued with meaning for remembering Kennedy were male, white, and in the Armed Forces. In imbuing athletes from the armed services with meaning, Smith implicitly defined his nation in a similar way that Roosevelt and Kennedy had: white masculinity, characterized by physical prowess, was projected as representative of the national identity in the context of war and racial oppression, the former given more emphasis.

Writing of Kennedy in relation to the Army–Navy game was not limited to the 1963 game, though. Specifically, Smith reinforced the construction of national strength and might by remembering the Army–Navy game that occurred a full year previous, in 1962. Then, Smith wrote that Kennedy was "hatless and without an overcoat in the November cold."[26] Painting Kennedy in the same cold-weather gear, Abramson wrote that "President Kennedy attended the last three Army–Navy games. . . . Two years ago the man of vigor shed his coat and sat in his shirt sleeves."[27] Likewise, Daley wrote that "recollection comes, too, of the President at the Army–Navy game, shunning an overcoat while everyone around him was well-bundled."[28] Hence, columnists implied Kennedy's toughness and vigor by describing his clothing. These descriptions constructed Kennedy in terms reminiscent of his inaugural address, where he cast his national identity as strong, virile, and moral. In that era of instability and in the context of a president's assassination, which threatened to expose that instability even further, Kennedy became columnists' symbol of national toughness and vigor; a symbol that repressed internal racial problems that the very president about whom they wrote worked to reveal.

Columnists further connected Kennedy to the military complex and national might by writing of their memories of his participation in the rituals associated with sport years earlier. Smith wrote of Kennedy's walking through a double-row of Navy and Army students during halftime of the 1962 Army–Navy game.[29] The Associated Press and Smith remembered Kennedy's flipping the coin at the beginning of the 1962 game while standing next to soldiers. Despite that Kennedy associated himself with many facets and levels of sport during his tenure as president, his memory was being constructed in terms of his attendance at the 1961 and 1962 Army–Navy game and his proximity to white male soldiers. These columnists situated Kennedy in their own nations through memory in his absence.[30]

In *The Queen of America Goes to Washington City*, Lauren Berlant argued that the experiences of blacks, women, and nonheterosexuals are often erased when politicians and national media attempt to define national identity. In short, minorities are denied a place in the national imagination. Such is the case in the columns referenced above. These columns in which writers remembered Kennedy in a stadium consisting of white males associated with the nation, in effect established their nations as white, virile, masculine, and associated with the Armed Forces. Because these columnists set limits to which identities would be represented in their nations they were engaged in a construction of national identity that would repress and marginalize the black and female body (and any political concerns therein) from the national identity they established.[31]

ALLOWING THE NFL TO PLAY: REMEMBERING HOW THE NATION WAS SHAMED

In the immediate aftermath of the Kennedy assassination, college and pro football leagues and conferences were uncertain of whether or not they should play their scheduled games. The NFL played all of its scheduled games on time while most other major sporting leagues or conferences postponed them. Columnists who wrote of the NFL games being played vilified National Football League Commissioner Pete Rozelle's decision to continue the season. Ultimately, though, columns about the NFL generally contrasted with those written about the Army–Navy game of 1963.

It is helpful to conceive of these columns that theorized sport's role in the aftermath of Kennedy's assassination as elegies. Peter M. Sacks defined the elegy to be a work of mourning in which the writer substitutes the deceased body with another object that survivors can use to move on from loss. Sacks's analysis of the genre extended from his reading of Freudian theory of trauma, substitution, and their relationship to language development. Although Sacks did not write specifically about the media's role in constructing the works of mourning that allow for a "healthy" recovery from cultural trauma or loss, he did suggest that there are moments in which death becomes "obscene, meaningless, or impersonal—an event either stupefyingly colossal in cases of large-scale war, or clinically concealed somewhere behind the technology of the hospital and the techniques of the funeral home."[32]

Kennedy's assassination fell into the colossal sort of which Sacks writes. The stadium(s) sports columnists wrote of were one of those technologies that clinically concealed death. In this case, columnists wrote successful elegies by reproducing what happened at games using people associated with the mythic, masculine, white national identity to catalyze a healing. Such columns could return the columnists' imagined nations to normalcy. The tragedy of Kennedy's death and the racism he worked to fix would altogether be avoided, and white, male, virile bodies associated with the nation-state that would also imply military strength and morality would again secure columnists' national identity.

For instance, in "D-Day Plus 11" Jack Mann of *The New York Herald Tribune* linked Kennedy with another president associated with athletics, white masculinity, and military might: He wrote of Roosevelt and his work during World War II.[33] He wrote that the news of Kennedy's assassination catalyzed the same feeling among spectators of Aqueduct (a race track in New York City) as when they first heard of President Roosevelt's death. He suggested that there was that feeling of "poured concrete in the lower intestine" which was "not exactly duplicated again . . . until news of Kennedy's death was learned of."[34]

The rest of his column underscored President Johnson's masculinity by comparing it to Kennedy and Franklin Roosevelt's, both of whom, Gary Gerstel showed in *American Crucible,* were raised to the level of mythic status in cultural memory through reference to war and toughness.[35] Mann compared the Roosevelt and Kennedy administrations through similar, significant events associated with nation that are characteristic of masculinity and strength: war and sport. Mann wrote, "This change of command [from Kennedy to Johnson] was not as frightening because the [soldiers] knew Lyndon Johnson, and he is not the longshot the new President Truman seemed to their political minds on D-plus-11, from 10,000 miles away, in a hot war."[36]

Mann then theorized that the change in command from Kennedy to Johnson would not be disrupting for the nation because Johnson had exhibited similar masculinity as the other two presidents. Although Johnson "never captained a PT boat, ordered an invasion of a continent or fisted a five-star general . . . he looked death in the eye and laughed at it. Stricken in 1955 by a heart attack," he was capable of toughness and humor. "That is all the Lyndon Johnson I know . . . it's encouraging."[37] Mann argued that Johnson was a known fighter. He imputed to Johnson the qualities of masculinity and strength, and implied a seamless transfer of command in the leadership of the nation-state as a result. In comparing Johnson and Kennedy's heroics, Mann created a story capable of supporting the national character of presidential toughness that would sustain the nation's strength in a period in which strength was questioned but deemed necessary.[38]

Daley, too, created a mythological national identity by writing of Kennedy's heroism in World War II. He wrote "the President's prowess as a swimmer made him a war hero after his torpedo boat was cut in two by a Japanese craft in the Pacific. He was for miles towing a wounded member of his crew, and later swam many miles in seeking the assistance he eventually obtained."[39] In the process he constructed an America in which citizens and heroes were masculine figures who fought in war and had athletic prowess. Framed in terms of the elegy and its conventions, these stories and substitutions allowed for a healthy mourning of and moving on from tragedy.

In contrast, other columnists' assertions that the NFL's decision to play games was distasteful to the nation can be seen as resulting from the fact that the people present at the NFL games upon which columnists focused were not associated with military strength or the nation-state. Hence, these games did not allow columnists to successfully reassert American strength and virility through substitution of bodies.

For example, many columnists constructed the nation as shamed when the NFL took the field. Irving T. Marsh of *The New York Herald Tribune* first acknowledged much of sport for carrying out actions he deemed appropriate: "[T]he sound of sports revelry was stilled yesterday as a nation mourned its martyred President."[40] He criticized the NFL for being the "only group which will carry out its schedule in full."[41] Smith wrote that the NFL lacked civility because it played games the weekend of Kennedy's assassination. The lead was:

> In the civilized world it was a day of mourning. In the National Football League, it was the 11th Sunday of the business year, a quarter-million dollar day in Yankee Stadium, a day for selling to television a show which that medium not always celebrated for sensitive taste— couldn't stomach.[42]

Smith later wrote of the NFL that "it is not encouraging to realize that a league with the foresight to make provisions for playing off ties cannot avoid shaming the nation."[43] However, Smith himself noted that the games were not televised. Hence, many people in the nation had no capacity to be offended by the games being played. Columnists' reaction to the nontelevised NFL games can be better framed in terms of what the games did not provide for writers, rather than for what they actually did to offend. This especially rings true when the offense columnists underscored was not the actual assassination, but the games being played.

For instance, Smith ended a column implying that the playing of games was tragic for the nation in this way: there was a "bad taste left when Pete Rozelle . . . hung up the business as usual sign. . . . For that exercise in tasteless stupidity there is neither excuse or defense."[44] Ziff regretted "that the whole NFL football season had not been set back one week," underscoring that "it was commissioner Pete Rozelle's decision."[45] The offended nation was one of Smith and Ziff's imaginations, where a sporting event seen by only a fraction of the citizenry could in fact shame the entire nation.

Daley wrote of the NFL games similarly and suggested that NFL players seemed out of place that day. He wrote the games were being played in the context of "a national nightmare."[46] He ended his column: the "feeling of disquietude never left completely. . . . That was why it was so difficult to concentrate on the game yesterday. Big men were playing a boy's sport at the wrong time."[47] Hence, these writers were incapable of spinning yarns that would substitute the deceased Kennedy with other men. Without people directly associated with nation-state and military might, columnists were incapable of producing works that would return their imagined nations to strength and virility after having lost their president in the context of the Cold War.

In contrast to the NFL games, however, the Army–Navy game did eventually provide the bodies and fodder for columnists to complete the elegiac convention of substitution that would allow the nation to be constructed in masculine, virile, and moral terms. Even before the game was played, many writers and columnists speculated as to whether the Army–Navy game should or would be cancelled or postponed. Jesse Abramson wrote that two teams being "subject to orders from the secretaries of the Army and Navy and the Defense Department" were yet waiting for word on whether the perennial game between the forces would take place. He continued, implying that if the game was played, the nation could heal, but because it had not, "the numbness of the nation continued."[48] Underpinning Abramson's column was the implication that the Army–Navy game would offer the material for columnists to create the elegiac story that would return the imagined masculine nations to stability and normalcy.

Ultimately, the Pentagon postponed the game, and set a date for December 7, 1963, for it to be played. In many of the columns regarding the game, the coincidental date that the Armed Forces resumed their season on the anniversary of the attack on Pearl Harbor, was not overlooked.[49] In a sports section that ran a header, "Dedicated to the Memory of President Kennedy," Abramson wrote that the game would be played on a "day which will live in infamy–the 22nd anniversary of the attack on Pearl Harbor which plunged the U.S. into World War II."[50] Abramson later wrote that the decision to postpone the Army–Navy game "was one that [was made so that] history would note that [it] was not played on the scheduled date after the assassination of the President."[51] He thereby anticipated that the game would be linked to cultural memory of Kennedy. Further on, Abramson connected the history of the game to World War II and to leaders of the nation-state. He mentioned that Philadelphia had been the site for the game "since the years of World War II, its attendants were to include leaders from the armed forces." He continued that "many leaders in the executive, legislative, and judicial branches of government, governors, and a cross-section of the public" were at the game.[52] The officials of nation present, the substitution of Kennedy was in the process of being completed through sport. That is, through the game and the officials present at it, Abramson substituted Kennedy with military and national officials would assure the nation's stability. In the column, that is, Abramson wrote of the officials and created a story of the nation's status, imagining its stability as a result of sport.

Emphasizing the bodies present, sports columnists wrote of the rituals at the Army–Navy game in terms of funeral ceremonies, which, Sacks suggested, can replace the body of the deceased to allow for a healthy mourning, closure, and stability. In his chronicle of the forthcoming game, Koppett wrote that the "usual festive displays will be dispensed with . . . Instead, a minute of silence will be observed . . . and other ceremonies will be of an appropriate nature."[53] Daley categorized the stadium as an "outdoor cathedral," thereby fitting the stadium into the category of one of those technologies that seals death from visibility, as Sacks wrote.[54] Ziff wrote that Los Angeles Rams owner Dan Reeves "quoted parts of [Kennedy's] eulogy that was uttered in his mass earlier that day [November 24]."[55] These rituals led to the closure of sports columnists' stories of tragedy and a return to normalcy: Smith and Daley suggested that the nation would soon "return to normalcy" through continuation of sport; Mann's "Big D" illustrated that Dallas had returned to normalcy in anticipation of the Cotton Bowl in which Navy would participate. With the Armed Forces' resumption of sport embodied in white, masculine, military players and officials, the nation returned to its normal, virile, moral state.

In these columns, writers fulfilled the conventions of the elegy and used the stadium to seal the reality of instability and tragedy beyond its walls. Ultimately, they suggested the presence of these bodies allowed a return to "normalcy." But these columnists' elegies offered closure by asserting a mythological notion of citizenship. They also implied that the problems of the nation-state were solved because the nation's military was secure. This construction of national stability and morality was an easy rhetorical maneuver when the racial realities of the nation-state were avoided.

There is further evidence that columnists closed their stories of Kennedy's assassination after they asserted their nations' strength and virility by writing of the Army–Navy game. Navy's win assured them a spot in what many columnists labeled the national championship game to be held in, of all places, Dallas, where Kennedy had been killed.[56] Daley, Danzig, and Jim Murray of the *Los Angeles Times* all wrote of the Cotton Bowl, but none referred to the death of Kennedy, even though it was held in the same city in which he fell. Hence a game held in the same site as the assassination and played by the same team associated with the president was not said to have significance for the nation or tragedy. But the mythological nation was further secured, at least by Daley: After Navy lost to Texas, Daley wrote that "at least one televiewer swelled with pride at that exhibition and thought how comforting it was to know that a nation's destinies would someday be in the hands of indomitable Navy officers like these."[57] The future of Daley's nation was safe in the hands of white males associated with the nation-state and a strong military complex—a message desired and offered over and again in the context of the Cold War.

These writers, collectively appearing in more than 200 papers throughout the country, used rhetoric quite similar to Kennedy's, which emphasized national strength and might through reference to the national military complex. Specifically, these columnists underscored the import of the Army–Navy game that year as meaningful to how Kennedy would be situated in cultural memory of national identity. However, none of these columnists, and few if any of their counterparts, mentioned the march or the civil rights movement that Kennedy supported that same year. Columnists' silence regarding civil rights in the wake of Kennedy's assassination reflected the Cold War rhetoric that touted American strength and morality while avoiding the reality of structural oppression of minorities. This rhetoric that avoided such realities was ironic, given that sport at that time was full of black men, many of whom supported civil rights.[58]

A LOSS OF INNOCENCE

The white and male national identity columnists espoused can be further discussed by examining the irony inherent in their use of memories of WWII to establish national identity as heroic, virile, and moral. Columns that linked the Army–Navy game to citizenship were rife with contradiction. They marginalized black citizens and concerns from their columns, despite that African Americans were a large part of the sporting arena and that Kennedy's administration did in fact concern itself with such minorities. Similarly, as cultural memories of World War II often emphasize American strength and virtue, this game was being established as significant to columnists' construction of Kennedy and national identity. But during World War II black soldiers were asked to fight against an oppressive Nazi regime, and they were not offered equal treatment within the forces. A similar marginalization of black identities occurred not only at the Army–Navy game but also in sports columns that suggested the teams and games represented the nation, and in mainstream media's Cold War rhetoric that implied the nation-state was moral and superior. This marginalization of black interests from sports columnists' memory of Kennedy occurred even though "not since the reconstruction had a

President of the United States so strongly linked his political fortunes to the fate of African-Americans."[59]

This marginalization of the civil rights movement from columns said to be written in memory of Kennedy, too, can be framed in the way in which the Kennedy assassination commonly serves as a cultural memory that signaled a loss of national innocence. Farber wrote that the assassination made people realize that not "all of America's possibilities were good" and that even today the baby boomer generation remembers the Kennedy assassination as signaling the loss of innocence for America.[60] But the perception that the nation was innocent prior to the assassination is indicative of a standpoint privileged by race, gender, class, and sexuality. To assume innocence existed prior to the Kennedy assassination requires not only the marginalization of black (and other minorities') concerns from definitions and memories of America, but also a simultaneous amnesia about Kennedy's work toward racial politics. If his assassination signaled a loss of national innocence, Kennedy's administration must be viewed in absence of its approach to racism.

The memory of Kennedy's assassination, with the result being an "end to innocence," is paradoxical in the way George Lipsitz highlighted the romanticization of the 1960s as a time of social and political activism is. Lipsitz argued that even though the mainstream out of America considered the Kennedy assassination as part of a matrix of events in which progress in the sphere of civil rights was evident, "a majority of Americans opposed almost all of the specific objectives of the civil rights movement."[61] Lipsitz remembered the activism of the 1960s to have occurred from "the self-worth and raised expectations resulting from participation in social movements by workers, women, military personnel, and members of aggrieved social groups," not participation of those already privileged by the power structures in America.[62]

The overwhelming absence of references to race in sports columnists' writing of Kennedy spoke loudly of the identities privileged in their imagined versions of America, not necessarily of Kennedy's administration or the actual, real nation. In this way, the nations that sports columnists wrote of were, in a very real sense, of their own imaginations. Given that the columnists writing for mainstream publications in 1963 were overwhelmingly white and male, the memories of Kennedy and nation they constructed can partially be attributed to their life experiences in an era in which the normalized national rhetoric privileged their identity and military strength. Their memories of Kennedy that celebrated the nation and the deceased president as virile and masculine disregarded race as an important part of either's story. That so many of these mainstream columnists omitted race from their stories reveals the lack of urgency and sincerity with which the writers and readers of their work approached race relations in the early 1960s, no matter how that time period is remembered now. In short, as columnists did not engage in an overt racial debate. They continued to normalize white masculinity, their own iden-tity, as the dominant national identity even as they wrote of sports, which was full of people of color. And it was that imaginary nation, one that was imagined in the absence of racial minorities, that experienced a re-turn to normalcy through the Army–Navy game.

The way we remember is partially how we currently perceive our-selves and our own identities in relation to power and privilege. Avoid-ing the reality that racial oppression was ignored by many whites even in the immediate aftermath of Kennedy's assassination allows them to ig-nore their own role in supporting structural racism. It is a memory strate-gy that perpetuates the national mythology of democracy and equality and is one that sports columnists demonstrably espoused and promoted after the Kennedy assassination.

NOTES

1. Using Freudian substitution theory, which this chapter builds on in terms of sports columns, Trevor and Shawn Parry-Giles argued that presidential candidates must carefully construct private and public selves to voters who are aware of cultural myths of the presidency and political rhetoric of the contemporary era. Clearly, in his image and the mythological national identity he constructed, Kennedy was aware of this dynamic. Parry-Giles, Shawn and Trevor, "Political Scopophilia, Presidential Campaigning, and The Intimacy Of American Politics," *Communication Studies*, 47, no. 3 (March 2001): 191–205.

2. Qtd. David Farber, *The Age of Great Dreams* (New York: Farrar, Straus & Giroux, 1994), 26.

3. Parry-Giles, "Political Scopophilia, Presidential Campaigning, and The Intimacy Of American Politics"; David Farber, *The Age of Great Dreams*.

4. Qtd, David Farber, *The Age of Great Dreams*, 26.

5. Max Frankel, *High Noon in the Cold War*, New York: Random House, 2004.

6. Shawn Parry-Giles, *The Rhetorical Presidency, Propaganda, and the Cold War, 1945–1955*, Westport: Greenwood, 2001.

7. Qtd, David Farber, *The Age of Great Dreams*, 26.

8. Qtd., Laurence Burd, "March to Aid Negro Cause, Kennedy Said," *Chicago Trib-une*, 29 August 1963.

9. Laurence Burd, "March to Aid Negro Cause, Kennedy Said."

10. Red Smith, "De Gustibus," *New York Herald*, 28 November 1963, sec. 4.

11. Sid Ziff, "And They Came Out," *Los Angeles Times*, 24 November 1963, sec. D.

12. Associated Press, "A Friend and Champion Is Missing from Sports," *New York Herald*, 24 November 1963, sec. 4.

13. Daley, "A Strange Afternoon."

14. Daley, "A Strange Afternoon."

15. Associated Press, "A Friend and Champion Is Missing from Sports."

16. W. W. Abbott, "The Papers of George Washington, Preface," 11 February 1999, http://gwpapers.virginia.edu/articles/abbot_3.html (retrieved 21 June 2007).

17. Gail Bederman, *Manliness and Civilization* (Chicago: University of Chicago Press, 1996), 215.

18. S. W. Pope, *Patriotic Games* (New York: Oxford University Press, 1997), 154.

19. Pope, *Patriotic Games*, 154.

20. In "Pro Football Attendance Unaffected," Koppett wrote that those in sport felt an acute sense of loss, not because Kennedy worked to desegregate sport, but because he attended games and "emphasi[zed] . . . physical fitness." The AP column cited

above claimed that Kennedy "was one of the best friends American sports ever had" and used his attendance at Army–Navy games as proof of its claim. In "One Drunk, Unarmed," Red Smith remembered that "John Kennedy enjoyed [football] games as a participant and spectator, and sports had his hearty official support as President."

21. Red Smith, "Five for Navy," *New York Herald Tribune*, 8 December 1963, sec. 4.

22. Jesse Abramson, "Army, Navy Squads Drill; For Nothing," *New York Herald Tribune*, 24 November 1963, sec. 4.

23. Leonard Koppett, "Pro Football Attendance Unaffected," *The New York Times*, 25 November 1963, sec. 4.

24. In 1964, flankerback Calvin Huey was the first African American to play on the varsity squad for Navy and in 1966 split end Calvin Steele was the first to play for Army. See Lincoln A. Werden, "Cahill's Plans for Army Eleven Include Its First Negro Regular," *The New York Times*, 4 June 1966.

25. Smith, "De Gustibus."

26. Red Smith, "One Drunk, Unarmed," *New York Herald Tribune*, 23 November 1963, sec. 4.

27. Jesse Abramson, "Sports Silent Tribute to President Kennedy—Most College Football Games Are Called Off," *New York Herald Tribune*, 23 November 1963, sec. 4.

28. Arthur Daley, "A Day of Mourning," *New York Times*, 26 November 1963, sec. L.

29. Smith, "One Drunk, Unarmed."

30. Associated Press, "A Friend and Champion Is Missing from Sports"; Red Smith, "One Drunk, Unarmed."

31. Lauren Berlant, *The Queen of America Goes to Washington City* (Durham, NC: Duke University Press, 1997), 238.

32. Peter M. Sacks, *The English Elegy: Studies in the Genre from Spenser to Yeats* (Baltimore: Johns Hopkins University Press, 1996), 299.

33. Jack Mann, "Reaction at Aqueduct—Tears, Shock, Disbelief," *New York Herald Tribune*, 24 November 1963, sec. 4.

34. Jack Mann, "D-Day Plus 11," *New York Herald Tribune*, 25 November 1963, sec. 4.

35. Gary Gerstle, *American Crucible* (Princeton: Princeton University Press, 2001).

36. Mann, "D-Day Plus 11."

37. Mann, "D-Day Plus 11."

38. Mann, "D-Day Plus 11."

39. Daley, "A Day of Mourning."

40. Irving T. Marsh "Weekend of Mourning–Most Sports Blacked Out," *New York Herald Tribune*, 23 November 1963, sec. 4.

41. Marsh "Weekend of Mourning–Most Sports Blacked Out."

42. Red Smith, "Carnival," *New York Herald Tribune*, 25 November 1963, sec. 4.

43. Smith, "De Gustibus."

44. Smith, "De Gustibus."

45. Ziff, "And They Came Out."

46. Daley, "A Strange Afternoon."

47. Daley, "A Strange Afternoon."

48. Abramson, "Army, Navy Squads Drill; For Nothing."

49. It may not have been a coincidence. The postponement of the Army–Navy game to this date may have been intentional and a product of Robert McNamara's desire to present the Kennedy administration, at the beginning of the Vietnam conflict, as fighting a war with the clean, moral decisions that presented themselves in the World War before it. Abramson, for instance, noted that the decision to play the game on that date "may have" been influenced by the White House and Secretary of Defense Robert McNamara.

50. Abramson, "Army, Navy Squads Drill; For Nothing." Later, Abramson would write that the Kennedy family requested the Army–Navy game take place, offering yet another connection of Kennedy, nation, and sport. Finally, it was the Secretary of the Army, Abramson recorded, who asserted that the game would be dedicated to the president's memory.

51. Abramson, "Army, Navy Squads Drill; For Nothing."

52. Abramson, "Army, Navy Squads Drill; For Nothing."

53. Leonard Koppett, "Decision Is Made by the Pentagon," *The New York Times*, 27 November 1963, sec. L.

54. Arthur Daley, "Philadelphia Thriller," *The New York Times*, 8 December 1963, sec. L.

55. Ziff, "And They Came Out."

56. See Arthur Daley, "A Strange Afternoon"; Allison Danzig, "Service Game Fitting Climax to Surprising Year," *The New York Times*, 9 December 1963, 50; Arthur Daley, "The Cotton Pickers," *The New York Times*, 1 January 1964; Jim Murray, "To Rule or Serve," *Los Angeles Times*, 3 January 1964, sec. B.

57. Daley, "Sunk Without a Trace."

58. Among the superstars who supported the civil rights movement were Bill Russell of the Boston Celtics, David Meggysey of the Saint Louis Cardinals, Jim Brown of the Cleveland Browns, Curt Flood of the St. Louis Cardinals, and many more.

59. Farber, *The Age of Great Dreams*, 89.

60. Farber, *The Age of Great Dreams*, 48.

61. George Lipsitz, *American Studies in a Moment of Danger* (Minneapolis: University of Minnesota Press, 2001), 61.

62. George Lipsitz, *American Studies in a Moment of Danger*, 64.

TWO

White National Tragedies

On December 16, 1967, Robert Lipsyte of the *New York Times* published a column in which he wrote of a press conference attended by Professor Harry Edwards and Dr. Martin Luther King Jr. During that conference Edwards and King linked sports to their civil rights agenda. Edwards argued that white Americans were generally oblivious to the oppression that inaction toward social justice implicitly accepted and perpetuated. In the context of the Vietnam War, Edwards argued that sport was the single site that had the potential to wake moderate white Americans up to the racist structures in the county and how they manifest in disproportionate numbers of African Americans dying in combat: "the Negro loves his country, fights for it in [the Vietnam] war. The tragedy here is that the country the Negro loves doesn't love him back."[1]

Herein, Edwards and King defined the systemic racial and classed oppression of African Americans as a tragedy of national proportions. In the process, they established sport as a vehicle through which to assert black masculinity.[2]

Through 1967 and up until his assassination in 1968, King was overtly critical of President Lyndon Johnson's policies regarding the Vietnam War, arguing that they were obstacles to racial equality. Four months after his press conference with Edwards, King pointed out that the war effort was "taking the young black men who have been crippled by our society and sending them 8,000 miles away to guarantee liberties in Southeast Asia which they had not found in southwest Georgia and East Harlem."[3] Exactly one year later, James Earl Ray gunned Martin Luther King Jr. down.

COLORBLIND NATION

A confluence of events, all associated with King's assassination, necessitated that Major League Baseball postpone its opening day scheduled for
April 8, 1968. First, upon hearing of Martin Luther King Jr.'s assassination, President Johnson called for a national day of mourning to be observed on Sunday, April 7, 1968. In his decree, he placed the onus of
racial oppression on white moderates, claiming that oppression was a
result of "inaction, of indifference, of injustice."[4] Second, Dr. King's funeral services took place on Tuesday, April 9, 1968. Hence, many baseball
players and officials wanted to wait to begin the season until after the
funeral services. Third, in many cities such as Baltimore, Washington,
D.C., Chicago, and New York, race riots broke out and necessitated that
the games be postponed.

Especially in the cities in which riots erupted, columnists constructed
the postponement and resumption of the season as meaningful to the
national recovery from tragedy. Bob Addie, who wrote for the *Washington Post* and *The Sporting News,* fulfilled the convention in the discourse of
tragedy that argues the nation is healed through sport. He wrote that
baseball provided a chance to "get back to the ordinary things of life . . . a
touch of normalcy . . . we all need so desperately."[5] Ironically, the "normal" condition of the nation was the problem and in fact the tragedy,
according to Drs. King and Edwards. The columnists also implicitly denied the existence of the ongoing, systemic oppression that Edwards,
King, and Johnson underscored as racist. That is, sport served the mythological function of presenting the nation as recovered from the tragedy
when in fact the nation was clearly plagued by the tragedy of racial
oppression.[6]

Moreover, prior to opening day, President Johnson made it clear that
his attendance at opening day in Washington, D.C., was in question. In a
column pondering who would toss out the ceremonial first pitch in Johnson's absence, Povich suggested that whoever did would offer a delivery:

> from the din of new words like reassess and divisiveness that have
> come into the language . . . [T]he charm of baseball is that everybody
> knows what it is all about. Every boy or girl who has ever caught a ball
> or bounced one has almost complete understanding of the American
> game . . . The ceremonial openers in baseball are a reminder that base-
> ball is the national pastime . . . It isn't certain if President Johnson or
> even Vice President Humphrey will throw out the first pitch because of
> other affairs. But that won't make much of a difference.[7]

Here, Povich established baseball and the ceremonial pitch as uniquely
American and capable of uniting everyone despite national, racial divi-
siveness. Such constructions of national unity developed through sport
served those privileged by race and solved the nation's racial problems

by simply ignoring their existence. Despite King's association of sport to his civil rights agenda, these columnists used his assassination and the resumption of sport after it to construct their nations as democratic. Given that the assassination of a race leader was the very impetus for emphasizing the game as significant, such rhetoric was especially ironic.

In a later column, Povich sought to praise American patriotism while denying the structural racism that led to the civil rights movement, King's assassination, and the riots that followed: He wrote that "in Washington, particularly, the opening game is an emotional affair, not merely because of the flourishing and ruffles that greet the Chief Executive and the bunting that may evoke a new flush of patriotism."[8] In this "new flush of patriotism" Povich implied a desire to turn what little focus there was on the assassination and riots to baseball and its connection with the nation-state's officials. The patriotism was for a nation privileged by race. That is, black and brown individuals would not likely view the American country—and so be patriotic—in the same way as their white counterparts. With the resumption of sport, the problems sports columnists wrote of were limited to the games. And the problems of racism and poverty that King identified as nationally tragic were altogether ignored in columns that were at the very least tangentially related to King's assassination. Hence, King's assassination was considered nationally significant to these columnists, but only on the condition that sport could heal the wounds of the nation through a simple turn away from them.

Moreover, a year prior to his death, King openly criticized President Johnson's allocation of funds and administrative attention to the Vietnam War as a major obstacle to the civil rights movement. King said the war was "playing such havoc with our domestic programs that [he was] forced into opposing it."[9] He continued to suggest that the war's funding was detracting from solving the fundamental "economic problems" facing African Americans and he promised to demonstrate to "expose the problems of the ghettos" as he openly opposed the War.[10] When riots tore through some of the very cities that King hoped to expose the poverty of through his demonstrations (namely Baltimore, Washington D.C., and Chicago) games were postponed.

Few columnists explained the reasoning behind these riots or the poverty that King worked to expose during his life. But they implicitly if not overtly endorsed Johnson's approach to the war in the context of King's assassination. For instance, Povich wrote that "President Johnson did not report to D.C. Stadium or the opening game, apparently giving priority to Ho Chi Minh, one of his newer and more pressing interests."[11] Despite Povich's suggestion that the nation was healing from the assassination of King, he avoided discussion of civil rights and their connection to the Vietnam War. He did so while underscoring the attention Johnson paid to that same war. He thus implicitly endorsed Johnson's approach to the Vietnam War. Povich continued and characterized the season opener as an end to violence: "the only violence is involved with the bat, against the cured and whitened hides of long-dead horses."[12] Hence, sport served Povich's nation by presenting it and its war as void of violence—racial or that in Vietnam. And later, after the game, Addie led another column by writing "Vice President Humphrey came out of the Presidential box at D.C. Stadium yesterday."[13] He finally expressed regret not at the assassination or riots or the reasons behind them, but that the president did not attend the game. In this way, sport served to remember King as an icon, but avoided his politics. Columnists also implicitly supported the war in Vietnam, to which King was overtly opposed. They did so by avoiding discussion of the ongoing violence in the nation associated with racial oppression, riots, and war. As such these columns used King as a figure to construct a democratic and just nation at war with an evil foe. They did this while denying the existence of the systemic oppression King fought against. In short, just as was the case with President Kennedy's assassination, here sports columnists used sport to tout a national identity of strength and justice even as inequality was clearly existent beyond sport.

Columnists also used their own memories of past opening days to construct a national identity that was implicitly mythological, white, and strong in war. In a column that appeared the day of the opener, Addie used memories of Presidents Kennedy, Eisenhower, and Johnson to discuss the service sport would pay to a nation experiencing tragedy. Addie recollected the strength of each man's throwing arm:

> Mr. Kennedy had a good arm. He threw with grace and form . . . President Johnson has a good arm. . . . Last year he threw four balls, which seems like a bit much even for the Great Society . . . Ike, of course, was no green pea with a baseball . . . General Eisenhower prided himself on baseball knowledge.[14]

Here, Addie created a mythological nation using baseball and its connection to Presidential ceremonies and the military as a means to do so. Similarly, Povich wrote "nice things could happen to a lesser light in government, like who gets to throw out the first ball. Back in 1917, an assistant secretary of the Navy did the honors. F. D. Roosevelt later was elected president of the United States four times."[15] In the same way that Jack Mann of *The New York Herald Tribune* created an elegiac myth of national strength and virility in 1963 by substituting the deceased Kennedy with the new President Johnson, Addie and Povich used the memory of white, male war heroes and presidents with which to substitute the deceased King. Through memory, politicians were made into athletes, and the nation constructed through them was strong and, ironically, white. That is, these games, meant to memorialize a race hero who opposed war, focused on white war heroes to "heal" the wounds of these columnists' versions of national identity. Moreover, prowess in war was championed over national policy regarding the civil rights movement.

These columnists writing of presidential ceremonies and the military complex in columns proclaiming to be about King were engaged in the form of nation that Lauren Berlant identified as problematic in *The Queen of America Goes to Washington City*. Such representations of nation constructed national identity in the absence of minorities while also proclaiming the nation to have untied after racial riots. Hence, these columns presenting the nation as racially united were ones of and privileging whiteness.

Some columnists, however, did write about the civil rights movement while using their memories of black males to do so. For example, Arthur Daley of the *New York Times* suggested King's assassination measured on the same scale as President Kennedy's assassination.[16] He then remembered and hailed Branch Rickey's selection of Jackie Robinson, a former World War II soldier, as the first black player in modern era Major League Baseball. He suggested that in times like racial assassinations and riots "a bow should be made to [Rickey,] the man who gave baseball the push supplying one irrevocable impetus."[17] Daley's focus on Rickey rather than Robinson or King, though, solidified a white point of view toward black masculinity's place in sport and the nation. Specifically, black males were allowed entrance into these columns only if granted entrance by a white male; only if the white male was made to be the hero. Daley, however, did not link sports to the world outside the stadium. He actually resisted the conventional rhetoric of tragedy and criticized the nation's approach to race relations in the process.

He overtly constructed sport as serving an example of how the nation could achieve equality. He wrote that "in sports the Negro gained the integration denied him elsewhere . . . The world of sports has not completed the job of integration, but it has made further advances than most segments of American life in approaching the still unrealized dream of Dr. Martin Luther King Jr."[18] He further wrote that there was a general "reluctance of the Negroes to believe everything they read in the white man's newspaper" except in the sports pages.[19] Hence, Daley argued that integration was not complete, and established sport as having progressed where other professional and social spheres in American had not. The implication was that blacks were offered agency in sports and its media. Daley also confronted the idea of national democracy being achieved and suggested that the limited democracy of sport was closer to achieving democracy than the nation itself.[20] In short, his column was quite critical of the current condition of racial oppression. Unlike his counterparts, then, Daley engaged in the same sort of argument Prof. Edwards and Dr. King desired. He criticized the nation's inequity in the sports pages—a sports page that reached white viewers because it was in the sort of media they consumed.

Daley was not alone in using Robinson and sport to construct a racially just nation through sport, however. Four months after King was assassinated, Robert Fitzgerald Kennedy was gunned down in California by Sirhan Sirhan. By then, Kennedy had already established his support for the civil rights movement and like King and Edwards, intertwined sports with race in an effort to draw whites' attention to their privilege. Like King, Edwards, and President Johnson, Robert Kennedy argued that "there is another kind of violence, slower, but just as deadly. This is the violence of institutional indifference and inattention and slow decay."[21] Again, columnists wrote of sport's service to the nation in the wake of this assassination, but avoided discussion of the structural racism that Robert Kennedy himself labeled as violent. This despite Kennedy and King's linking race and sports.

Specifically, Addie called Robert Kennedy's assassination a "tragedy" and wrote that "the late Sen. Kennedy belonged as much to the sports scene as he did to the political scene."[22] He then suggested that Jackie Robinson could be a seamless substitute for Robert Kennedy in the Senate. "Jackie Robinson, former Brooklyn Dodger . . . is among those being considered by New York Gov., Nelson Rockefeller, to fill the U.S. Senate vacancy caused by the death of Sen. Robert F. Kennedy."[23] Dave Brady of the *Washington Post* chronicled the role Rosey Grier, a Los Angeles Rams defensive tackle, played in wresting a gun from Robert Kennedy's assassin. He then wrote that "even before Kennedy had entered the race for the Democratic presidential nomination, Grier served at functions with which the Senator was associated."[24] These sports columnists remembered Robert Kennedy as a friend to sport and also suggested that sports figures themselves were friends and capable of entering the political sphere. In mentioning Grier and Robinson, too, these columnists implicitly represented their nations as democratic and racially just by introducing black athletes into the political sphere. However, they presented that political sphere and their versions of national identity to be quite like the sporting arena: black masculinity was represented, but only in one dimension, one that paid a service to a racially just nation, and where racial discord was not a reality.

Likewise, columnists throughout the nation used their memories of Robert Kennedy to construct athletes and political figures as part of "the American family"; a construct that itself was racialized and masculine. Ross Newhan of the *Los Angeles Times* remembered Robert Kennedy through the tragedy of his brother's assassination.[25] He remembered Robert Kennedy as a "man, like his brother, for all seasons," and then chronicled all of the sports he played.[26] Dave Brady of the *Washington Post* underscored Robert Kennedy's association with Don Drysdale and George Plimpton, sports figures themselves. Steve Cady of the *New York Times* wrote that Robert Kennedy's assassination was the second time in two months that "large segments of the sports world w[ould] call time out . . . for a slain national leader."[27] He led his column by writing of how John Glenn played touch football with Robert Kennedy's son David the day after his death.[28] He then chronicled the many pro football players, national politicians, and Army officials that played touch football on the White House lawn with Robert Kennedy. The column culminated when he quoted Sam Huff of the Washington Redskins as saying "this is a terrible thing, like the death of a member of the family."[29] Daley wrote of Rusty Staub and Bob Aspromonte's refusal to play the day of Robert Kennedy's services and argued that "less than two months earlier they went through similar shock, the assassination of Martin Luther King, Jr."[30] He continued to write:

> insubordination on the part of a player is a violation of his contract and lays him open to penalty. But these were unusual circumstances. They almost would seem to call for the same understanding that would normally be forthcoming if it had been the death of a close relation. Millions regarded Bobby Kennedy in that light.[31]

These columnists constructed Kennedy as sports-loving and part of the "American" family. More specifically, in the context of the Vietnam War and civil rights movement these columnists represented the nation in similar ways as they had in the aftermath of President Kennedy's assassination: when a young, virile, white, athletic politician died, it was, to these columnists, a national tragedy.[32]

All of these columnists used sport to construct mythological nations in the context of tragedy. These nations were white and/or predicated on entrance of a particular form of black masculinity into their nations. They also used the construct of the family to establish white males as central to their national identity.

Finally, these columnists labeled violent acts tragedies only if they were constructed as single events, like an assassination or riot. The term tragedy, however, was not reserved for ongoing cyclical oppression in the nation that Edwards labeled tragic and President Johnson and Robert Kennedy labeled as violent. These same oppressions kept raced, gendered, and sexed identities from getting jobs working for mainstream sports pages. Those benefitting from structural racism were also those defining tragedy and subsequently constructing national identity. Generally, tragedies could only happen to a nation capable of healing or returning to normalcy through sport. The nation constructed in these columns was one that tautologically constructed national identity in ways that did not challenge the structures that privileged whites because, in part, those constructing it were white.

AMERICAN RELIGIONS

Fully aware of the mythological nation mainstream media constructed through sport and its representation of black masculinity, Harry Edwards, in organizing a protest at the 1968 Olympics, said that "if there is a religion in this country, it is athletics."[33] In an attempt to shatter the mainstream media's mythological construction of national identity, Edwards organized many black athletes who were competing in the 1968 Olympics in a protest, with the hope of "affect[ing] . . . a substantial portion of the country in the stadium or in front of the television. We want to get to those people, to affect them, to wake them up to what's happening in this country, because otherwise they won't care."[34] His goal was, in short, to resist the way in which black masculinity in sport was often used to represent a democratic and racially just nation. His strategy for doing so was to use a forum that already attracted whites' attention toward black males, sport. The most significant event that columnists wrote of regarding Edward's activist intentions occurred when, in Mexico City, two black Olympians, Tommie Smith and John Carlos, thrust their fists high in the air against the backdrop of the American flag and the national anthem. What was unique about Smith and Carlos's protest was that it was made by athletes on the field of play, not political leaders associated with sport. Hence, columnists had no choice but to write about the protest in terms of black masculinity and its relationship to the mythological construction of national identity that sport historically served and that privileged whiteness.

However, the protest was not just about American race relations. It was also about America's role in the global community. For instance, the men's protest was a climactic moment in African American athletes' year-long threat to boycott the Olympic Games if South Africa, with its state-legislated policy of apartheid, was allowed to participate. And by the time the protest took place, Smith and Carlos extended their political motives to include global racism. Many columnists, however, forced their stories of Carlos and Smith into the frame of American equality.[35]

For instance, Red Smith of the *New York Times* conflated Smith and Carlos's protest with the civil rights movement, thereby limiting its motives to American race relations. He wrote that the raised fists were a gesture meaning "we shall overcome" and then condemned the act for taking place at an inappropriate time.[36] Likewise, Povich's first column about the protest connected it to the civil rights movement in America, despite that the athletes' project was global in nature. Although Povich's defense of the athletes is reflective of a commendable point of view, Povich's narrative limited the controversy of the protest to its appropriateness. He wrote that Smith and Carlos

> did not disrupt any Olympic event by their actions on the ceremonial stand. Their sin was a technical one. . . . If it was unpatriotic in the view of most observers, the courage and dignity of their revolt gesture was inescapable. . . . Even those who would deplore the time and place of their demonstration will concede that a right of protest was theirs.

Passage of the Civil Rights Acts by Congress affirmed the Negroes' complaint of 300 years.[37]

Clearly, Povich's column supports Smith and Carlos's right to expression and racial progress in general. Despite this support, Smith and Povich wrote of the single event—the athletes raising their fists—as if it, not the structural oppression, sparked the protest and was the controversy. Again in this way, tragedy and controversies were single events, not systemic oppressions.

In a later column, Povich adopted a standpoint that characterized many of his counterparts' approach to the protest. Povich contrasted Carlos and Smith with black males who adopted stances toward America that resembled Jessie Owens's; stances Povich had established as patriotic. He wrote that "America's boxing-basketball Negroes appear a different breed than the raging militants on the track team."[38] Povich categorized African American males of the "boxing and basketball" and the "track and field" teams by behavior. Other columnists extended on the categories of which Povich wrote. Cady marginalized Smith and Carlos by juxtaposing them with Owens. He wrote that Owens, "Working for the Mutual Broadcasting System said that he had been disturbed by the boycotts. "[39] Similarly, Neil Amdur of the *New York Times* wrote of Bobby Douglass, a black wrestler, by implying that black males should be quiet and passive. Amdur quoted Douglass as saying, "'I want to prove that Prof. Harry Edwards is wrong. I want to prove that I can do more by competing than by sitting on the sidelines yelling black power.'"[40] He established that black athletes should be represented, but not heard, on the field. Similarly, Daley championed George Foreman for his patriotism and by implication condemned Carlos and Smith for their protest.[41] These columnists, then, categorized black people who did not confront or protest oppression as "American," and the act in which Smith and Carlos engaged as inappropriate and unworthy of further examination. In this way, black athletes on the field of play allowed columnists to argue the country was democratic while disciplining those black men who challenged the virile, strong, and white nation historically supported through sport.

Columnists eventually vilified Carlos and Smith for behavior they deemed unpatriotic and/or raised the protest to the level of national tragedy. For example, Povich criticized the shock the protest catalyzed, but did not examine the reasons for the protest. "The shock at the actions of Smith and Carlos was great, but the surprise needn't have been. . . . [They] gave advanced warning that they were unreliable . . . [because] they fail[ed] . . . to respect the American flag and the National Anthem."[42] Again defending their right to free speech, but reprimanding their use of it, Povich wrote that the athletes were "unpatriotic" but also "courag[eous]."[43] William Carsley of the *Chicago Tribune* wrote that the event was tragic because "Smith and Carlos, who obviously achieved no satisfaction from competing for their country, occupied places on the United States team that could have gone to athletes who care"; meaning athletes who would not speak out against the nation.[44] He wrote that the two "perform[ed] like a pair of boorish refugees from a motorcycle gang" and further vilified both for their seeming lack of patriotism.[45] Daley further criticized the protest because it occurred "where it did not belong and created a shattering situation that shook this international sports carnival to its very core. It was also divisive."[46] Of course, the act itself was not divisive; it only drew attention to the actual conditions of the nation and globe that was divided. And the reason people argued the protest did not belong on the field of play was that sport had established its normal condition as one that denied the social realities of oppression, despite that many of the athletes in the sporting world were victims of this very oppression. Perhaps better stated: because the protest happened on the field of play, the rhetoric of a return to normalcy could not be used. By protesting on the field of play, Smith and Carlos drew attention to the fact that normalcy was indeed the problem. Addie condoned the comparison in mainstream media at the time between the protest and Nazis. He wrote that:

> There has been a parallel suggested between the snub of Owens by Adolph Hitler . . . and the two current athletes. . . . The shock came not that the two angry young men had a right to protest, but at the stage they used for their theatrical performance, which was embarrassing to the United States. Some of us are getting too old to think of somebody tearing up the Constitution or spitting on the flag—else what would happen to such stirring moments in our history as the flag raised at Iwo Jima?[47]

Here, Addie used the memory of Owens competing at the Olympics for America and another memory of World War II to prove Smith and Carlos's lack of patriotism. Whereas Owens was a black American who proved American superiority over an enemy in terms of athletic prowess and in the context of war, Smith and Carlos drew attention to the white nation's lack of morality in terms of its approach to race, also in the context of war. The difference between Owens's protest and Carlos and Smith's, however, was that Owens's protest was in the name of American patriotism in the context of a war generally accepted as morally just. In contrast, Carlos and Smith protested American participation in global oppression. In short, black athletes who supported the American nation were welcomed into the American family while those who did not were not. Smith and Carlos, not racial oppression, were constructed as national embarrassments.

Povich even revealed an ideological connection between disdain for the sprinters and support for the war. He reported that U.S. Olympians on the shooting team hung signs out of a window in their dorm that supported the International Olympic Committee's decision to kick "the two sprinters out of Olympic Village and off the American team . . . [They also hung a sign to] win the war in Vietnam."[48] Whereas Edwards and King linked assertions of black masculinity to sport and the resistance of the Vietnam War, the mainstream sport media was certain to vilify black Americans who protested that war. Likewise, sports columnists did not tolerate any questioning of the nation, either in its approach to race or the Vietnam War. As was the case with the two assassinations, then, mainstream columnists generally constructed this single moment, the protest, a tragedy. In the process, they refused to draw attention to the cyclical, long-standing and structural oppressions within and beyond the nation-state that these athletes were attempting to expose and that Edwards, King, Kennedy, and Johnson labeled tragedies themselves.

Columnists situated black masculinity in their versions of national identity by opining of athletes' standpoints regarding Vietnam prior to the 1968 Olympics, however. Just a year earlier, for instance, Muhammad Ali refused to enlist in the Army after being drafted. One of the many reasons Ali cited for refusing to enlist was the racial imbalance of power in both the nation and the war. Two days prior to his official refusal to enlist, Ali said:

> You want me to do what the white man says and go and fight a war against some people I don't know nothing about—get some freedom for some other people when my own people can't get theirs here? You want me to be so scared of the white man that I'll go and get two arms shot off and ten medals so you can give me a small salary and pat me on the head and say "good boy, he fought for his country?"[49]

Hence, Ali established his refusal to join the war as a resistance of what he perceived to be a white power structure. He also suggested that his refusal to enlist was a choice that asserted his humanity and opposed the passive role whites generally required of their black male athletes or "good boys."

Inevitably, columnists established Ali's stance as un-American, as it did not conform to the role of the passive or patriotic black male. Sid Ziff of the *Los Angeles Times* contrasted Ali's approach to Vietnam with Floyd Patterson's, implying that Patterson's desire to enlist in the Army was more admirable.[50] In a later column, he wrote that "Ali could have avoided all of his draft troubles by enlisting in the reserves . . . he would be [rich and] carefree as a lark."[51] Ziff limited the discussion of Ali's objection to Vietnam to financial matters, never broaching the issue of structural injustice or the War itself. He also, by implication, approved of black males supporting the nation and its war, while disdaining those drawing attention to its racial problems.

It was again Daley who took a different approach than his counter-parts. He made clear the connection he saw between sport, national iden-tity, and memory:

> Yet a couple of memories keep intruding on that jarring supposition, flashbacks to the games at Rome in the 1960 Olympics. It's always an emotional moment when an Olympic champion stands on the topmost part of the three-part pedestal and the flag of his country rises on the center staff while the band plays his country's national anthem. . . . None stood at attention with more pride than Cassius Marcellus Clay. Sure he had won for himself, but he had also won for his country. Even when he returned to the States he went wandering around Times Square in his pullover uniform with USA lettered across his chest. He was proud to wear it and to show it off. . . . That's why there's a tragic feeling here. . . . Actually, it's a greater offshoot of the tragedy of Viet-nam.[52]

Here Daley argued that Ali's decision in 1967 to object to the war tar-nished his own memory of Ali's 1960 Olympic win. For Daley, though, the tragedy was not in Ali's refusal to enlist. Rather, it was the war and its tactical and racial problems that underpinned Ali's decision. Daley even rejected Floyd Patterson's categorization of Ali as un-American. He quoted Ali saying, "Floyd says he's gonna bring the title back to America. If you don't believe the title is already in America, just look at who I pay taxes to."[53]

As a solution to this problematic construction of the games, and in contrast to his counterparts' vilification of Smith and Carlos, Lipsyte underscored the motives behind the protest, even more so than Daley did. He mentioned that the Olympics took place in the context of contro-versy—that of the "murderous snuffing-out of Mexican student riot-ing . . . and the admission of South Africa" to compete despite its policies of apartheid. Both, he argued, were examples of deplorable actions gen-erally ignored by the mainstream sport media.[54] Whereas his counter-parts generally wrote of the controversy and the protest to be about its appropriateness, Lipsyte illustrated that the controversial protest oc-curred because racism and poverty were global and national problems.

Similarly, in the context of King's assassination and its potential effect on the 1968 Olympics, Lipsyte suggested American policy toward race had an effect globally. The common link between the assassination and the potential boycott of the Olympics, Lipsyte allegorically argued, was that both offered evidence that racism does not know national borders. According to Lipsyte, in not pressuring South Africa to halt its apartheid policies, the American political system tacitly endorsed them, and there-by also supported and was part of a globalized form of racism. Here, Lipsyte illustrated that violence was not a single act, but systemic and ongoing as a result of general complacency in the policies of America. In the process, he illustrated that nations' borders do not limit the reach of their racial policies.[55] This insight underpinned his writing about Ali as well. Lipsyte's work through 1968 could be summarized in a quote from Ali that served as the title of Lipsyte's culminating piece on the champ:

> On February 26, 1964, Ali first confirmed the rumor of his membership [of the Nation of Islam] by repeating that parable to a shocked and angry white press. Clay turned back their arguments with a soft and deadly "I don't want to be what you want me to be I'm free to be who I want."[56]

The column continued to chronicle Ali's criticism of the racial imbalance in the Vietnam War and at home. Hence, throughout the late 1960s, Lipsyte implicitly criticized the notion that athletes and black males in general were expected to submit to a preconceived stereotype of patriotic athlete.[57] Lipsyte even implicitly criticized officials in the nation-state who attempted to discipline black athletes for not conforming to that patriotic stereotype. Implying the same hypocrisy in then-Governor Ronald Reagan of California, Lipsyte wrote that "Edwards' activism . . . has brought . . . a demand by Governor Ronald Reagan that Edwards be dismissed from his" professorship at San Jose State College.[58]

Ultimately, then, when athletes challenged the nation-state, columnists wrote of their acts in one of three ways. One was to avoid discussion of the racial oppression by focusing on sport's ability to return a nation to normalcy. The other was to label black males' acts of protests tragic, un-American, or some other such derivation. This approach, however, denied the tragedy of systemic oppression in the nation. The final, least used, was to allow athletes who protested American oppression into their versions of "American" and thereby challenge the current condition of racial and political privilege. Hence, all of these columnists were commenting on national identity and providing potential for readers to change or reinforce their beliefs regarding race and the war. Twenty years later, however, a black male who had been accepted as a member of the "American family" contracted HIV, a disease that had been associated with gay identities; gay identities who had been stigmatized in mainstream media and culture. Mainstream sports columnists, as a result, had to negotiate between the mythological and pathological as they wrote of Ervin "Magic" Johnson.

THE ALL-AMERICAN FAMILY

In his "Proclamation of AIDS Awareness Month," President Ronald Reagan said "both medicine and morality teach the same lesson of AIDS . . . the best way to prevent AIDS is to abstain from sexual activity until adulthood and restrict sex to a monogamous, faithful relationship . . . [and to know] the blessings of stable family life."[59] In *The Queen of Ameri-*

ca Goes to Washington City, Lauren Berlant identified the Reagan administration and mainstream media as fundamental in reducing political rhetoric of the 1980s and 1990s to consist of topics associated with private life.
According to Berlant, politicians and mainstream media referred to sexual practices, family values, and moral character, rather than policies and
deeds in determining who would be considered "American."[60] Berlant
also suggested that this connection of sexuality with morality defined
American identity narrowly.[61]

However, on November 7, 1991, Magic Johnson announced that he
had contracted HIV, and for columnists, this did change their meaning of
"American."

When Magic contracted HIV, he was a young, masculine figure associated with sport; much like Robert Kennedy. As a result, he was, as
Thomas Boswell of the *Washington Post* put it, "a part of almost every
American family. And, now, we can't get him out of the family. He's
everybody's brother or son who may get AIDS."[62] In an era characterized
by political rhetoric calling forth family values, and in sports pages that
had a history of constructing the family as central to their nations, such a
statement held further significance than may first appear on the surface.
Citizenship was being redefined, as a member of the sexually moral
"family" contracted HIV. Hence, sports columnists would not redefine
black masculinity or the construct of the family through Magic. Rather,
sports columnists' nations and their relationship to HIV/AIDS would be
redefined as a member of their national family and democratic nation
had contracted HIV/AIDS.

For example, Alison Muscatine of the *Washington Post* placed Magic's
infection in the realm of national tragedy and in the process also constructed HIV and AIDS as an issue for her national identity. She wrote
that sport was central to the manner in which nation was imagined:
"Tragedies that befall athletes seem to penetrate the American consciousness more than any others, unleashing a wave of emotion and shock that
crosses class, race, gender and generational lines. Most people, it seems,
know and love Magic. Now, it seems, most people are worried about
him."[63] Muscatine was involved in a definition of citizenship, claiming
"most people" cared about Magic. But Muscatine separated HIV/AIDS
from homosexuality. There was no mention of homosexuality in the categories of people to whom sport news transcended despite that she was
writing of HIV/AIDS in the early 1990s. Hence, the people comprising
"most people" in her nation were assumed to be heterosexual; Magic's
contraction was a tragedy of national proportions because a major,
heterosexual figure contracted HIV.

Bob Verdi of the *Chicago Tribune* wrote:

> Magic was special, Magic is special, and that explains why the world
> grieves at his crisis. That is why President Bush sends prayers from

Rome, that is why Dan Rather's news program begins with the press conference at the Great Western Forum, that is why kids whom Magic touched without ever patting their heads or shaking their hands dribble in gymnasiums now with no particular energy or direction.

Verdi associated the virus with national officials and mainstream media figures who shaped and were part of the mainstream versions of national identity. Hence, HIV/AIDS, through Magic's body, was entering the mainstream's version of national identity.[64] Mike Conklin of the *Chicago Tribune* established Magic in national mythology through referencing Reagan's role in *Knute Rockne All-American:*

> Maybe the earliest, most publicized example of an athlete battling disease was George Gipp, the Notre Dame football player who was injured in his final season with the Fighting Irish, developed pneumonia, and died in 1920 at age 25. Coach Knute Rockne's "win one for the Gipper" speech would become a legend, enhanced later in the movies.[65]

Conklin placed Magic in the same mythological narrative line as both Reagan, who played Gipp, and the All-American young athlete who tragically dies too early.[66] Finally, Tony Kornheiser of the *Washington Post* communicated Magic's contraction of HIV/AIDS by referring to a cultural memory sports columnists had set in their mythological national identity of masculinity: "I felt the same stunned reaction that I remembered having 28 years before, when I was in a seventh-period math class, and word of John Kennedy's assassination spread through the school like a bad dream."[67] Magic was already being constructed as a young, virile, male figure hero who would die too early. He was, in short, set in similar narrative lines as both Kennedys were after their assassinations; or in the Gipp, a sports figure, now associated with Reagan, who met an early death.

In columns like Boswell, Verdi, Muscatine, and Conklin's, HIV/AIDS was allowed in their nations, but only on the condition that the sexual norms of the All-American family would not be challenged. Black males were used to support the myth of equality and assumed to be heterosexual. These columnists limited the tragedy to be about Magic's contraction, rather than the epidemic of HIV/AIDS or Reagan's general neglect of it: By 1985, Reagan had yet to mention HIV/AIDS in any speech. By that date, nearly 15,000 Americans had died; most of them were homosexual.[68] Moreover, these columnists who limited the tragedy included a woman, Muscatine. Throughout her career, Muscatine had a close connection to official rhetoric of the nation. In 1993, Muscatine joined President William Jefferson Clinton's White House, which accepted Congress' Don't Ask, Don't Tell policy, one that continued the closeting of gay people.[69] Hence, her gender and sex did not equate to a resistance of rigid definitions of national identity that historically oppressed homosexuality. The mythology of sport and its connection to a similar national identity, in short, affects and is affected by people other than those white males who are often privileged by both.

But Muscatine was not the only minority columnist who defined black masculinity rigidly despite not being white. For instance, Michael Wilbon, a black columnist of the *Washington Post* who generally adopts a liberal standpoint in his work, wrote that "Magic became angered at one newspaper column that cited the incredibly low percentage of men who become infected by women."[70] Wilbon continued to establish Johnson and NBA athletes as heterosexual and justified in promiscuity. Wilbon wrote on November 10, 1991, that:

> If you've ever left an NBA arena late, real late, say an hour after the game is over, or followed a team back to the hotel and seen the literally dozens of women waiting outside both locker rooms, you understand that players don't have to go looking for sex; it's staring most of them in the face. Not only is it not easy to say no, it's almost impossible. To abstain, we're talking about a level of self-control that I, certainly, for one, would not have under similar circumstances.[71]

Wilbon implied that male athletes were powerless to the wiles of women. Wilbon also wrote that if Magic proclaimed he was heterosexual that that was good enough for to him believe it and so limited discussion of HIV/ AIDS to heterosexual terms. As a result, Wilbon established blackness in narrow, heterosexual terms. The notion that black writers would establish black masculinity in more diverse terms than white ones, then, was not proven through Wilbon's columns on Magic.

In fact, Wilbon's construction of black masculinity resembled many of his counterpart white columnists': Dave Anderson limited his concern about HIV to heterosexuals. He wrote that Magic:

> has been labeled by many as a "hero" when hedonist might be the better word. . . . While insisting that he has "never had a homosexual relationship" . . . [he also] did "his best to accommodate as many women as [he] could . . ." Anybody with a sense of heterosexual responsibility isn't likely to get the HIV virus.

Anderson, that is, argued that Magic's promiscuity was a problem, but also seemed quite protective of heterosexual (not homosexual) health.[72] Sport served a heterosexual nation and its health concerns.[73] Finally, Jim Murray of the *Los Angeles Times* wrote, "Wait a minute . . . Magic doesn't deserve this . . . [Magic is] not going to let HIV get away with it."[74] Underpinning Murray's assertion was the assumption that Magic's infection was different from that of others, that HIV invaded a place in which it did not belong—Magic's heterosexual body. The tragedy, then, was that HIV invaded a place imagined as American, part of the heterosexual family. The tragedy was not that tens-of-thousands of Americans who happened to be homosexual were dying.

A complex narrative of national identity manifested through sports columnists' writing on Magic Johnson, then. They worked to alter the traditional definition of national identity to include HIV/AIDS. Indeed, they were part of a mainstream media that produced what was later called the "Magic effect"—where HIV clinics across the nation reported a significant increase in testing thousands more heterosexuals within weeks after Magic's press conference. However, they also wrote of HIV/AIDS and black masculinity in rigid fashion.[75] The national identities these columnists constructed were not much more inclusive than those before. Rather, when Magic, a member of the American and "sexually moral" family, contracted the virus generally associated with homosexuality, columnists did not redefine their nations to include homosexual identities. Instead, they redefined their nation to include the imagined possibility of the virus entering heterosexual bodies that were already considered part of the family. And the tragedy was that the virus could now enter the people generally accepted as "American," and not that homosexuals were already dying in the thousands. Moreover, the minority columnists cited in this section did not challenge the historic heteronormativity of sports pages as they wrote of Magic. This illustrated that nonwhites and women may yet construct "Americanness" in a way that lacks diversity, especially if they do not see the intersectional nature of identity: even though Muscatine is a woman and Wilbon black, they are both heterosexuals, and so in writing of HIV/AIDS, may have done so from their own experiences, experiences that melded with mainstream America's heteronormative approach to identity. Likewise, the inclusion of minority identities in sports pages does not necessarily equate to resistance of white, patriarchal, heteronormative points of view. While inclusion of diverse identities in institutions is quite important, so is inclusion of those with political standpoints that would resist mythologies.

For instance, it was again Lipsyte who challenged the heterosexual assumptions that underpinned mainstream media's writing of Magic's contraction of HIV. He wrote that sports columnists were generally in "an obscene rush to declare [Magic] heterosexual."[76] He wrote that there was no "devil's advocate" in the "media blitz and disappearance of Magic," after his press conference.[77] The whole event, he wrote, seemed like a "Magic Kingdom ride."[78] The reference to and implied criticism of the event and its Disney aesthetics was more critical of mainstream media and conservative officials' conceptions of black masculinity and national identity than may appear on the surface. Sharon Zukin and Douglas Kellner wrote that Disney aesthetics privilege the white, middle-class—identities that Reagan and George Herbert Walker Bush put at the center of their nations through rhetoric of sexual morality and family values.[79] Hence, Lipsyte criticized mainstream media's construction of black masculinity and national identity through Magic as heterosexual. The ramifications of columnists' general heteronormativity should not be overlooked: In "Eloquence and Epitaph" Phillip Brian Harper chronicled news media coverage of news reporter Max Robinson's death resulting from AIDS. Harper explained that political leaders and media outlets spoke of Robinson and AIDS with language that avoided the possibility of a black male homosexual and potentially limited education about the virus.[80] Likewise sports columnists' establishment of Magic's contraction as a national tragedy occurred only as they situated Magic, and so the disease, as heterosexual. Such constructions of Magic, the disease, and the nation marginalized homosexuality and potentially limited education about the virus and its relationship to sexual practices, thereby potentially causing material harm.

LIPSYTE AND DALEY'S RESISTANCE AND SPORT MEDIA

Beginning in the 1960s, and through 2007, Lipsyte and Daley continuously resisted rigid constructions of black masculinity and national identity in which his counterparts engaged. They did this in one of the outlets most responsible for establishing dominant national identities, mainstream sport media. Moreover, they wrote for the *New York Times* sports section, the same outlet for which many of the columnists constructing national identity through rigid definitions of black masculinity worked. They thereby adopted the rhetorical strategy of what George Lipsitz identified as the spider that works within the structures of oppression to use them as means for liberation. This move enables a particular group "to focus attention on the actions of those doing the discriminatings rather than solely on the victims of discrimination."[81] That is, their work potentially reached out to readers who accepted rigid constructions of black masculinity as "normal." In the process, they potentially taught whites the problem with "normal." In the sports pages, then, Lipsyte and Daley potentially performed the work of activists who reach out to people different from them in order to change minds. They, in short, performed the work both Dr. King and Dr. Edwards called for in the press conference cited at the beginning of this chapter.

Likewise, Lipsyte and Daley's careers offer an example regarding the import of studies of sport media: It potentially changes minds that once embraced rigid conceptions of race and national identity. Through teaching of their careers, too, scholars may be able to exert a great amount of power by revealing the problematic connection between sport and national identity that many columnists, even quite liberal ones like Povich, Muscatine, and Wilbon, often make. Lipsyte and Daley, two white, male, heterosexual authors took a more liberal and critical approach to writing about black masculinity than their counterparts had. Their careers thus offer proof that one's race, gender, class, religion, nation, and/or sexuality does not indicate or predict one's values.

NATIONAL MEMORIES

Over time, memories of black males' overt criticism of the nation-state have experienced a sort of shading that presents American inclusion and democracy as having progressed, if not achieved. For instance, the columnists writing of King in this chapter were part of a mainstream media that has held King to the status of national hero. Today, King is remembered as a leader who was embraced throughout his life. But this is misremembering how he was perceived when he was alive. Few columns cited above mentioned King's politics and his continuous criticism of white moderates, the Vietnam War, and/or the white press. But, King appeared on CIA watch lists and was vilified by many whites throughout the 1960s. The Martin Luther King Jr. Memorial makes no mention of King's criticism of the Vietnam War, nor his overt censuring of America. It rather constructs King and his memory as a man committed to hope and peace. While this may indeed capture King's attitude, the way his memory is reframed neglects to confront Americans with the reality of their resistance to King when he was alive. He was, in short, perceived as a threat to the white power structure. However, in these columns he was used to remember the nation as diverse and/or patriotic. Likewise, today he is remembered as having been accepted and embraced by the white public throughout the 1960s.

Similarly, Smith and Carlos's protest has been framed as heroic, brave, and indicative of American civil disobedience. For instance, *Sports Illustrated* and *HBO Films* have recently published or showed memory projects about American sports that tout the protest as a significant moment in national history. Neither project, however, articulated the motives behind the protest. *Sports Illustrated* merely stated that the men "shocked America."[82] This is the extent of the project's story on Carlos and Smith, and it thereby equates shock to activism and heroism without explaining the protest or the structural racism that catalyzed it. In this way, Smith and Carlos have been raised to the level of national heroes in the same way I suggested King has.

Memories of Ali also serve a similar national identity by misremembering the way much of mainstream media and citizens of the nation originally reacted to the boxer. Take, for instance, George Vecsey's construction of a diverse America through Ali's lighting of the ceremonial flame at the 1996 Olympics: "the lighting of the Olympic flame in the heart of Dixie was performed by a man, Muhammad Ali, who had traded his self-styled slave name for a Muslim name, and had somehow emerged from shunned draft dodger to national, as well as global, hero."[83] Vecsey performed the same trick of memory much of mainstream media has with Ali: Holding him up as a hero, and referencing the change in how many perceive him, does not require people to change their stance about black males criticizing the war or race relations. It merely requires people to accept Ali's now-Parkinson-ridden body as part of their national identity. This use of Ali to define the nation as having progressed, however, is a nifty trick of memory that presents a physically and orally weakened Ali as representative of the national identity's inclusive spirit.

Hence, columnists, mainstream media, and many American citizens represented these black males who challenged the nation-state as part of their national identity, but in the process, repressed from memory their overt criticism of these civil rights figures. These memories privilege whiteness. As black males who were once vilified are held up as iconic heroes of the nation, those embracing oppressive ideology do not have to shift their standpoints, although they are assured that their approach to race relations has progressed. Moreover, remembering black males like Smith, Carlos, and Ali as American heroes without placing the way they were initially condemned front and center avoids placing blame on whites for being protective of their privilege in the past. In *Possessive Investment in Whiteness* George Lipsitz wrote that perceiving one's own race as innocent is a power move. Remembering whites' stance toward black males as innocent is a manner in which privilege maintains its power. For again, we learn from our past, unless that past is cleansed of its failures.

NOTES

1. Robert Lipsyte, "Striking Nerves," *New York Times*, 16 December 1967.
2. *New York Times*, "The Draft: Cassius versus the Army," April 30, 1967.
3. Martin Luther King Jr., "Black Soldiers in Vietnam," 4 April 1967, http://www.socialistworker.org/2003-2/464/464_08_BlackAthletes.shtml (4 March 2007).
4. Lyndon Johnson, "Address to the Nation upon Proclaiming a Day of Mourning," 5 April 1968, *American Experience*, http://www.pbs.org/wgbh/amex/presidents/36_l_johnson/psources/ps_mourning.html (20 April, 2007).
5. Bob Addie, "Golden Arms Abound," *Washington Post*, 7 April 1968, sec. E; Bob Addie, "Muted Ceremonies Likely on Tuesday," *Washington Post*, 6 April 1968, sec. E.
6. David Voigt, *America through Baseball* (Burnham Publishing, 1976).
7. Shirley Povich, "This Morning," *Washington Post*, 10 April 1968, sec. D.
8. Povich, "This Morning," *Washington Post*, 10 April 1968, sec. D.
9. Qtd. Associated Press, "Dr. King to Press Anti-War Stand," *New York Times*, 24 March 1967, sec. A
10. Associated Press, "Dr. King to Press Anti-War Stand."
11. Povich, "This Morning," *Washington Post*, 11 April 1968, sec. C.
12. Povich, "This Morning," *Washington Post*, 11 April 1968, sec. C.
13. Bob Addie, "HHH Ignores Protest," *Washington Post*, 11 April 1968, sec. E.
14. Bob Addie, "Opening-Day Memories," *Washington Post*, 10 April 1968, sec. D.
15. Shirley Povich, "This Morning," *Washington Post*, 10 April 1968, sec. D.
16. Arthur Daley, "The Long Season Begins," *New York Times*, 6 April 1968, sec. 5. See Arthur Daley, "Strange Feeling."
17. Daley, "The Long Season Begins," *New York Times*, 6 April 1968, sec. 5. See Arthur Daley, "Strange Feeling."
18. Arthur Daley, "The Trail Blazer," *New York Times*, 9 April 1968, sec. 5.

19. Daley, "The Trail Blazer."

20. As Daley wrote of Robinson in the context of King's assassination, sport was paying a service to his white nation. In "Whose Broad Stripes and Bright Stars," Amy Bass argued that mainstream sports writers of the 1960s used many black athletes to "validate . . . democratic ideals" without drawing attention to the nation's racism that King and Edwards cited at the beginning of this chapter worked to dismantle. Amy Bass, "Whose Broad Stripe and Bright Stars," *Sports Matters*, John Bloom and Michael Willard (New York: New York University Press, 2002) 184–204, 187.

21. Robert Kennedy, "On the Mindless Menace of Violence," *Robert F. Kennedy Memorial*, 4 April 1968, http://www.rfkmemorial.org/lifevision/onthemindlessmenaceofviolence/ (23 March 2006).

22. Bob Addie, "Senatorial Possibility," *Washington Post*, 9 June 1968, sec. C.

23. Addie, "Senatorial Possibility."

24. Dave Brady, "Sport Figures Surrounded RFK," *Washington Post*, 6 June 1968, sec. C.

25. Ross Newhan, "Kennedy Recalled as a Man for All Seasons," *Los Angeles Times*, 7 June 1968, sec. F.

26. Newhan, "Kennedy Recalled as a Man for All Seasons."

27. Steve Cady, "Many Sports Events This Weekend Put Off in Respect to Senator Kennedy," *New York Times*, 7 June 1968, sec. L.

28. Dave Brady, "A Kennedy Friend Keeps Boys Busy," *Washington Post*, 7 June 1968, sec. D. Brady also wrote that Robert Kennedy was responsible for popularizing touch football as a game throughout the nation.

29. Brady, "A Kennedy Friend Keeps Boys Busy."

30. Daley, "Compounding a Felony."

31. Daley, "Compounding a Felony."

32. Lauren Berlant, *The Queen of America Goes to Washington City*, 136. I elaborated upon this in the introduction and chapter 1.

33. Qtd, Robert Lipsyte, "Strinking Nerves."

34. Qtd, Robert Lipsyte, "Strinking Nerves."

35. In a press conference immediately following their race, Smith and Carlos asserted that their protest was to represent "black unity" across national and class lines. Carlos said the protest was to confront whites who perceived black people "as animals" if they did something "bad." But if "we do something good . . . they'll throw us some peanuts or pat us on the back and say 'Good Boy.'" Here Smith and Carlos suggested the protest was to assert black masculinity and draw attention to the rigid roles that were expected of black men in America. See "2 Accept Medals Wearing Black Gloves," *New York Times*, 17 October 1968, sec. S. Moreover, these two athletes were known to be members of Prof. Harry Edwards' social movement articulated through sport prior to the Olympics. That movement was not just one in the "nation's racial struggle, [but was one] . . . by colored people all over the world against a white man's lingering colonialism," and the war effort. Edwards said, "I refuse to be drafted so George Wallace can be safe." See Arnold Hano, "The Black Rebel Who Whitelists the Olympics; The Black Rebel," *New York Times*, 12 May 1968, sec. SM.

36. Red Smith, "Olympic Emotions Reach All Levels," *Washington Post*, 18 October 1968, sec. D.

37. Shirley Povich, "This Morning . . ." *Washington Post*, 19 October 1968, sec. C.

38. Shirley Povich. "This Morning . . ." *Washington Post*, 24 October 1968, sec. K.

39. Steve Cady, "Owens Recalls 1936 Sprinter's Ordeal," *New York Times*, 17 October 1968, sec. C.

40. Neil Amdur, "Negro Hopes to Pin Down Medal, *New York Times*, 12 October 1968,sec. L.

41. Arthur Daley, "The Incident," *New York Times*, 10 October, 1968, sec. S.

42. Shirley Povich, "This Morning . . . " *Washington Post*, 24 October 1968, sec. K, p 1.

43. Shirley Povich, "This Morning . . . " *Washington Post*, 19 October 1968, sec. C.

44. William Carsley, "Athletes Who Care and Those Who Don't," *Chicago Tribune*, 25 October 1968.

45. William Carsley, "Athletes Who Care and Those Who Don't."

46. Arthur Daley, "The Incident."

47. Bob Addie, "An Affair of State?" *Washington Post*, 19 October 1968, sec. C.

48. Addie, "An Affair of State?"

49. Qtd, Robert Lipsyte, "I'm Free to Be Who I Want," *New York Times*, 29 May 1967.

50. Sid Ziff, "Floyd is New Man," *Los Angeles Times*, 4 June 1967, sec. H.

51. Sid Ziff, "Big Sports Stories," *Los Angeles Times*, 29 May1967, sec. C.

52. Shirely Povich, "Clay Defended as Boxer, not American Patriot."

53. Povich, "Clay Defended as Boxer, not American Patriot."

54. Povich, "Clay Defended as Boxer, not American Patriot."

55. Robert Lipsyte, "One Who Got Away."

56. Robert Lipsyte, "I'm Free to Be Who I Want," *New York Times*, 29 May 1967.

57. See Lipsyte, "I'm Free to Be Who I Want"; "Striking Nerves," "Case Closed," *New York Times*, 1 July 1978; "Fighter Charges Board with Bias," *New York Times*, 18 February 1966; "Instant Bile," *New York Times*.

58. Lipsyte, "Striking Nerves."

59. Ronald Reagan, "Proclamation 5709: AIDS Awareness Month," 29 September 1987, http://www.reagan.utexas.edu/archives/speeches/1987/092987e.htm. 4 February 2007.

60. Berlant, *The Queen of America Goes to Washington City*, 1.

61. Berlant, *The Queen of America Goes to Washington City*, 177.

62. Thomas Boswell, "Magic Opens the Doors," *Washington Post*, 15 November 1992, sec. C.

63. Alison Muscatine, "Magic's Revelation Transcends Sports; Athletes' Tragedies Have Greater Impact," *Washington Post*, 10 November 1991, sec. D.

64. Bob Verdi, "A Collective Smile Turns to Sorrow," *Chicago Tribune*, 9 November 1992, sec. S.

65. Mike Conklin, "Magic Lesson: Disease Doesn't Play Favorites," *Chicago Tribune*, 8 November 1991, sec. S.

66. Through the spectacle of Hollywood film, the role of the football player representing "All American" values set Reagan in the realm of national mythology and served his politics that privileged white heterosexuality well. Reagan even embraced the nickname "Gipper" throughout his governorship of California and presidency, suggesting that mainstream consumers enjoyed the national mythologies of sport and conservativism in which Reagan had engaged.

67. Tony Kornheiser, "A Hero's Message of Hope," *Washington Post*, 8 November 1991, sec. C.

68. See Daniel Began, "Study Says Reagan Has Shown Little Concern over AIDS," Associated Press, 19 September 1985.While campaigns such as ACT UP were working hard to elicit federal and state funds to care for HIV/AIDS victims, Reagan's presidency was marked by a general neglect of the HIV/AIDS epidemic as a political concern, so much so that in February of 1990, he apologized for not making it a priority during his administration See Bruce Hilton, "AIDS Week: Better Late that Never?" *San Francisco Chronicle*, 4 February 1990, sec. A.

69. She was Senator Hillary Rodham Clinton's head speech writer in 2007.

70. Michael Wilbon, "Available at Your Peril," *Washington Post*, 10 November 1991, sec. D.

71. Wilbon, "Available at Your Peril."

72. Dave Anderson, "Sorry, But Magic Isn't a Hero," *New York Times*, 14 November 1991, sec. B.

73. Shari Dwarkin and Faye Linda Wachs ultimately claimed that the discourse surrounding Magic lead to the conclusion that "'bad' (gay, black, or working-class) sexuality is juxtaposed against the unstated norms of . . . white, middle-class, heterosexual men [who] are left out of the picture and are absolved altogether from any

involvement with HIV/AIDS promiscuity." See Shari Dwarkin and Faye Linda Wachs, "Disciplining the Body," edited by Susan Birrell and Mary G. McDonald, 258–69 (Boston: Northeastern University Press, 2000), 264.

74. Jim Murray, "Warning HIV: No Hiding Now," *Los Angeles Times*, 10 November 1991, sec. C.

75. Chase wrote that "Last evening, AIDS hotlines around the country were flooded with calls. Hotline volunteers said many people who thought they may be at risk of infection were calling for testing information, while others called specifically to voice support for Mr. Johnson and offer donations to AIDS-related organizations." See Marilyn Chase, "Johnson Disclosure Underscores Facts of AIDS in Heterosexual Population," *The Wall Street Journal*, 11 November 1991, sec. B.

76. Robert Lipsyte, "Magic as Hero: It's Not the Most Comfortable Fit," *New York Times*, 15 November 1991, sec. D.

77. Lipsyte, "Magic as Hero: It's Not the Most Comfortable Fit."

78. Lipsyte, "Magic as Hero: It's Not the Most Comfortable Fit."

79. See Sharon Zukin, *Landscapes of Power: From Detroit to Disney World* (Berkeley: University of California Press, 1991). Douglas Kellner, *Media Culture* (New York: Routledge, 1995).

80. Philip Brian Harper, "Eloquence and Epitaph: Black Nationalism and the Homophobic Impulse in Responses to the Death of Max Robinson," *Fear of a Queer Planet*, Ed. Michael Warner (Minneapolis: University of Minnesota, 1993), 239–63.

81. George Lipsitz, *American Studies in a Moment of Danger*, 125.

82. *Sports Illustrated* (Time Warner Books, New York, 2001); Frank Deford, *Picture Perfect: The Stories Behind the Greatest Photos in Sports*, 2002.

83. George Vecsey, "Sydney 2000: A Symbol More Than a Gesture," *New York Times*, 16 September 2000.

THREE

Bombs Bursting, but Not Here

Under a firework-lit sky, and in front of a full capacity crowd at Turner Field, Muhammad Ali waited to light the 1996 Olympic flame that would blaze during the two-week competition held in Atlanta, Georgia. Columnists were quick to emphasize Atlanta's being the home of the 1996 Olympics. Mike Downey of the *Los Angeles Times* constructed a vision of global and national diversity based on Atlanta's being both the birthplace of Martin Luther King Jr. and former President James Carter:

> They came from everywhere, from Hong Kong to Congo to Tonga, runners and punchers and tumblers, cycle and horse riders, arrow and gun shooters, iron pumpers and canoe paddlers, to a corner of America that had produced a President of the United States and a King who championed civil rights, but never the Olympic Games.[1]

Dave Kindred of *The Sporting News* also referred to Martin Luther King's association with Atlanta in his summary of the opening ceremonies. He cited Muhammad Ali in his rendition of the games as marking a moment of "mankind coming together [in] Martin Luther King's home."[2]

In contrast to how columnists wrote of Ali in 1968, however, Kindred and Downey used this now-American-icon as a vehicle for establishing their respective nations as having achieved racial equality. Kindred wrote that "[s]wimmer Janet Evans carried the flame up a long ramp to the stadium rim, there touching her torch to Ali's, and then the 1960 Olympic gold medalist raised high the flame in his right hand."[3] Downey wrote similarly, but drew attention to the weakened condition of Ali's Parkinson-ridden body: "A strong Janet Evans passed the torch to the once mighty Ali's trembling hand, this was Atlanta's night to let civilization know that a city that once burned to the ground was now eager to be illuminated by an eternal flame."[4] As Downey highlighted the weakened state of Ali's body against Evans's white and strong one, he constructed

Ali as the patriotic athlete—a far cry from the threatening black male he was constructed as a few decades earlier. Hence, these columnists transformed the meaning of Ali to conform to rigid expectations that sport and mainstream media required of its black males, which were elaborated upon in the last chapter.

Both of these writers ended their columns by chronicling how President William Jefferson Clinton was "misty-eyed" when he saw Ali light the flame. In representing Clinton, they connected Ali's lighting of the flame to the nation itself.[5] In drawing attention to Atlanta's being King's birthplace and using rhetoric to associate Ali with national identity, Clinton, and diversity, these columnists focused on Ali's love of country but offered no substantive discussion of whites' racism in the past or in the present. Kindred wrote:

> Clay said to the Russian [who, in 1960, asked him about racial intolerance in the United States,] 'Tell your readers we got qualified people working on that problem, and I'm not worried about the outcome. To me, the USA is the best country in the world, including yours." That was then, this is now. . . . Now this man who once refused induction into the U.S. Army—"I ain't got no quarrel with them Viet Cong," he said—has lit the Olympic flame.[6]

Downey wrote:

> And who better than their old Kentucky neighbor Muhammad Ali to usher in the new South in this, our republic's bid for a brighter tomorrow? America is a far different place from the one he represented 36 years ago as Cassius Marcellus Clay Jr., still imperfect, still impoverished, yet dedicated to be a better land than the one that once so discouraged a young prizefighter from Louisville that he hurled his gold medal into a nearby river.[7]

Both columnists established Ali as nationally heroic as a result of his patriotism in 1996. Kindred wrote of Ali's criticism of the Vietnam War, which, by 1996, was generally recognized as a problematic conflict in the nation's history. Likewise, Downey wrote of poverty, not race, in establishing Ali as a national hero. Hence, the memories these columnists evoked in writing of Ali were ones that would not necessarily confront or challenge rigid standpoints of race, despite that Ali himself was made famous by challenging such standpoints in the past. In fitting Ali into the rigid construction of patriotic black male; remembering the Vietnam War; or discussing class instead of race, these columnists avoided memories of white racism and racism in the past that, if raised in 1996, might have confronted those with latently racist attitudes.

These columnists' writing of Clinton and Ali's interaction at the 1996 Olympics was typical given their avoidance of explicit discussions of race while representing a racially progressive nation through Ali. For instance, in his first inaugural address, Clinton cited "deep divisions among our people" and "power and privilege" that "shut down the voice of the people."[8] But not a single reference to race was made. Weeks later, Clinton established what was then considered to be the nation's most racially diverse presidential cabinet, proclaiming that it was the first "that [would] look like America."[9] In short, Clinton was well aware of racial injustice and worked to alleviate it, but was loathe to mention it. However, in the final chapter of *Racial Formation in the United States*, Michael Omi and Howard Winant examined the national identity Clinton and other politicians established through rhetorical practices that avoided overt discussion of race but that also represented a socially just nation. Clinton utilized "universal" language of poverty, health care, disease, "'personal responsibility,' and 'family values' . . . [he] w[o]n back white suburbanites. . . . In [his] use of racially coded language, [Clinton and] the 'new Democrats' chose to remain silent on any explicit discussion of race and its overall meaning for politics."[10] As well, Omi and Winant established that racial euphemisms, in alluding to class and colorblindness, "perpetuat[ed] the same type of differential, racist treatment" that existed in the past by defining "'American identity' as white."[11] Hence, as these columnists used sport, Ali, memory, and Clinton to construct their nations as diverse, their work was produced by and producing the normal condition of both sport and nation as white. And when a white terrorist bombed the 1996 Olympics the connection between and among sport, memory, and white privilege became all the more clear.[12]

Specifically, by 1996, sports columnists' voices were hardly monolithic. The writers comprising of mainstream sports columnists in 1996 constructed not a single nation. Rather, their columns can be characterized as engaged in a contest for how white supremacy and terrorism would be situated and/or remembered in cultural definitions of "American." Subsequently, two kinds of nations existed in sports columnists' recordings of the bombing at the 1996 Olympics. One camp of columnists first presented the nation as "diverse" in Clintonian fashion while also avoiding the real and significant history of white privilege in the nation. Such constructions of national identity avoided any rhetoric that would draw attention to the existence of white terrorism and white racism in the nation's history or in its present. Another camp of columnists confronted white privilege and recognized and warned against the history and future dangers of white terror in the nation. The existence of these two camps of columnists in sports pages across the nation equated to a contest for what would be considered legitimate memories for the mainstream reading public.

WHITE DIVERSITY

A day after Ali lit the Olympic flame, a pipe bomb killed two and injured 111 at Centennial Park, the public space constructed for the 1996 Atlanta Olympics. Immediately, U.S. intelligence officials theorized the bombing to have been carried out by a white supremacist, most likely of the Georgia Militia.[13]

Peter Appelbome of the *New York Times* labeled the bombing a "tragedy."[14] Thomas Boswell of the *Washington Post* first categorized the terrorist act a "tragedy" and lifted it to national proportions, suggesting that when the Olympics carried on, "the nation turned bad into good."[15] Ken Rosenthal,[16] J. A. Adande, and Jennifer Frey of the *Washington Post* labeled the games "tragedy-stricken."[17] Bill Plaschke and Mike Downey of the *Los Angeles Times* and Tony Kornheiser of the *Washington Post* all worked to establish the 1996 Olympics as a memory for the nation by writing of the bombing.[18] Downey even wrote that "Atlanta would be remembered for its violence."[19] In the context of national and racial constructions that defined American identity as white, sports columnists who wrote about this terrorist act, which was theorized to be carried out by a white supremacist, revealed the distinction and connections between what I call white priviledge and white supremacy that many media pundits and scholars problematically conflate.

For instance, columnists wrote about Centennial Park, the site created for the general public to gather during the Olympics, as if it was a space where people from all backgrounds could meet. However, that space was created after black and impoverished people were banished from the park. Still, these Olympics and the park were, as Thomas Boswell wrote, to show an "appreciation for diversity."[20] Brian Duffy of *U.S. News & World Report* wrote that Centennial Park was "open to those who could not afford tickets [to the games]."[21] Applebome emphasized that Centennial Park was quite "[u]nlike the [other] Olympic venues, the park [wa]s free, open to all, and not subject to security checks."[22] Rosenthal wrote "celebrity worshippers, religious zealots, corporate acolytes—they were all on hand for the re-opening of Centennial Park." He also cited a school teacher Mary Jenkins: "The park has created a physical and psychological space that Atlanta hasn't had. . . . This is a very segregated city, a very suburban city. This park is the kind of space that makes cities come alive. . . . The whole notion of shared experience. . . . People can come here." Rosenthal continued: "The park belongs to the people."[23]

These columnists all emphasized the park's being open to "the public" or "the people" and representing "our sense of diversity." But the people and public to whom the park was open established "our diversity" in very narrow terms—terms that defined diversity in similar ways Clinton's rhetoric and columns about the opening ceremonies did. Few if any columnists mentioned the gentrification, antipanhandling laws, and arrest sweeps of black people that occurred in the weeks leading up to the games, and in conjunction with the International Olympic Committee's visits in choosing Atlanta as a host city.[24] Gerald Weber, legal director of the ACLU of Georgia, and Anita Beatty, co-president of the Atlanta Task Force for the Homeless, argued that there were a number of city policies that coincided with Atlanta's being awarded host-city status that also threatened the civil rights of the city's black impoverished:

> Among them were sweeps of homeless camps and gathering areas, particularly before conventions arrived in Atlanta. . . . [And] [t]he demolition of old buildings that might have been used as affordable housing. . . . In addition, the Atlanta city government passed a series of ordinances that, for all intents and purposes, made homelessness illegal. These new laws prohibited aggressive panhandling, lying down on a public park bench, either remaining in or walking across a public parking lot unless one had a car parked in that lot, and occupying vacant buildings.[25]

Under these ordinances, African American homeless people were by far the most arrested, according to a study conducted by the agencies of which both leaders were a part. Few if any columnists noted the subsequent absence of people experiencing the intersection of poverty and racism at the park, even as they underscored its diversity.

Even those columnists who mentioned that the park was built in a place that once was inhabited by black impoverished people used euphemisms that avoided drawing attention to the fact that the place's "diversity" was underpinned by a displacement of black impoverishment. For instance, Dave Anderson of the *New York Times* wrote, "to construct Olympic Park and Coca-Cola Olympic City as an Olympic playground, Atlanta leveled a shabby area of downtown."[26] Anderson reduced the significance of the lives of those displaced, and black poverty in general, through the euphemism "shabby." This euphemism hid the power of and bought into the white privilege that considers diversity to exist, even in the absence of black poverty. Hence, Centennial Park and the columns that emphasized its diversity were both products of and producing white privilege. Those identities believed to be of the people were those that spoke to white middle-class versions of diversity, and were manifest through a sweeping away of the colored poverty and overt discussions of race. In a roundtable discussion with Mark Dyreson, Steve Gietshcier, S. W. Pope, and many others, Dyreson revealed the coverage of the 1996 Olympics projected the nation as a place where "everyone share[d] the same suburban values and spr[u]ng from the same ethnic cultures."[27] The voices of the people displaced to make room for the park and "our diversity" were, to borrow from President Clinton, "shut down" by "power and privilege."[28]

In an insightful column, however, Kornheiser underscored the extent to which the Olympics had been commodified to support the selling of products. He noted:

> [T]he crush of people in Centennial Park waiting in line in the heat for hours to get into "The Super Store," a schlockery where you can buy the same official Olympic merchandise you can buy in the Kansas City airport. Speaking of Centennial Park, there is a statue there of Baron de Coubertin. He is facing "Bud World" and "Coca-Cola City," and the look on his face indicates that if he'd known what the Olympics would turn into, he'd have bought Anheuser-Busch and Coke stock.[29]

Similarly, Rosenthal wrote of the memorial service following the bombing: "The memorial service gave the same number of mentions to AT&T (one) as it did to the two people who died. The moment of silence lasted all of nine seconds."[30] In short, Kornheiser and Rosenthal played the role of cultural critics, condemning international corporations for participating in what Paul Lauter called the "triumph of commodification."[31] The national identity projected through the park was a product like AT&T or Coke. It was projected through mainstream media and national politicians which, in underscoring diversity without presenting black poverty, catered to the aesthetics of white, middle-class tastes, tastes indicative of white priviledge.

A TRICK OF MEMORY

In writing of the terror attack, columnists' narratives constructed the 1996 Olympics as a memory proving their nations' strength, resiliency, and diversity. Kindred wrote the resumption of the games after tragedy demonstrated "the people's" resiliency in the aftermath of tragedy. He wrote that when the fans returned to Centennial Park, the act of a single foolish terrorist was overcome.[32] Downey wrote that:

> In one morbid way, the bomb did Atlanta a great service. There are many—myself very included—who forever would have painted Atlanta as the biggest loser of the Olympics. . . . Instead, I and others will go home telling of an Atlanta that overcame an adversity . . . Atlanta will be remembered for its violence. Atlanta will also be remembered for its valiance . . . the Olympics turned out to be about: rising after a fall, envisioning a brighter tomorrow, getting there to give everything you got, and remembering where you are.[33]

Don Markus of the *Baltimore Sun* quoted Georgia Governor George Zell Miller as saying the bombing would not be remembered as the significant moment of the Olympics. "While we will always remember in our hearts the loss, the reclaiming of our city, the defiance the entire Olympic family showed is a more powerful story that will ultimately be the way these

Games will be remembered."[34] Boswell wrote that "when these Games are remembered, it probably will be as a stubborn triumph for the Olympics."[35] These columns were, in the present, establishing the tragedy at the 1996 Olympics as a memory for their nations. However, these columnists established this memory as speaking to national strength and resiliency in the face of adversity, not indication that the nation-state had terrorists inside its borders.

Moreover, utilizing the rhetoric of tragedy, columnists defined their nations as strong when sport resumed in the stadia and sites of contest. Kindred wrote that "somehow, the Games moved to moments of triumph when athletes went on with the work that brought them to a field of dreams that became a nightmare."[36] Boswell chronicled Donovan Bailey's record win in the 100-meter dash and American Gail Devers's win in the same event. He then wrote that "the Olympic flame still burned brightly."[37] Dave Anderson of the *New York Times* engaged in the rhetoric of tragedy by debating whether the games should have continued. He quoted Francois Carrad, deputy general of the International Olympic Committee saying, "The games will go on." Anderson then wrote, "And they should. To cancel these Summer Games would be surrender to the evil cowards who planted the pipe bomb that exploded early yesterday morning among revelers in Centennial Park, the Olympic party land [sic]."[38] Anderson presented national strength in the act of athletes' and civilians' returning to the Olympics. In short, Boswell, Kindred, and Anderson suggested that the resumption of sport equated to a national overcoming of terrorism. Such rhetoric, however, limited discussion of white terror, and should be viewed as a symptom of the narrowly-defined diversity characteristic of the nation this camp of columnists and federal politicians in general constructed in 1996.

For example, in a further attempt to demonstrate how the nation overcame adversity in the context of a terrorist attack, Kornheiser, Plaschke, and Boswell used the story of U.S. silver medalist winner in wrestling, Matt Ghaffari. Through him, they created the 1996 Olympics as significant cultural memories for a resilient America. All three asserted that what they would remember most was not the bombing, but moments of compassion Ghaffari showed after winning the medal. Kornheiser wrote:

> What do you [think you will] remember most about the Atlanta Olympics? For some it will be the bomb, of course . . . I'll think of the tender moments, like swimmer Angel Martino giving her bronze medal to a friend who has cancer, and wrestler Kurt Angle weeping through the playing of 'The Star-Spangled Banner' at the medal ceremony, after placing his gold medal around his mom's neck. . . . In my mind the most compassionate act of all was Ghaffari going to the hospital to visit Fallon Stubbs, teenage daughter of Alice Hawthorne, who was killed in the bomb.[39]

Here, Kornheiser tied Ghaffari's compassion and the patriotic moment of "The Star Spangled Banner" being sung to how he (and so his readers) would remember the 1996 Olympics. Similarly, Plaschke suggested that Ghaffari's medal had "magic" and that "he ha[d] spread that feeling throughout a city that badly needed to believe these Olympics still had magic left."[40] Plaschke suggested that Ghaffari's medal allowed Atlanta and the nation projected through it to recover from the terror. Plaschke then assigned the label of "American" to Ghaffari by chronicling the athlete's trek from Iran to America and quoting him as saying, "I've worked my butt off to be an American."[41] Boswell explained that Ghaffari was afraid that the American public would chastise him for not winning the gold. He then quoted Ghaffari as saying, "After my match, the people showed me how to turn a negative into a positive. . . . A few days later, we had the bomb. . . . Again, this great nation turned bad into good. Everyone put humanity ahead of sport."[42] While Kornheiser, Plaschke, and Boswell paid homage to the dead, they also began to set their version of the Olympics in the realm of the mythological through the good acts of Ghaffari. That is, these stories attributed this unique man's admirable and heroic internal qualities to their nations' compassionate character, democratic ideal, and its subsequent ability to heal. The compassionate national character these columnists constructed through Ghaffari necessarily avoided the reality that white terror lurked within the nation-state's borders, even when that terror was what their nations were healing from. Finally, the healing would be for those lucky enough to have witnessed the stories of the 1996 Olympics unfold through media, not those in the park, or those who would be or had been threatened by white terror in other places.

But the terrorist acts that columnists suggested the nation overcame through sport extended beyond those at the 1996 Olympics. For instance, Elizabeth Levitan Spaid of *The Christian Science Monitor* tangled tragedies and constructed her nation as having a unique character in the process.

> The blast, which comes eight days after the downing of TWA Flight 800, continues to keep world's attention riveted on terrorism. Two months ago, 19 US personnel died after a bomb blew up barracks in Saudi Arabia. Fifteen months ago, Oklahoma City was the target, and before that, the World Trade Center in New York. . . . "We celebrate freedom here," says Eleanor Pemberton of Conyers, Ga., a spectator at a women's basketball contest Saturday. . . . "We need to stand tall. This could have happened anywhere in America," former Mayor Maynard Jackson said Saturday. "This is a convenient place for someone to do something as awful and tragic as this. . . . The show must go on."[43]

Spaid suggested that through the Olympics, the acts of terror that had been exacted upon American soil and people from 1994–1996 would be overcome. Her reason for this claim was that America was the land of the free and people here could "stand tall." Similarly, Boswell referred to the aforementioned tragedies as well as the 1972 Olympics in Munich. He argued that "death and terror did not stop the Olympics today."[44] He then equated sport and the Olympics with what he labeled American diversity and character:

> This was not really the Atlanta Games so much as it was the American Olympics—the first true one, with the whole world aboard, since 1924. As such, it celebrated our diversity and hospitality, our gaucherie and our generosity . . . and our general decency.[45]

Boswell constructed America as strong, resilient, diverse, and unique.

Collectively these columnists established their nations in the mythological, arguing terrorism was overcome through athletes' acts on and/or off the field. They also established their nations as diverse, despite that the diversity espoused through the Olympics was one serving and underpinned by white privilege. That privilege not only belied Atlanta's and the nation's actual conditions by marginalizing black poverty. It also denied substantive discussion of white terror that may have complicated the construction of the nation as democratic and embracing diversity. Adande, a black man, and Spaid, a woman who often wrote of discriminatory practices in the nation-state, touted American ideals as representative of the nation-state, despite their own identities and their historic writings that confronted white privilege.[46] The denial of black poverty and white supremacy existing in the nation suggested that when national identity is discussed through sport, the mythologies of both are normalized to such an extent that columnists who would seemingly resist both do not. Moreover, the dearth of female columnists of color in 1996 illustrated the white masculine privilege in the make-up of the mainstream press. Still, the dearth of such columnists would not necessarily explain the fashion in which this camp of columnists constructed the Olympics as proof of their nations' strength, resiliency, good character, and diversity. The diversity represented through these columns privileged middle-class identities, and subsequently white versions of blackness—that is, the black and impoverished were altogether dismissed.

However, this camp's general avoidance of discussion of white terror is best explained as buying into mythological national identities supported through sport. Specifically, of memory and nation, Lauren Berlant wrote that the mainstream media assure the future of white privilege by avoiding realities and memories of oppression.[47] Hence, in establishing cultural memories of the 1996 Olympics to tout national diversity, democracy, strength, and resiliency while avoiding discussion of white terror, these columnists were assuring a diverse and strong future for their nations, a future that would not require whites to confront their own privileged approaches to race in the present or past, a future that would deny the existence of terror groups in the nation.

AVOIDING MEMORY OF TERROR

The definition of the nation as diverse was established in how some columnists remembered their national history through the games. Many columnists used the bombing to remember their nations having been historically free from terror. In "Triumph over Terror," Jerry Adler wrote that "the Atlanta games will be forever remembered for the first fatal terror attack directed at civilians."[48] William Booth of the *Washington Post* wrote that the blasts at Oklahoma and Atlanta signaled "the end of [national] innocence" from terror.[49] Boswell wrote of Matthew Britt, a doctor in Oklahoma, who suggested the bombings at Oklahoma City and Atlanta indicated the nation's children were losing their innocence.[50] Michael Grunwald of the *New York Times* suggested the nation was "no longer immune to terror."[51] Lance Morrow of *Time* wrote:

> The Atlanta bomb was not Munich 1972, which was Black September's awful masterpiece. By comparison, Atlanta was amateur night. But Atlanta came in the immediate aftermath of TWA Flight 800, and close enough in history to Oklahoma City, to leave in Americans' minds a conviction, developing like a Polaroid picture, that their nation is somehow in the process of losing whatever may be left of its old immunity. . . . Terror was an evil native to other lands.[52]

Brian Duffy wrote of Oklahoma City, Atlanta, and violence and wondered what "evil had suddenly become us."[53] Kindred distinguished between American citizens' reaction to terror and those from Northern Ireland. Whereas in Ireland and Northern Ireland terrorism had existed for the better part of two centuries, Kindred argued that it was just now visiting America—America was losing its innocent identity.[54]

Collectively, these columnists established their nations as historically lacking terror, which was revealing of the identities privileged in those nations. These columns altogether avoided the historical reality that homegrown white terrorism had long been part of American history. It existed in lynching of black and gay identities for as long as the nation was officially an independent state.[55] Such repressions in memory were similar to those that avoided the historical reality that many whites vilified King and Ali. These repressions were also similar to those that failed to realize that the displacement of black impoverished people from the site where Centennial Park belied the Park's claim to be public. In short, the construction of a diverse nation had been predicated on columnists' avoiding memories of moments when overt white racism in the nation's history and the social realities that underpinned the actual construction of Centennial Park. Even if the whites reading or writing these columns did not participate in such racism, it was part of the nation's history that was being omitted in these stories. By avoiding these memories, columnists could hold up the nation as democratic and experiencing a momentary lapse in terror.

Moreover, as the columnists represented diversity through Centennial Park, they tacitly privileged whites and whiteness as always progressing toward establishing democracy for all identities, rather than being obstacles to it. Hence, they supported and were affected by white privilege.

Specifically, columnists constructed their nations as currently void of a network of white terror through the games. They suggested that a single individual carried out the terror at Centennial Park, glossing over the fact that a network of white supremacist/terror organizations existed in the nation-state. Boswell wrote that the terror was carried out by an "isolated lunatic"; Kindred wrote that it was the act of a single foolish terrorist.[56] These pieces suggesting that the bombing was carried out by a single individual presented terror as an anomaly to the nation-state, rather than a result of its terrorist networks, themselves with a robust history. The repression of white terrorism's history and present status was what Cynthia-Levine Rasky called the "denial and legitimation of white hegemony."[57] For if the nation was constructed as lacking terror and racial oppression, then white versions of diversity, progress, and history were justified.

Finally, Downey and Boswell continued their stories of the bombing and chronicled mainstream media's accusation of Richard Jewell as the terrorist. (Jewell was the security guard first hailed as a hero for evacuating Centennial Park in the moments before the bomb detonated. His profile of a police officer wannabe, according to numerous reports, would explain his desire to set off a bomb in public while also being the one to "save" many civilians). Many media outlets immediately used Jewell's profile to convict him in the court of public opinion. Ultimately, however, Jewell was never arrested and the media's focus on Jewell made him a strawman victim. Downey referred to Jewell's being accused as a lynching. "This was the year I saw a man lynched and not with a rope [but by the media] . . . I don't know if . . . Timothy McVeigh blew up that Oklahoma City office building . . . but one thing I do know: [He] was charged with a crime: Richard Jewell was not."[58] Downey's use of lynching to describe Jewell's experience was the only reference to terrorism specifically linked to white supremacy in his work. This was despite that the Atlanta bombing and lynching were and had been, in no uncertain terms, connected to white supremacy. Boswell was much tamer with his language, but still focused on media rather than white terrorism as the culprit in the tragedy: "An innocent man was made infamous around the world, his life put under a cruel microscope for months. How will that damage ever be undone?"[59] The damage was to a single white male, not the many at Centennial Park.[60] Moreover, the permanent damage was exacted by the amorphously defined media, not the ongoing white terror groups in the nation; not the white privilege defining "diversity" in very narrow terms.

Hence, one camp of columns about the 1996 Olympics generally constructed their nations as representing diversity, as resilient and strong, as compassionate or historically lacking terror and in the process were produced by and producing white privilege.

Some writers, however, did use their position in mainstream media to remember the history of white terrorism in the nation-state. They thus potentially resisted the mythological of national identity that many of their counterparts constructed. For example, Coleman McCarthy's work appeared in the *Washington Post,* and although it was not a sports column, it was a text about the Olympics that was overtly critical of the sort of rhetoric cited in the first camp's columns. He challenged the notion that terror was a foreign entity:

> That was much the reaction to the Oklahoma City bombing: Germs of terrorism, once an infectious poison quarantined among car-bombers in Belfast or suicide-bombers in Israel, are now invading the serenity of America. Why us. . . . This expression of shock that suddenly it is happening here ignores a few facts, starting with those supplied by the FBI's Bomb Data Center. In 1984, 803 bombings or attempted bombings occurred, a number that soared to 3,163 in 1994. From 1990 to 1994, California was the nation's bomb capital, with 2,424 attempted or actual explosions.[61]

Here McCarthy argued that white terrorism had been part of the nation-state for a long time prior to the 1996 Olympics. His feature worked to establish the history of white terrorism in the nation, which many of his counterparts repressed from their memories of national history. He even underscored the irony of a national anthem at the Atlanta Olympics and its lyrics of exploding bombs. He wrote "a bomb-loving government can expect to have a bomb-loving citizenry. It does."[62] Hence, McCarthy resisted sports columnists' tendency to construct their national identities as innocent from violence and so diverse. He even suggested that violence was part of his national identity.

S. L. Price of *Sports Illustrated* underscored the national network of white terrorist groups and their capability and threats to exact violence on the games:

> Court records reveal that the last time a Summer Games was held in the U.S., in L.A. in 1984, a right-wing "Aryan" paramilitary group called the Order made elaborate plans to bomb several Olympic sites. When members of the group were arrested that year, several like-minded militias vowed to continue what they saw as the Order's 'unfinished business,' though no incidents related to that threat were reported. Last April federal agents near Macon, Ga., arrested two members of the Georgia Republic Militia with bombmaking materials in

their possession. It was widely reported at the time that the group was planning a "war" on the '96 Olympics, though authorities denied it.[63]

Both writers criticized their counterparts' identities by remembering some of the acts of white terrorism that had occurred before 1996. Each thereby challenged the construction of a national history characterized by white benevolence and that catered to white, middle-class sense of racial progress.

Similarly, Boswell's most insightful column rejected the notion that America was exceptional and innocent of terror and racial oppression. He argued that terror existed in many nations, and is not a racial construct, but an ideology related to extremists of all races and nations, including America:

> Our whole range of Parliamentary militarists make the shortlist of [potential guilty parties]. . . . Skinheads and Klansmen make the shortlist too. . . . Next time we hear about a bomb in Belfast or a famine in Africa, perhaps the suffering will seem less remote and harder to ignore.[64]

This column, quite a contrast to the other two he wrote on the 1996 Olympics, implicitly illustrated that terrorism is not naturally connected to race, but is an ideology. He similarly demonstrated that nations are constructs with direct connections to how cultures perceive terrorism and each other. He wrote that "all those who . . . c[ould] deny that [terrorists] exist among us" are part of the problem.[65] Hence, Boswell confronted white privilege by suggesting that passively ignoring the reality of white terrorism in the nation is a symptom of privilege and a false notion of whites' innocence.[66] Interestingly, in some columns, Boswell embraced a standpoint that constructed his nation in ways that privileged white mythologies; while in others he confronted that mythology. Like all of us, his identity is complex, and his ideas change over time, as does his focus. As he wrote of athletes' feats in sport, he constructed a mythological nation. When he wrote specifically of terrorism and diversity, he underscored race problems in the nation. Boswell's straddling of the two camps of columnists writing of the terror at the Olympics indicates that individual columnists' work is not singular in nature, and cannot be categorized without analysis of the context, event, and themes in and about which the column was written.

Ultimately, columnists who acknowledged the existence of white terrorist groups in the nation confronted the nations their counterparts constructed; nations that were implicitly defined as democratic and with an innocent past. They began the process of deconstructing privileged nationhoods by challenging the notion of national diversity that mainstream media, through politics and sport, was in the practice of celebrating. They also resisted the tendency of mainstream media to hide the reality of white terrorism from memories of the nation. These columns resisted the presentations of nation and tricks of memory that were prevalent in mainstream media at the time. Finally, these columnists demonstrated that white privilege can be resisted by drawing attention to the existence, dangers, and history of white terror and racism in the nation-state.

Given that columns from both camps this chapter identifies appeared in the same publications—indeed, in Boswell's case, were written by the same author—it is hardly a far leap to argue that readers of different standpoints read work from both. In this way, these columns were collectively contesting for how diversity, black poverty, and the history of terrorism in the nation would be remembered through the 1996 Olympics. Likewise, these sports columns had the capacity to shift cultural conceptions of national identity to include knowledge of how white privilege works for those who embraced privileged stances toward race, terror, and national identity. It works, at times, by emphasizing a narrow form of diversity and/or denying the existence and history of white terror providing knowledge of the mechanisms of white privilege, finally, potentially educates readers by requiring them to examine their rigid definitions of diversity, nation, and terror. Showing the existence of racism and white terrorism has the potential to confront those embracing white privilege with the reality that racism, even in its passive form, is a violent and continuous problem in the nation. Moreover, by confronting those who embrace white-privileged approaches to nation or diversity, the columnists in the second camp worked within the mainstream media, an outlet often blamed for producing privilege, in order to deconstruct it.

NOTES

1. Mike Downey, "Putting a New Georgia on Their Minds," *Los Angeles Times*, 28 July 1996, special section S.
2. Dave Kindred, "Muhammad Ali Will Always Be the Greatest," *The Sporting News*, 28 July 1996.
3. Kindred, "Muhammad Ali Will Always Be the Greatest."
4. Downey, "Putting a New Georgia on Their Minds."
5. Downey, "Putting a New Georgia on Their Minds."
6. Kindred, "Muhammad Ali Will Always Be the Greatest."
7. Downey, "Putting a New Georgia on Their Minds."
8. William Jefferson Clinton, "First Inaugural Address," Bartleby Books, 2 February 2006, http://www.bartleby.com/124/pres64. html (22 January 1996).
9. William Jefferson Clinton, "First Inaugural Address."
10. Michael Omi and Howard Winant, *Racial Formations in the United States* (New York: Routledge, 1996), 147–50.
11. Omi and Winant, *Racial Formations in the United States*, 60, 66.
12. Throughout the book, I accept the definition of terror generated by terrorism experts A. P. Schmid and A. J. Longman and generally accepted by social scientists: "Terrorism is an anxiety-inspiring method of repeated violent action, employed by (semi-) clandestine individual, group or state actors, for idiosyncratic, criminal or political reasons, whereby—in contrast to assassination—the direct targets of violence

are not the main targets. The immediate human victims of violence are generally chosen randomly (targets of opportunity) or selectively (representative or symbolic targets) from a target population, and serve as message generators. Threat- and violence-based communication processes between terrorist (organization), (imperiled) victims, and main targets are used to manipulate the main target (audience[s]), turning it into a target of terror, a target of demands, or a target of attention, depending on whether intimidation, coercion, or propaganda is primarily sought." See A. P. Schmid and A. J. Longman, *Political Terrorism, A New Guide to Actors, Authors, Concepts, Data Bases, Theories, and Literature* (Amsterdam, Transaction Books, 1988), 28. This bombing was not only the first of many by Eric Rudolph, but was immediately suspected to have been carried out by white supremacists, as shown below. As such, the repetitive nature required of an act to fit into this definition of terror was fulfilled; likewise, the act was clearly an act of communication to threaten the nation-state in its approach to race, abortion, and homosexuality.

13. See "Who Planted the Bomb?" CNN, 27 July 1996.

14. Peter Applebome, "Grim Reality Doesn't Scare Most Fans from Games," *New York Times*, 28 July1996.

15. Thomas Boswell, "Beyond the Quest for Gold, Games Have a Silver Lining," *Washington Post*, 5 August 1996, sec. D.

16. J. A. Adande and Jennifer Frey, "Security Tightens in Village, but Athletes Still Come Out to Play," *Washington Post*, 28 July 1996, sec. A.

17. Ken Rosenthal, "Glitz, Hype Overshadow Real Tragedy," *Baltimore Sun*, 31 July 1996, sec. D.

18. See Tony Kornheiser, "The End Is Such a Deflating Experience, *Washington Post*, 5 August 1996, sec. C; Mike Downey, "The Bittersweet End," *Los Angeles Times*, 5 August 1996, special section; Bill Plaschke, "Looking for Right Spirit? Begin List with Ghaffari," *Los Angeles Times*, 5 August 1996, sec. S.

19. Downey, "The Bittersweet End."

20. Boswell, "Beyond the Quest for Gold, Games Have a Silver Lining."

21. Brian Duffy, "Terror at the Olympics," *U.S. News & World Report*, 5 August 1996, (121):5, 121–127; 125.

22. Applebome, "Grim Reality Doesn't Scare Most Fans from Games."

23. Rosenthal, "Glitz, Hype Overshadow Real Tragedy."

24. See Karen Denton, "The Olympics, Homelessness, and Civil Rights," *The ACLU Reporter*, Fall 1999.

25. Steve Gietschier noted that "American cities that bid for the Games typically make a guaranteed, lucrative television deal part of their proposal to the IOC . . . based on the assumption that the events would be telecast live." See Pope, S. W. et. al., "Virtual Games: The Media Coverage of the 1996 Olympics," *Journal of Sports History* (27):1, 1997 63–73. See also Seth M. Low, "The Anthropology of Cities," *Annual Review of Anthropology*, 1996 (25): 383–409.

26. Dave Anderson, "Olympics Not Games Anymore," *New York Times*, 28 July 1996, sec. D.

27. S. W. Pope et al., "Virtual Games: The Media Coverage of the 1996 Olympics," *Journal of Sports History*, 63–73.

28. William Jefferson Clinton, "First Inaugural Address."

29. Kornheiser, "The End Is Such a Deflating Experience."

30. Rosenthal, "Glitz, Hype Overshadow Real Tragedy."

31. Paul Lauter, *From Walden Pond to Jurassic Park*, (Durham, NC: Duke University Press, 2001), 109.

32. Dave Kindred, "Georgia Will Always Be on Our Mind?" *The Sporting News*, 12 August 1996.

33. Downey, "The Bittersweet End."

34. Don Markus, "Spirited Ceremony Brings Games to a Close," *Baltimore Sun*, 5 August 1996, sec. C.

35. Boswell, "Beyond the Quest for Gold, Games Have a Silver Lining."

36. Kindred, "What Is It with These Fools?" *The Sporting News*, 5 August 1996.
37. Thomas Boswell, "Terror Leaves Games in Somber Mood," *Washington Post*, 28 July 1996, sec. D.
38. Anderson, "Olympics Not Games Anymore."
39. Kornheiser, "The End Is Such a Deflating Experience."
40. Plaschke, "Looking for Right Spirit? Begin List with Ghaffari."
41. Plaschke, "Looking for Right Spirit? Begin List with Ghaffari."
42. Boswell, "Beyond the Quest for Gold, Games Have a Silver Lining."
43. Elizabeth Levitan Spaid, "Blast Quiets but Can't Quiet Olympic Spirit," *The Christian Science Monitor*, 29 July 1996, sec. D.
44. Boswell, "Terror Leaves Games in Somber Mood."
45. Boswell, "Terror Leaves Games in Somber Mood."
46. See Elizabeth Levitan Spaid, "Churches Still Struggling to Cross Racial Divide," *The Christian Science Monitor*, 10 April 1993, p. 6; "Atlanta's Freaknik a Symbol of Atlanta's Racial Divide, or Just a Party?" *The Christian Science Monitor*, 18 April 1997, p. 4; "Georgia Contests Test What Pulls Votes: Race or Party?" *The Christian Science Monitor*, 1 October 1996, p. 1.
47. Lauren Berlant, *The Queen of America Goes to Washington City*, 56.
48. Jerry Adler, "Terror and Triumph," *Newsweek*, 5 August 1996: 24–33.
49. William Booth, "Blast Hit Heart of Party," *Washington Post*, 28 July 1996, sec. A.
50. Boswell, "Terror Leaves Games in Somber Mood."
51. Michael Grunwald, "FBI Charges Fugitive in Atlanta, Olympic Bombings," *Washington Post*, 15 October 1996, sec. A.
52. Lance Morrow, "An Equal and Opposite Darkness," *Time*, 5 August 1996, 148(7): 72.
53. Duffy, "Terror at the Olympics," 121.
54. Kindred, "What Is It with These Fools?"
55. *Autobiography of an Ex-Colored Man, Cane,* and many other texts by African American authors demonstrate that public lynchings were forms of social control that were geared toward intimidating entire groups of people, not toward exacting violence against specific people. They hence fit into the definition of terror cited at the beginning of this chapter. See James Weldon Johnson, *The Autobiography of an Ex-Colored Man* (New York: Penguin Books, 1990); Jean Toomer, *Cane* (Penguin Books: New York, 1993).
56. Boswell, "Beyond the Quest for Gold, Games Have Silver Lining."
57. Qtd, Mary G. McDonald, "Mapping Whiteness," *Sociology of Sport Journal* 22, no. 3 (2005): 245–55; 249, 397–408.
58. Mike Downey, "It Was Clear Case of Rush to Judgment," *Los Angeles Times*, 28 October 1996, sec. C.
59. Thomas Boswell, "Reassuring Our Convictions," *Washington Post,* 28 January 1998, sec. D.
60. Moreover, the perpetrators of violence were the unidentified and amorphous "media." According to Joel Black, the practice of condemning media for its leading to moral decline is a means of escaping real, harmful issues such as gun violence, and, I would suggest, white terrorism. (See Joel Black, *Reality Effect* [New York: Routledge, 2002]). This is not an argument about who should have been blamed for terror, but an observation that white hegemony garners power by repressing historic and current manifestations of white terrorism.
61. Coleman McCarthy, "Residue from Rockets' Red Glare," *Washington Post*, 20 August 1996, sec. D.
62. Coleman McCarthy, "Residue from Rockets' Red Glare."
63. S. L. Price, "Stained Games," *Sports Illustrated*, 5 August 1996 (85):6, 22-28.
64. Boswell, "A Bond Linking Us All." *Washington Post*, 28 July 1996, sec. C.
65. Boswell, "A Bond Linking Us All."
66. Likewise, Rosenthal argued that terror was an ideology without a nation. Ken Rosenthal, "Glitz, Hype Overshadow Real Tragedy."

FOUR

Counter Wars

Against the backdrop of a clear blue sky, United Airlines flight 175 and American Airlines flight 11 plunged into the World Trade Center. Smoke plumed. Debris-caked New Yorkers flooded the city streets. In Washington, D.C., United Airlines flight 77 dove into the Pentagon wall. Like in New York, innocent Americans lost their lives. Family members frantically dialed their loved ones' cell phones. But the cell towers were saturated with calls. News of the terror traveled quickly. En route to the White House, United Airlines flight 93 was downed in Shanksville, Pennsylvania, by a few heroic citizens. A gaping hole where the plane crashed served as the temporary grave for those on that plane. Across the nation, anxious citizens, themselves targets and victims of the terror, read and watched news stories about the acts of violence.

Later that afternoon, President George W. Bush addressed the country. With aplomb he established his nation as full of citizens resolved to exact revenge against the terrorists. He said, "This is a day when all Americans from every walk of life unite in our resolve for justice and peace. America has stood down enemies before, and we will do so this time."[1] Three days later, with the Twin Towers still smoldering and bodies being unearthed from the rubble, President Bush wrapped his arm around a rescue fireman and sounded off through a bull horn: "I can hear you. The rest of the world can hear you. And the people who knocked these buildings down will hear all of us soon."[2] On September 20, 2001, Bush delivered the "Address to a Joint Session of Congress and American People," in which he established his national identity in anticipation of war:

> On September 11th, the enemies of freedom committed an act of war against our country. Americans have known wars—but for the past 136 years, they have been wars on foreign soil, except for one Sunday in

1941. As long as the United States of America is determined and strong, this will not be an age of terror; this will be an age of liberty, here and across the world. We will rally the world to this cause by our efforts, by our courage. We will not tire, we will not falter, and we will not fail. It is my hope that in the months and years ahead, life will return almost to normal.[3]

In the ten days after the attacks, Bush constructed his national identity as one that had historically been attacked by "enemies of freedom." He also explained that the nation would return to normalcy when revenge was exacted for the attacks, and through a courageous and strong commitment to freedom.

Sport was quick to tie its doings to that of the nation's: Three hours after the attacks, Major League Baseball Commissioner Allan Huber "Bud" Selig postponed the baseball season. In writing of sport's service to national identity in the context of terror and the subsequent War on Terror, columnists adopted three kinds of standpoints, which I define as "camps." Writers in the first camp asserted that sport had historically served the nation in the context of war, and would do so in the aftermath of 9/11's terrorism. This camp reflected the very sort of national identity Bush constructed, defining their individual nations as strong, virile, and ready to avenge the terrorist attacks.

The second camp resisted the traditional use of sport to construct a mythological national identity. This camp distinguished between sport and national identity, claiming that everyday citizens' problems should not be overlooked through rhetoric related to sport. The final camp was critical of and confronted the nation's and the first camp's construction of a mythological national identity and War on Terror. This camp represented a counternarrative to the national mythology traditional in sports columns written in the context of tragedy.

The very existence of three divergent political standpoints regarding national identity in the context of war illustrated a significant shift in the voices that, by 2001, comprised mainstream sports columnists. While columnists from earlier eras generally marginalized voices critical of the nation's policy, especially in the context of war, in the post-9/11 era sports columnists themselves were among those most critical of it. In writing of 9/11 and the subsequent War on Terror, then, the collective voices of sports columnists were much more representative of the many political views of citizens in the nation than before. Moreover, these voices reflected a contestation for how 9/11 and the War on Terror would be constructed in the dominant national identity and its memory.

SPORT'S MYTHS AND ITS NATION

After Selig postponed the season, many sports columnists engaged in the rhetoric of tragedy by theorizing that sport would heal or serve the nation by resuming the games. These columnists established 9/11 in a grand patriotic narrative about sport's historic role in delivering stability to a nation under attack. Steve Buckley of the *Boston Herald* wrote, "All you need to know about the study of sport in America is that, during World War II, President Roosevelt insisted that Major League Baseball continue to operate. Roosevelt believed the games would buoy the spirits of Americans, and he was right."[4] Walter Shapiro of *USA Today* wrote of Major League Baseball Commissioner Kennesaw Mountain Landis's worry that baseball, in the wake of the attacks on Pearl Harbor, would be acting in an unpatriotic fashion by beginning its season on time—months after the attacks. He summarized a letter Landis wrote to President Roosevelt:

> Landis and the 16 team owners were prepared to halt the sport for the duration of the war if that was what the president deemed proper. But thanks to Roosevelt's sagacious letter of approval, the 1942 season was played in its 154-game entirety, climaxing with a World Series in which the upstart St. Louis Cardinals upended the New York Yankees, four games to one.[5]

George Vecsey of the *New York Times*, citing baseball's continuing its (truncated) schedule during both world wars, argued that sport was a social institution offering stability to the nation in times of crisis.[6]

Columnists argued that the resumption of sporting events after 9/11 would lead to the nation's return to normalcy and lift its national spirit. Vecsey wrote a column entitled, "Can American Sports Ever Get Back to Normal?" in which he labeled 9/11 a "tragedy." He continued to write that "we will get back to some semblance of normalcy. We need our games."[7] Hal Bodley of *USA Today* chronicled that Selig "talked to the White House," thereby associating the decision with Bush's nation.[8] Mike Tierney of the *Atlanta Journal Constitution* wrote:

> America's pro athletes vacated playing fields once more Wednesday as sports joined hands with a nation healing from a terrorist assault on two cities. . . . Measuring a line between respect and resilience, Selig is considering resumption on Friday, when the Braves are supposed to welcome the Marlins.[9]

These columnists linked sport to a national recovery from the terror of 9/11. The places and athletes they used to construct their nations as recovered or in the process of being so, however, revealed the identities privileged in their nations.

For example, Scott Ostler's column in *The San Francisco Chronicle* engaged in the same convention in the rhetoric of tragedy as those columns cited above. But he also associated the tragedy with New York:

> Commissioner Bud Selig shut down the game for three days so far, and even though the Sportswriter Code demands criticism of Selig for every decision, that seems about right. Who really knows? . . . If nothing else, the Yankees deserve a chance to provide New York with a diversion and a spiritual boost. [10]

Ostler was only one of many columnists who secured the tragedy as specific to New York while also constructing a nation ready for war. Ostler suggested that sport could provide a seemingly contradictory purpose: It could offer New Yorkers a diversion from the reality of terror while also elevating the spirits of fans, which had been depressed by the terrorist attacks. Steve Wilstein of the Associated Press linked New York, national identity, the Yankees, and citizenship:

> Sports is the most parochial and national of our institutions, touching our identities as citizens deeper than other entertainments. We come together for our cities and our regions and we root for the home team. For a while, after 9-11, New York became America's home team. [11]

Here New York was a trope for Wilstein's nation and how it would recover from 9/11. [12] Likewise, Dan Barry of the *New York Times* quoted Steven Cohen, Vice Dean of Public Affairs at Columbia University, as having said that New York was then seen by the rest of the country "as the most American of cities. . . . We're tough, we're resilient, we fight back, and we're undaunted.'" [13] Joe Lapointe of the *New York Times* conflated New York with his national identity suggesting that the T-shirts "God Bless America" and "Don't Mess with New York" signaled the same sort of strength in national identity. [14] These columnists constructed New York as a place reflective of their resilient and courageous national identities. They also constructed New York as a place willing to retaliate against an enemy, thereby conflating resiliency and war with sport, New York, and national identity.

Like Ostler, many columnists suggested that baseball players and the Yankees specifically reflected the values and character of their nations. Roger Angell of the *New Yorker* wrote:

> The Yankee players had been on the scene, so to speak, on the morning of September 11th, when the bad news for the country arrived, and how they felt and how they would fare now mattered. And millions here in the city felt the connection: the Yanks were us. [15]

Bodley wrote, "Despite a lifetime of ingrained Yankee-hating, I'm going to root for them. . . . Let's think about us. Go team America. [16]

Diane Pucin of the *Los Angeles Times* quoted Harrison Mitchell, who once worked in one of the Twin Towers: "Baseball is our national pastime, right? Baseball is part of America and we need to be Americans right now." Pucin ended her piece stating that "we will" watch baseball again. "It's who we are. We're Americans."[17] A year after the attacks, Wilstein remembered the nation's recovery through resumption of sport:

> Fans came back quickly when the baseball and football games resumed after Sept. 11. They chose to stand together, defy the terrorists and show they were not afraid. In coming to the games, the fans declared that their lives will go on and they would not hide in their homes as the terrorists hid in caves.[18]

These columnists thus constructed their nations through a conflation of New York and baseball while implying that patriotism equated to a support of retaliation. Against whom that retaliation was to come was left unclear, and that lack of clarity was the same sort that the Bush administration utilized as it carried out a mismanaged war, while co-opting sport as a mechanism to support that war.

Columnists' writing of New York, though, was part of a construction of national identity in which male sports figures, firemen, and policemen came to represent national response to the terrorist attacks. That is, columnists anchored a patriotic national identity in a matrix of New York service *men* and ballplayers, both of whom were present at Yankee games. Josh Dubow of the Associated Press established all the citizens in his nation as supportive of New York baseball and New York servicemen as a result of the terrorist attacks. "Everybody seemed to be cheering for New York's baseball teams after Sept. 11. The interlocking 'NY' on the teams' caps symbolized the perseverance of the city and the country in the wake of the worst terrorist attacks in the nation's history."[19] Angell likewise associated the Yankees with firemen and policemen and constructed his national identity in very narrow terms:

> Ceremonials and long minutes of silence, players in Fire and Police Department caps (and the "PAPD" version, for the Port Authority's cops), plus attending groups of policemen and firemen, vociferously cheered, greeted the resumption of play after a week's suspension. . . .[20]

Writing of the Yankees, Tyler Kepner of the *New York Times* chronicled of New York fans: "unscripted and uninhibited, they filled the silence with a chant. 'U-S-A! U-S-A!' they cheered, and a few minutes later they applauded and waved flags."[21] These columnists lifted the Yankees, policemen, and firemen to the status of American heroes while using sport to assert an overly patriotic national identity.

However, the athletes that columnists associated with a masculine and patriotic national identity in the context of terrorism and war extended beyond baseball. One year after the attacks Bill Plaschke and David Wharton of the *Los Angeles Times* placed a single athlete, Pat Tillman, Arizona Cardinals safety who left a $3.6 million contract to join the armed forces, in the same grand narrative of sport's service to nation. They wrote of Tillman and referred to the many "heroic" athletes who served in World War II.[22] Both columnists ultimately suggested that Tillman was proof the nation was still full of "men of honor."[23] Plaschke noted that Tillman exemplified "what was best about America."[24] All of these columnists used cultural memories of World War II to align athletic prowess with war heroics, and the correct form of patriotism in the context of war. Gary Smith of *Sports Illustrated* and Plaschke told the same stories of Tillman, stories whose content were reminiscent of other symbols of American mythology. Tillman's hard work ethic in college, evidenced in his refusal to redshirt his freshman year, was reminiscent of the values stories of John Crevecoeur and Ben Franklin purport in defining "the American character." His fortitude even in the face of legal punishment during a high school trip to Mexico was reminiscent of President George Washington's cherry tree and President Abraham Lincoln's honesty. And his penchant to camp alone was reminiscent of Thoreau's Walden Pond.[25] Similarly, Jason Cowley linked Tillman's story to President Kennedy's life and suggested constancy to American identity:

> It was as if the words of John F Kennedy, resounding across the decades, had spoken directly to [Tillman]. He knew that, following the events of 11 September 2001, his mission no longer lay on the football fields of America, where he played for the Arizona Cardinals.[26]

These columnists used the athlete-turned-soldier Tillman to anchor 9/11 and the war in a grand narrative of American history, or at least the values that are characteristic of that grand narrative. They suggested that the nation's identity was always found in exceptional men like Kennedy and now Tillman. Hence, Tillman served these columnists' construction of a mythic national identity that was represented in stories with moral endings familiar to American mythology, itself full of white male patriots.[27] This construction of national identity through white males, coupled with the acceptance of war reflected a tradition in mainstream sports columns, as shown in chapters 2 and 3.

Similarly, Mortimer Zuckerman of *U.S. News & World Report* wrote of Tillman: "But, every now and then, there's a moment that gives a face and a name to those who are fighting and puts the patina of courage" on it.[28] Tillman "put his ideals into action and, in so doing, reminded all of us what those overused terms in sports–'guts,' 'courage,' and 'tough'— really mean."[29] Plaschke wrote "the real tackles weren't the ones made to inspire your team, but to save our neighborhoods."[30] Tillman, who was in Afghanistan, but whose actual day-to-day experiences were not known, became a construct of sports columnists' imaginations where the enemy was altogether absent and participation in war equated to courage, honor, and patriotism.

Likewise, many columnists' descriptions of President Bush's ceremonial first pitch at the third game of the Yankee-Diamondback World Series implicitly supported war. Angell wrote, "President Bush threw the ceremonial first pitch of game three for a strike, from the full distance, and the Yankees and the weather seemed to take it from there."[31] Wilstein used Bush's pitch as a way to juxtapose his national identity with terror:

> That was the same message President Bush delivered when he threw out the first pitch of Game 3 at the World Series. It was a perfect strike, literally and symbolically. Seeing that, how many Americans hoped Osama bin Laden was watching on a satellite TV in his cave, wondering what it takes to defeat the spirit of this country?

Describing Bush's bullet-proof gear, Dana Milbank associated Bush with a soldier and found a matrix of national identity, war, masculinity, sport, and unthinking patriotism by which to define his nation's response to terror. His column ended by stating that Bush "tossed a strike and he . . . left the field to chants of 'U-S-A,' it appeared his message got through. 'USA Fears Nobody,' proclaimed a banner hanging from an upper deck."[32] All of these columnists represented national response to terror through Bush's presence and used rhetoric that established their national identities as masculine, patriotic, and implicitly supportive of war. They did so, partially, by playing on the word "strike" to associate the strength of the president's throw with the anticipated bombings of Afghanistan.[33] Again, however, these narratives about retaliation lacked the nuances that could distinguish between terrorists and Afghani citizens, reactionary versus reasoned war.

Ultimately, columnists tied sport to tragedy in memory of the 9/11 terrorist attacks by mythologizing Tillman and projecting the strength of Bush's pitch into the realm of national heroics. This memory of terrorism and the nation's reaction to it, however, cleansed both of their violence. The cleansing, moreover, was predicated on a substitution of places and people that experienced violence (the Twin Towers, Pentagon, and Shanksville) with places and bodies that would allow columnists to use rhetoric of national masculinity, courage, and retaliation. In terms of Peter Sacks's theory of the elegy, columnists dispelled the mourning by composing elegies that substituted for the deceased a more palatable object, person, or place.[34] Sacks further argued that funeral ceremonies associated with death perform such work. Hence, Edward Wong of the *New York Times,* writing of the resumption of the baseball season, suggested that "the mourning was far from over, but the healing took a different form last night."[35] William Rhoden of the *New York Times* argued that Yankee Stadium served as "an open-air cathedral," for those who died on 9/11.[36] These columnists substituted Yankee Stadium and the fans for the sites of terror and Afghanistan. Similarly, columnists writing of Tillman's joining the Marines were characterized by the fact that his actual body was not present. Tillman's body was absent from columnists' view when they wrote of him and his experiences in war. Hence, columnists again established their national ideals by elegizing the absent Tillman. In turn they allowed a "healthy" or palatable mourning and a subsequent celebration of national ideals. Tillman had not yet been killed, but his movement from the football field to Afghanistan allowed columnists to substitute his absence with rhetoric of mythological national identity.

All of these columnists claiming that athletes and politicians and the locations they were in served the nation revealed the conditions under which masculine, courageous, and vengeance-seeking national identities could be established in the context of terror and war. In short, columnists replaced images and sites that would require reflection on the implications of globalized war with people and places that allowed a reassertion of patriotism: Ground Zero was where the war was promised, and Yankee Stadium and Tillman were the places sports columnists cleansed that promise of its violence. The problem with such tactics as substitution and cleansing is that they advocate for war in columns about sporting events and sports figures without imagining the consequences or the necessary preparation for war. Moreover, sports columnists' practices of avoiding the realities of war can be explained through trauma theory. The *DSM-IV*, the psychiatric handbook used to diagnose mental disorders, defined "efforts to avoid activities, places or people that arouse recollections of the trauma" as a major symptom of posttraumatic stress disorder. [37]

Ultimately, then, there were three ways in which these columns about the Yankees and Tillman engaged in constructing a mythological national identity. First, American heroes were white males. Second, these columnists wrote of war without writing of the actual soldiers' experiences in the war. Rather, they wrote of the sports figures in New York or of Tillman, all of whom became vessels through which columnists constructed their imagined nations as male, brave, strong, and just. Third, and as a result, patriotic responses to these males were equated to support of a mythological nationalism that made the consequences of patriotic fervor and war invisible. Hence, the unthinking patriotism these columnists advocated was also a precursor to public support of a mismanaged and falsely advertised war. [38] The potential consequences and reach of the War on Terror were invisible in all these columns. These columnists, like the Bush administration that prohibited soldiers' coffins from being on shown on television, then, constructed what Patricia Zimmerman called the war in the air: where bodies of the injured and dead are avoided by mainstream media and the consequences of war are dislocated from the stories about it. [39]

While white males were overwhelmingly the ones constructing mythological and masculine national identities in the context of 9/11, they were not the only ones. Columnists in this mostly white-male camp included Diane Pucin, a woman; William Rhoden, a black male; and Edward Wong, an Asian American male. A masculine national identity that implicitly supported a war in which mainly people of color and of little means would die, together with the enemy, was seen in columns by writers of a variety of races and both genders. But the inclusion of minority voices in sports pages did not automatically equate to differing points of view regarding national identity. Instead it was differing concepts regarding sport's relationship to national identity that brought forth these differing views of national identity.

A DIVERSION, BUT NOT A MYTHOLOGY

Many columnists, however, resisted the traditional rhetoric of tragedy and exposed the problems in assuming a linkage between sport and national identity in the context of forthcoming war. Jason Whitlock of the *Kansas City Star* exposed some of the racism that manifested itself within the nation-state after 9/11. Whitlock summarized his experiences on a plane ride after the Broncos-Chiefs game he attended on September 23, 2001:

> I sat next to a man who appeared to be of Arab descent. All sorts of silly, stupid thoughts danced through my pea-sized brain. I actually considered getting off the plane. And then I remembered I would be letting the terrorists win. They want us to change our routines. They want to ruin the pleasures, such as easy travel and sporting events that we take for granted. They want us to bow to our racist tendencies.[40]

Whitlock, a black columnist and former college athlete who often takes a well-reasoned, racial lens to his writing, warned against the racial stereotypes that were being constructed and accepted after 9/11.

Whitlock and Mitch Albom, a white columnist of the *Detroit Free Press*, both argued that the connection between sport and national identity in the context of war was tenuous. Whitlock wrote:

> While our government began its retaliatory campaign against terrorism, I sat inside Denver's Invesco Field at Mile High and watched the Broncos slap our Chiefs. I made a point not to look at the press-box televisions showing details of our bombing of Afghanistan. I didn't want to be updated. I wanted to escape for a few hours. Sports played its role beautifully Sunday. . . . The marching orders we've been given since Sept. 11 have been rather simple. President Bush and his staff told us that we were going to conduct a long, bloody war against terrorism and that we must have the courage to go on with our lives.[41]

Unlike his counterparts, Whitlock did not use sport as a means to tout war or unthinking support of it. In contrast, he drew attention to the fact that sport serves as a manner in which culture dissociates from the traumatic event, as the *DSM-IV* suggests. He also underscored the potential bloodiness of the forthcoming war. In the process, he suggested sport had a place in everyday citizens' routines, but that place was quite separate from the War on Terror; sport did not return the nation to stability, either. Similarly, Albom summarized a van trip he took from Detroit to Cleveland to attend the Lions–Browns game on September 23, 2001. He wrote:

> Normally, I fly to games. But "normal" disappeared 13 days ago when terrorists captured the skies for one awful morning and threw America over a cliff. . . . The terror mongers had nudged most of us off our paths. This was how they nudged me. I was in a van for a four-hour commute.[42]

Here, the concept of normalcy was destabilized by terror, and, he argued, sport did not reestablish that normalcy. He continued to write that "on the all-news radio stations they spoke of America's coming military action and Afghanistan's refusal to turn over Osama bin Laden. For the first time in a long time, however, we did not immediately turn on the news."[43] Like Whitlock, then, Albom subverted the conventions of the rhetoric of tragedy and distinguished among sport, national identity, patriotism, and support of the war. The remainder of his column deconstructed the rituals at the game meant to represent patriotism while arguing that national stability and strength was not associated with them.[44] Instead, he argued that everyday people's return to their routines was a sign of recovery from the terrorist attacks. In making these claims while referencing the War on Terror in their work, both columnists implied that sport was a diversion from the realities of war, not a proper means to support it; that a return to normalcy was not predicated on sport or rhetoric of strength, retaliation, or virility. These columnists, in short, not only resisted using sport to construct a mythological, masculine national identity but they also deconstructed the narratives that did so. In the process, they potentially served to highlight to readers that the connection between sport and nation was tenuous at best.

A year after the terror Christine Brennan of *USA Today* challenged the way baseball was linked to cultural memories of patriotism in the context of 9/11. She wrote:

> If you listen to the sports talk shows, you know that baseball and Sept. 11 have somehow become linked. . . . Even though last year's World Series gave the nation's sports fans something to enjoy in the days and weeks after the terrorist attacks, I see absolutely no relationship between baseball and Sept. 11, 2002. . . . What facet of baseball is so redeeming and worthwhile to deserve this kind of patriotic kinship with Sept. 11?[45]

That Whitlock is black, Albom white, and Brennan a white woman is of utmost importance to underscore in arguing that resisting national mythology is a matter of standpoint, not skin color or gender. Just as male columnists of color and women columnists in the first camp supported national mythologies through sport, white, black, and women columnists resisted that mythology here. Hence, while it is clear and obvious that including all minorities in social, cultural, and political institutions is necessary to achieve social justice, so too is including different points of view regarding race, nation, gender, and sexuality. The inclusion of racial, gendered, sexed, and/or classed diversity in institutions does not equate to diversity in standpoints regarding identity, nation, and/or social justice. Yet kinds of diversity are necessary to manifest true diversity.

A NEW KIND OF SERVICE

There was, too, a subgroup of columnists that focused on how athletes served other citizens in a time of need. In so doing, this subgroup dislocated sport from the national identity and resisted the mythology of the first camp. For instance, referring to Pearl Harbor and to Pete Rozelle's decision to allow the games to continue just days after President Kennedy's assassination, Paul Attner of *The Sporting News* quoted the Jets head coach as saying, "'If (people) want a diversion, [sports isn't it,] go to church, pray.'"[46] He then listed the many relatives of athletes in the NFL who were harmed or nearly killed during the terrorist attacks. Attner continued, specifying that many NFL teams such as the Redskins, Giants, Eagles, 49ers, Titans, and Steelers donated blood, attended services, and/or visited victims and servicemen in the days following the attacks. Similarly, Kepner wrote a column about the first game the Mets played after the attacks, resisted the construction of athletes as national heroes, and also illustrated the potential activism inherent in sports columns. Rather than focusing on hits or runs, he wrote that Mets Manager Bobby Valentine "stayed at Shea [Stadium in New York] until 3 a.m., directing volunteers who were loading relief supplies for victims of the World Trade Center attacks. 'It was my diversion,' Valentine said."[47] Throughout the column, Kepner described the general malaise among players, showing that athletics did not serve a nation of strength and virility. In later columns about the Mets, Kepner resisted the tendency to link sport to a healing process and even suggested that the city and nation may not heal from the terror. He also highlighted that the Mets donated their time and some of their pay to victims of the attack.[48]

These two columnists, then, showed that sport was of little value to the nation in the context of 9/11. But they also emphasized the humanity of the people in professional sport and showed that sport could serve the nation when athletes volunteered for the Red Cross, visited the injured, and donated money or time or both. The potential power in such columns should not be overlooked. Just as those columns that constructed a virile and revenge-seeking nation through sport wielded substantial power, those columns that emphasized service and monetary contributions as exemplary responses to terror potentially moved citizens to help others when in need.

This camp of columnists played an activist role by resisting mythological narratives about nation, sport, and war. In this resistance was the potential to reach readers who would otherwise buy into the mythological national identities the first camp of columnists constructed.

COUNTERNARRATIVE: MAKING THE WAR VISIBLE

While the 2001 season ended, the War on Terror did not. Eventually, columnists began to dislocate sport and Tillman from their national identity and in the process question the effectiveness of the Bush administration's approach to the War on Terror.

Rick Reilly of *Sports Illustrated* confronted the mythological national identity and clean War on Terror his counterparts in the first camp and federal officials constructed. He did so by writing about soldiers playing sport in Afghanistan and acknowledging that people were dying in the War on Terror. Chronicling how the Delta Company Desperados built a baseball field for entertainment during down time, Reilly contrasted Yankees games with the games the soldiers played in Afghanistan. He wrote that "instead of New York cops providing security, they have infantry posted on all sides, which is what you need in a war with no front against an enemy who doesn't care about saving his own flesh, only splattering yours."[49] These baseball players/soldiers were in a war zone, experiencing the violence of war, not in New York playing games nine miles away from the site of the terrorist attacks and half a world away from the war. Reilly then brought to mainstream media knowledge of the war's violence occurring—even though President Bush had claimed the conflict to have ended. In bringing this violence to light, Reilly used the very people his counterparts used to repress it:

> Since the war began in March, 10 soldiers have committed suicide and another 15 deaths are being investigated as possible suicides. Hopelessness comes with this kind of conflict: You can't quite figure out how it can end, but guys are getting sent home in body bags in between. More American soldiers have been killed since President Bush declared an end to major combat operations on May 1 than died in the war itself.[50]

In describing the deaths by suicide and from enemy fire, Reilly challenged his counterparts' construction of the war and the mythological nationalism that underpinned it. Reilly also illustrated that more deaths had occurred since President Bush, dressed in Air Force gear, descended on the *USS Abraham Lincoln* to offer a speech beneath the "Mission Accomplished" banner as the backdrop than prior to this moment. Overtly, too, Reilly criticized the war's goals, suggesting that there was no end point, even as young men were dying. Unlike his predecessors writing of Muhammad Ali and Vietnam and unlike his contemporary counterparts, Reilly used sport to criticize the president and the war.

It would take a year after that column until Reilly would find allies among other sports columnists. On April 22, 2004, Pat Tillman's unit was ordered, against their wishes, to tow a broken Humvee along the south-eastern border of Afghanistan. (The order came against the platoon's wishes and from a commander at a base far from where the platoon was). When the platoon came through a rocky ravine, fire came down upon them from the two canyon walls above. Confusion ensued. At the end of fight, Pat Tillman, American hero through whom the "war without casualty" was partially constructed, lay dead, a victim of friendly fire.

Immediately after news of Tillman's death was relayed to the Pentagon, however, the official press release read in part:

> The former Arizona Cardinals safety Pat Tillman was posthumously awarded the Silver Star for gallantry on the battlefield for leading his Army Rangers unit to the rescue of comrades caught in an ambush. Tillman was shot and killed in Afghanistan on April 22 while fighting "without regard for his personal safety."[51]

As with the first pitch of game three and the "Mission Accomplished" banner, national officials worked to control the narrative of the War on Terror by manipulating Tillman's story to fit their themes and scripts. Their manipulation of Tillman's story extended beyond the press release, though. Tillman's fellow platoon mates, including Russell Baer, a friend to Pat and his brother Kevin, were told to keep knowledge of the fratricide repressed.[52] Marines in Tillman's unit were ordered to burn his uniform and body armor. And ultimately, an "initial investigator's report" was "buried and redone after he recommended that 'certain leaders be investigated' for 'gross negligence.'"[53]

Frank Rich of the *New York Times* argued that through the Tillman story the Pentagon and Bush administration attempted not just a cover-up but also a re-creation of the national identity established in sports stadiums after 9/11.[54] According to him the Bush administration went out of its way to "script a narrative" of Tillman and the war that would support the "myths" of national identity.[55] Rich wrote, "Mary Tillman [Pat's mother], was offended to discover that even President Bush wanted a cameo role in this screenplay: she told *The Post* that he had offered to tape a memorial to her son for a Cardinals game that would be televised shortly before Election Day. (She said no)."[56] Despite her refusal, however, Bush taped the memorial and it was aired during the game. Given the precedent set by his appearance at game three of the Yankees Series in 2001, Bush's having the video play in Cardinal Stadium worked to fit the story of Iraq and Afghanistan back into the realm of national strength and resiliency, back into a space—the stadium—that would cleanse the war and the story of Tillman of violence while praising and glorifying his heroism.[57]

This time, however, columnists chronicled Tillman's experiences in Afghanistan and Iraq as a means to resist the mythological national identity Bush worked to create. In writing of Tillman's death, Steve Coll of the *Washington Post* maintained the soldier's status as a hero, but deconstructed the national mythology established through him. Coll wrote:

> Myths shaped Pat Tillman's reputation, and mystery shrouded his death. . . . Many Americans mourned his death last April 22 [2004] and embraced his sacrifice as a rare example of courage and national service. . . . The records show that Tillman fought bravely. . . . They also show that his supervisors exaggerated his actions and burnished his legend in public.[58]

Coll chronicled how the Pentagon's press release about Tillman's death knowingly misled the public because he was "the Army's most famous volunteer on terrorism . . . [who], for many Americans [captured] the best aspects of the country's post-September 11 character."[59]

Rick Morrissey of the *Chicago Tribune* characterized the cover-up a tragedy of national proportions. He also said that Tillman, like many soldiers, was a hero, and the true "dark side of the Tillman tragedy [wa]s the danger of his sacrifice being shaped and twisted for other purposes."[60] Morrissey then went on to criticize the unthinking patriotism that sports columnists supported in the aftermath of 9/11 and in doing this reframed Tillman's story as one about the current War on Terror. He wrote, "Nobody wants [Tillman's death] to become a tribute to the NFL's sense of patriotism, the way many of the post-9/11 ballpark ceremonies by Major League Baseball became" ones.[61] Similarly, Terry McDonnell, editor of *Sports Illustrated*, introduced a commemorative issue on Tillman and 9/11 by underscoring the problematic mythology that sports columnists constructed in the aftermath of 9/11.[62] He wrote that after 9/11, "The games resumed, and the nation came together around sports. Stadiums became places to find strength; what had been diversion now felt like ritual. It was tribal. We were going to war." But McDonnell did not stop there. He also worked to deconstruct the Bush administration's narratives of the war in the air. He wrote that "[a]s of September 11, [2005] at least 272 members of the U.S. military have died in Afghanistan, Pakistan, and Uzbekistan. . . . In Iraq at least 2,643 members of the U.S. military have died since the beginning of March 2003."[63] Both of these writers told the story of Tillman's death and his actual experiences in war to reframe the way 9/11 and the nation-state's response to it were remembered. That is, through Tillman, they were working to unlink memory of 9/11 from sport and tie it to the death that occurred when a mismanaged war was supported through an unthinking patriotism. Hence, these writers overtly criticized the Bush administration, the War on Terror, and sports columns from the first camp as they wrote of Tillman's death. They ultimately created a counternarrative to the national mythology that had been traditional of sports pages in the context of any war, even in many columns just one year earlier.

Similarly, Gary Smith wrote a feature article that recorded Tillman's thoughts concerning the distinction between Afghanistan and Iraq: "'This war is so f— illegal' Pat said of the Iraq War."[64] Smith wrote that Tillman sat upon a bunker and realized that he was in a war that he did not sign up for.[65] Smith dislocated the current war in Iraq from the myths associated with Tillman and in the process suggested that the War on Terror was two wars, the one in Iraq being illegal.[66] Hence, Smith remembered Tillman's actual experiences in Afghanistan and Iraq, and the nation-state's attempt to cover them up, rather than bolstering the national mythology through Tillman, the dead American hero. Smith also worked to reframe how Tillman and 9/11 would be remembered. He suggested that 9/11 should be remembered through the terror of 9/11 and the actual wars in Afghanistan and Iraq, not New York, the Yankees, or mythologies of Tillman.

Collectively, this last camp of columnists situated soldiers' themselves in the war, thereby working to reframe the way their counterparts remembered 9/11 and Tillman. This reframing also permitted a criticism of the current War on Terror, for in chronicling Tillman's war experience, they showed that the patriotic and vengeful national identity constructed in sports stadiums and columns after 9/11 had global implications, and dire consequences for even the most "American" of heroes. And in writing of men who died in war, these columnists resisted the construction of the war without casualty. They did not suggest people on an American field of competition represented the nation or its reaction to terror. They also refused to fulfill the conventions in the discourse of tragedy that cleansed the war of its violence.

The final of the three camps of columnists, too, represented a major shift in the role sports columnists traditionally played in writing of national identity through sport. This camp challenged not only the mythological construction of nation that was traditional of sports columns written in the context of tragedy, but also the nation-state's officials. As such, some sports columnists were now involved in contesting with official constructions of national identity, and in the process, engaged in an overtly political discussion.

9/11: NEVER FORGET

From California to New York, Minnesota to Arizona, American citizens gathered in stadiums and in front of televisions in almost ritual fashion to witness, once again, the mechanisms by which sport and nation come to narrate something of our own history. Perhaps Robert Blum summarized the NFL's memorialization of 9/11's ten-year anniversary best:

> On September 11, 2011 . . . American flags as large as football fields were unfurled inside stadiums and fans of all ages sang the national anthem with gusto Sunday in a red-white-and-blue observance marking the 10th anniversary of the Sept. 11 terrorist attacks and start of the country's most popular sport: the NFL.[67]

What was overwhelmingly absent in the stories of heroism and memories of trauma, however, was context to the memories. In short, while memories of first responders abounded, very little, if any, memories about the fervor for war in 2001 were represented. Likewise, very little if any reference to Pat Tillman, one of the NFL's very own heroes, was made.

Among the columnists, and, dare I say, among many Americans, the rituals at games that were played the week after the terror attacks in 2001 still hold a special place in their memory. Ethan J. Sklonick of the *Palm Beach Post* wrote:

> A decade ago, the NFL skipped one weekend and then resumed its games to help give fans an escape from reality. Now, it is recognizing the significance of that period . . . The football? That mostly got forgotten, although the events surrounding it remain memorable to many playing at the time.[68]

Here Sklonick acknowledged that the rituals, not the games themselves, led to a sort of healing or catharsis for those watching the televised events unfold.[69] These ceremonies with their "American flags" and first responders' clothing, allowed "the season [to] settle back into normalcy. A new normalcy. . . . It was just a little of what 9/11 changed forever." That is, the new normalcy was the sports' pageantry which led to a patriotism that deflected the realities of war away from the stadium and consciousness.[70]

But the rituals were fit into a narrative frame cultivated by the NFL, both on televisions and in stadiums:

> A recorded message from actor Robert DeNiro was broadcast on videoboards reminding fans that we honor those brave men and women by continuing to show our unity and strength as a country. "We remember our great country and the people that died in this tragic incident, the first responders and their families and all the people that kept our country safe," he told FOX from the sidelines of the Giants-Redskins game. "This is a chance for everyone to come together and feel great about our country, the sacrifices so many people have had and what we all have in front of us. We've got a lot to be proud of."[71]

In the same recorded message, President George W. Bush, who capitalized on the connection mainstream media cultivated among sport, politics, war, first responders, and patriotism, appeared. He "praised the rescue workers of that day in a televised pregame show segment prior to the openers."[72] Bush, whose legacy is tied to 9/11, along with DeNiro, a national icon who has also come to represent New York, both limited their discussion of 9/11 to first responders. While it is clear that the first responders were the heroes of that day and that praising them is not only admirable, but also the right thing to do, the way 9/11 was remembered was through people who, in no uncertain terms cleansed 9/11 of some of its otherwise messy elements.

The only reference to the war came out of former Miami Dolphins received Orande Gadsden. He said "You got a sense, it's the same thing you feel in the Olympics, 'Let's go get 'em.' If you had sent 32 teams with all their players to go find Osama bin Laden, someone would find him. Just give us our equipment, and drop us off."[73] As a result, sports' role in advocating for what was generally accepted as a mismanaged war was altogether dismissed from memory. In fact, the only controversy that arose in columns about the anniversary of 9/11 came in Bill Plaschke's column. Plaschke wrote about Major League Baseball's decision to pro-hibit its players from wearing hats with fire and police department logos on them. Plaschke wrote:

> You know those first-responder caps worn by National Football League sideline figures Sunday in honour of the 10th anniversary of 9/11? Rex Ryan of the New York Jets wore a cap honouring the New York fire department? Tom Coughlin of the New York Giants wore a New York police department cap? As you probably know by now, a group of Major League Baseball players wanted to do the same thing, but the league said no.[74]

Plaschke then underscored that the caps themselves reflected something uniquely "American" and as a result, prohibiting their use was un-American. "The whole point of sports is to be a rich part of the American fabric, and throughout the last century baseball enjoyed that unique part of Americana," Plaschke said. "But in not allowing those hats to be worn, baseball totally stepped away from cultural relevance."[75]

The point here is that 9/11 was reduced to a ritualization of honoring first responders. To be sure, such honor is well-deserved. However, the phrase, "Never Forget," that has stamped 9/11, coupled with the honor-ing of first-responders, does raise the question what it is that Americans are "never forgetting." The memories that columnists and the NFL underscored were those of patriotism and uplift, not terror or war. Like-wise, the controversy that Plaschke spent his column on was that certain hats were prohibited from being worn. Meanwhile, at the time, America was yet engaged in a war that originated as result of the attacks on 9/11, and the controversy these columnists focused on was reduced to cloth-ing. Hence, the memories of 9/11, at least those elicited by sports, were those that were cleansed of violence. They also were those that lifted American identity to benevolence and bravery as exemplified in the first responders. Even Plaschke, one of Tillman's greatest advocates just years earlier, did not use this occasion to remember the athlete-turned soldier. Hence, memories of 9/11 initiated through sport were used to mythologize the nation and to repress any memories of the war on terror and Iraq in which Tillman and thousands of others died or were injured.

MEMORIALIZE, DON'T REMEMBER

In *Tangled Memories,* Sturken looked at "how histories are told through popular culture" from the media to memorials.[76] Sturken argued that there is an interplay between the individual's witnessing of an event and mainstream media's representation of it. This interplay, over time, can transform the factual occurrence of an event to fit into narrative frames dictated by mainstream media. Sturken also argued that individuals can resist the mainstream media's representation of these moments. In the case of remembering 9/11, however, mainstream sport media seemed more interested in portraying the national identity as virile and strong rather than engaged, at that moment in time, in a ten-year ill-planned war, one of the catalysts for which was sport's reaction to 9/11. Likewise, just as was the case immediately after the terror attacks, the mainstream sport media seemed to privilege an overly masculine form of national identity.

In "Masculinity, Courage, and Sacrifice," Sturken argued that the stories of heroism on September 11 rarely included women, for "the stories of the women who died on those planes, in the Pentagon, and in the World Trade Center have not moved us as a public to the same degree."[77] A quick review of the narrators of 9/11—the NFL, President Bush, and Robert DeNiro—confirm Sturken's point. Susan J. Brison examined the images and narratives that presented themselves in relation to 9/11 as telling of a penchant toward unification mandated through spectacle and sport. The outburst of patriotism and nationalism that coupled 9/11 was evident, Brison writes, in the oft-repeated "We are all New Yorkers" and "We are all Yankees" that deluged the media in the days and weeks immediately following those attacks. She then wrote, "I don't really think we're all New Yorkers, and I'm not a fan of the Yankees"[78]

Even ten years after the attacks, the masculine heroes of fire departments and professional sport were people through which a return to a seemingly stabilized world could occur. This was a world where the people on screen were associated with virility not only because of the narratives that coupled them, but also because of the space they inhabited—a baseball/football field—and the city of New York, the most phallic and capitalist of American cities. This indicates a return to a national identity that existed prior to war and terror. But this stabilized identity also denies that the nation was engaged in wars that had no definable purpose, and that the way 9/11 would be remembered would be for an emotional response, not the concrete and real tragedy that occurred to innocent citizens in New York, Pennsylvania, and Washington, D.C.; nor those in the mismanaged wars already mentioned.

Sport most likely did provide some respite or allowance of recovery from trauma to those who experienced it in a mediated form—those who watched the events of 9/11 unfold on television. However, the trauma was not fully escapable for the many people who suffered at the towers, in D.C., or Pennsylvania. Because those who experienced the trauma through television did not have the severe reminders of trauma, closure could be possible through a game. Put another way, after the stories of masculine heroism are told, and the landscape of New York shown to still be properly memorializing the dead, closure or healing is possible for those who are interested in reasserting America's place in the global landscape. The stories of American courage, sacrifice, and virility, all told, shows that 9/11 had been properly memorialized. The memories of terror and misguided war properly repressed, sports' role—from patriotic fervor to Pat Tillman—in catalyzing such a war could be simply avoided. Hence, on the ten-year anniversary of 9/11, we memorialized through sport, but we did not remember.

NOTES

1. George W. Bush, "President Bush's Address to the Nation on 11 September 2001," September 11, 2001, http://www.whitehouse.gov/news/releases/2001/09/20010911-16.html (20 September 2004).

2. George W. Bush, CNN News, September 14, 2001.

3. George W. Bush, "President Bush's Address to the Nation on 11 September 2001."

4. Steve Buckley, "Thankfully, Games Go On," *Boston Herald,* 22 November 2001, p. 92.

5. Walter Shapiro, "Baseball Strike Talk Cheapens Post-Sept. 11 Patriotism," *USA TODAY*, 28 August 2002, sec. A.

6. George Vecsey, "Can American Sports Ever Get Back to Normal?" *New York Times,* 16 September 2001, sec. 1.

7. Vescey, "Can American Sports Ever Get Back to Normal?"

8. Hal Bodley, "Selig Facing Difficult Decision on Resuming Games," *USA Today,* 13 September 2001, sec. C.

9. Mike Tierney, "Another Day Off as Nation Mourns," *Atlanta Journal Constitution*, 13 September 2001, sec. F.

10. Scott Ostler, "The Question Is How, Not When to Play," *San Francisco Chronicle*, 13 September 2001, sec. E.

11. Steve Wilstein, "Patriotism and Protest at Yankee Stadium," *The Associated Press,* 22 July 2004, http://www.lexisnexis.com .

12. Wilstein, "Patriotism and Protest at Yankee Stadium."

13. Dan Barry, "New York Carries On, but Test of Its Grit Has Just Begun," *New York Times*, 11 October 2001, sec. B.

14. Joe Lapointe, "Baseball: Fans Wear Their Emotions," *New York Times,* 12 September 2002, sec. D.

15. Roger Angell, "Can You Believe It?" *New Yorker,* 26 November 2001.

16. Bodley, "Selig Facing Difficult Decision on Resuming Games."

17. Diane Pucin, "Terrorism Can't Defeat Heroism," *Los Angeles Times,* 16 September 2001, sec. D.

18. Wilstein, "Patriotism and Protest at Yankee Stadium."

19. Josh Dubow, "Booing New York Means Baseball's Back to Normal," 15 March 2002, http://www.lexisnexis.com

20. Angell, "Can You Believe It?"

21. Tyler Kepner, "At Yankee Stadium, Tributes and a Monument to Heroism," *New York Times,* 12 September 2002, sec. D.

22. David Wharton, "War Isn't Their Kind of Game," *Los Angeles Times,* 24 April 2004, sec. A.

23. Wharton, "War Isn't Their Kind of Game."

24. Bill Plaschke, "The True Meaning of Sacrifice," *Los Angeles Times,* 24 April 2004, sec. D.

25. See Gary Smith, "Remember his Name," *Sports Illustrated,* 5 September 2006, 88–101; Plaschke, "The True Meaning of Sacrifice."

26. Jason Cowley, "Sport," *New Statesman,* 24 May 2004, http://www.proquest.com.

27. See Plaschke, "The True Meaning of Sacrifice"; Cowley, "Sport."

28. Mortimer Zuckerman, "A Hero's Parting Message," *U.S. News & World Report,* 10 May 2004: 72.

29. Zuckerman, "A Hero's Parting Message"; 72.

30. Plaschke, "The True Meaning of Sacrifice."

31. Angell, "Can You Believe It?"

32. Dana Milbank, "At Yankee Stadium, President Makes a Pitch for Normalcy; Bush Calls for Americans to Find 'Balance' of Caution and Defiance," *Washington Post,* 31 October 2001 sec. A.

33. Greg Stoda wrote of another political figure at Yankee games; a figure that, because of his association with New York, was quickly vaulted to national significance in a similar way that Reagan was through his association with California and film. Stoda wrote that "[Rudolph Giuliani] was one of baseball's most prominent faces last autumn. . . . So, too, were the dynastic Yankees from The Bronx in World Series defeat." See Greg Stoda, "Symbolic Home Run Helped a City's Healing Piazza Embodied September 11 Recovery." A few writers were invested in using Rudy Giuliani's rhetoric as a mechanism by which to heal their nations. In "A Nation Challenged: The Mayor," Jennifer Steinhauer wrote of a press conference in which Giuliani argued for a return to normalcy and invoked the Yankees as integral to the return. "At news conferences filled with questions about fear, he still talks about the Yankees, encourages people to go to restaurants and peppers the conversation with joking asides." Jennifer Steinhauer, "In Uncharted Territory, Guiliani Campaigns against Fear," *New York Times,* 18 October 2001, sec. B.

34. Peter M. Sacks, *The English Elegy: Studies in the Genre from Spenser to Yeats* (Baltimore: Johns Hopkins University Press, 1996), 299.

35. Edward Wong, "Runs, Hits, and Healing at Stadium," *New York Times,* 26 September 2001.

36. William C. Rhoden, "This Time, a Deeper Appreciation," *New York Times,* 24 October 2001, sec. S.

37. American Psychiatric Association, *DSM-IV* (American Psychiatric Publishing: Washington, DC, 2000), 468.

38. See Gavin Smith, "The Ending Is Up to You," *Film Comment,* July–August 2004, 22.

39. Patricia Zimmerman, *States of Emergency: Documentaries, Wars, Democracies* (Minnesota: University of Minnesota Press, 2004), 57.

40. Jason Whitlock. "We Can't Be Afraid to Watch and Enjoy Sports," *Kansas City Star*, 8 October 2001.

41. Whitlock. "We Can't Be Afraid to Watch and Enjoy Sports."

42. Mitch Albom, "Road to Recovery Takes Unlikely Turn," *Detroit Free Press*, 23 September 2001.

43. Albom, "Road to Recovery Takes Unlikely Turn."

44. Albom, "Road to Recovery Takes Unlikely Turn."

45. Christine Brennan, "Thoughts of 9/11 Override Baseball," *USA Today*, 11 September 2002, sec. 3.

46. Paul Attner, "The League Will Go On, but so Will Its Grief," *The Sporting News*, 24 September 2001.

47. Tyler Kepner, "Patriotism Does Not Erase the Trepidation," *New York Times*, 18 September 2001, sec. C.

48. See Tyler Kepner, "Emotional Return Home for the Mets," *New York Times*, 21 September 2001, sec. C.

49. Rick Reilly, "War Games," *Hate Mail from Cheerleaders*, New York: Sports Illustrated Books, 2007, 314.

50. Rick Reilly, "War Games," *Hate Mail from Cheerleaders*, 315.

51. Steve Coll, "Barrage of Bullets Drowned Our Cries of Comrades," *Washington Post*, 1 May 2005, sec. A; Frank Rich, "It's All *Newsweek*'s Fault," *New York Times*, 22 May 2005: 4, 13; Dave Zirin, "Pat Tillman, Our Hero," *U.S. News & World Report*, 10 May 2004, http://www.proquest.com.

52. See Steve Coll, "Barrage of Bullets Drowned Out Cries of Comrades" (New York: Houghton Mifflin, 2005), 181–99; 182; Dave Zirin, "Pat Tillman, Our Hero," *U.S. News & World Report*, 10 May 2004, p. 72; Frank Rich, "It's All *Newsweek*'s Fault," *New York Times*, 22 May 2005, c. 4, p. 13; Gary Smith, "Remember His Name," *Sports Illustrated*, 5 September, 2006, 88–101; Terry McDonnell, "Brothers," *Sports Illustrated*, 5 September 2006.

53. Smith, "Remember His Name."

54. Although Rich's column was not a sports column, it was a column written about this event. Hence, I include it here.

55. Rich, "It's All *Newsweek*'s Fault."

56. Rich, "It's All *Newsweek*'s Fault."

57. Smith, "Remember His Name," 100.

58. Steve Coll, "Barrage of Bullets Drowned Out Cries of Comrades"; 181–82. Although his work initially appeared in the News section of *Washington Post*, Mike Lupica selected Steve Coll's "Barrage of Bullets Drowned Out Cries of Comrades" for inclusion in the annual version of *Best American Sports Writing*.

59. Coll, "Barrage of Bullets Drowned Our Cries of Comrades," 191.

60. Rick Morrissey, "Well-Known Soldier a Hero, Plain and Simple," *Chicago Tribune*, 31 May 2004, sec. S.

61. Morrissey, "Well-Known Soldier a Hero, Plain and Simple."

62. Hence, the commemorative issue of *Sports Illustrated* clearly was geared at reframing the way sports and 9/11 had been tied in cultural memory. Like Morrissey's column, though, this reframing occurred though memory of Tillman. On the cover was Tillman in fatigues, and the issue's title was "Remember His Name."

63. Terry McDonnell, "Brothers," *Sports Illustrated*, 5 September 2006.

64. Smith, "Remember His Name," 91.

65. Smith, "Remember His Name," 91.

66. Smith, "Remember His Name," 91.

67. Robert Blum, "Sports World Remembers 9/11 Attacks," *Telegraph*, 12 September 2011, B. 3.

68. Ethan J. Sklonick, "NFL Opening Weekend," *Palm Beach Post*, 11 Sept. 2011.

69. Sklonick, "NFL Opening Weekend."

70. Blum, "Sports World Remembers 9/11 Attacks."

71. Blum, "Sports World Remembers 9/11 Attacks."

72. Blum, "Sports World Remembers 9/11 Attacks."

73. Blum, "Sports World Remembers 9/11 Attacks."

74. Bill Plaschke. "MLB's Blunder Caps 'em all; 9/11 Fiasco Shows How Game Has Been Diminished by Its Arrogant Sense of Tradition," *The Gazette*, 15 September 2011.

75. Bill Plaschke. "MLB's Blunder Caps 'em All; 9/11 Fiasco Shows How Game Has Been Diminished by Its Arrogant Sense of Tradition."

76. Marita Sturken, *Tangled Memories* (Los Angeles: University of California Press, 1997), 5.

77. Marita Storken, "Masculinity, Courage, and Sacrifice." *Signs* 1 (Autumn 2002), 444–445.

78. Susan J. Brison, "Gender, Terrorism, and War." *Signs* 1 (August 2002), 427.

FIVE

Patrons of the Saints

On August 27, 2005, Hurricane Katrina, then a category one storm, rumbled across the Gulf of Mexico. Twenty-four hours later, it reached category five status and neared the Mississippi delta region. Not a single federal official warned Gulf Coast residents of the storm's potential danger.

When the storm hit land on August 30th, many New Orleans citizens—the majority of them black and impoverished—sought shelter in the Superdome, home of the New Orleans Saints. Water ravaged the city, submerged homes, cars, and the region. As late as September 4th, the George W. Bush administration had yet to send federal assistance to evacuate the dome despite that the survivors, by then, were hungry, scared, and surviving in an oven amidst human waste.

The slow response of the Bush administration, however, was indicative of federal politicians' historic neglect of that region's black and poor people. In *Development Arrested*, Clyde Woods illustrated that beginning with the slave trade and continuing to the current era, white plantation and farm owners, as well as federal politicians and their policies, exploited the black laborer. The region, as a result, has remained impoverished for centuries.[1] Similarly, in "The Broken Contract," Michael Ignatieff wrote that politicians of the nation have historically neglected the black and impoverished citizens of New Orleans and its surrounding areas. "Public officials simply didn't bother to cross the social distances that divided them from the true poverty of the New Orleans population."[2]

In writing of Hurricane Katrina, sports columnists initially revealed the nation's neglect of the black and impoverished in New Orleans. However, when the NFL season began, only two weeks after the storm, a significant portion of columnists suggested the New Orleans Saints paid a service to New Orleans and the nation. Using rhetoric of national unifi-

cation, many columnists suggested the nation and/or region was represented through sport and in the process avoided discussion of race and
class oppression initially exposed through the tragedy.

There was one other camp of columnists, though. This camp demanded that the black and impoverished citizens be remembered as part
of Katrina's story and the nation's responsibility. These columnists not
only refused to embrace their counterparts' mythological construction of
national identity, but also confronted white privilege in the sports pages
that traditionally privileged that identity. These columnists engaged in a
contest for how the black impoverished population of New Orleans
would be remembered not only as part of Katrina's story, but the dominant national identity as well. The contest began another robust debate
about the place of race and class in mainstream sports media.

THE TRAGEDY IN THE DOME AND THE MYTHS AFTERWARD

In writing of the citizens left to toil in the Superdome, many columnists
constructed the stadium as a metonym for the suffering of New Orleans
citizens whom the Bush administration, like other administrations before
it, neglected. Stephan Fatsis of *The Wall Street Journal* wrote that in the
Superdome structural poverty and racism were clearly visible, and that
"Katrina ha[d] turned the Saints' stadium, the Superdome, into a national
symbol of squalor."[3] David Weiss of *The New York Daily News* wrote that
"the Superdome was turned into a relief center and virtually left condemned."[4] Michael Silver, a feature writer for *Sports Illustrated*, wrote
that "[a]ll the stadiums and arenas, the houses of glory, had been turned
inside out into houses of suffering."[5] The Superdome was, according to
Gary Smith of *Sports Illustrated* "now the site of riots, murders and rapes,
even an apparent suicide by a man who couldn't bare another moment of
the stench."[6]

Collectively, these columnists constructed the Superdome as the site
of national tragedy. To them, it was not the storm that was the tragedy;
Katrina was merely the catalyst that exposed it. The tragedy was the
suffering that occurred within the dome and the consequences of racial
and economic oppression. In short, these columnists redefined the Superdome's cultural meaning from the festive location of Super Bowls to a
visible trope for failed American ideals. Sport columnists, then, served to
deconstruct the national mythology of achieved democracy, one that
sport often supported in its representations of the Superdome.

By the NFL's opening day in 2005, however, a majority of the citizens
who had been left to fester in the Superdome had been transferred to two
other sports stadiums—the Astrodome in Houston, Texas, and the Alamodome in San Antonio, Texas. Still, with the season underway, columnists used sport, and specifically the New Orleans Saints, to pay a service

to the traditional, mythological national identity. Michael Wilbon of the *Washington Post* wrote, "'America's Team' is playing tonight, you know. No, I'm not talking about the Cowboys. The Saints are the team so many of us root for now."[7] Dave Anderson of the *New York Times* wrote that "[w]hether the Dallas Cowboys like it or not, the Saints are now America's Team, at least until they can go home again."[8] An editorial in the *New York Times* argued that the Saints were now "everybody's favorite team."[9] Anderson wrote of Jim Haslett, Saints' coach, who said: "The best thing we can do as a football team to keep New Orleans alive is win games. . . . The best thing to keep the city and the Gulf Coast region out there is win games."[10] Silver wrote that the Saints were "the torchbearers for a city and a region."[11] He later suggested of the Saints' first game that they had the ability to "heal a reeling nation."[12]

As columnists suggested the Saints were America's team and ascribed healing qualities to its players, they imbued athletes' feats (not those of New Orleans citizens in sports stadiums across the nation) with meaning for how Katrina would be situated in national memory. Only when the neglected citizenry associated with New Orleans entered places that would *not* draw attention to the nation's failures did they become representative of these sports columnists' construction of national identity, Hurricane Katrina, and/or New Orleans. In contrast, people still in the Alamodome and Astrodome, people in places that would represent the nation's failures and were substituted with NFL players playing games in Carolina and later, New York.

In telling the story of Katrina, then, columnists fulfilled the convention in the rhetoric of tragedy that substitutes the places and people that experienced tragedy with those of sport. Just as columnists established their mythological nation by representing the post-9/11 nation through athletes and servicemen, columnists writing of Katrina used only those capable of fitting into a similar kind of nation in post-Katrina narratives.

The first game the Saints played in 2005 was against the Carolina Panthers on, of all dates, September 11. Their second game, a "home game," was played against the New York Giants at Meadowlands Stadium in New Jersey. Columnists used these temporal and spatial connections to 9/11 in writing of the Saints' service to the nation in the context of Hurricane Katrina. Silver wrote that "by kickoff Sunday—after a standing ovation for the New Orleans players from the crowd of nearly 73,000, a prayer in remembrance of Sept. 11 and an F-16 flyover—the Saints were determined to make an immediate statement."[13] Lisa Olson of the *New York Daily News*, in an otherwise astute and complex column, associated 9/11 with this tragedy while highlighting the heroics of "firemen and policemen" in both.[14] Anderson evoked memories of 9/11. He quoted New Orleans wide receiver Joe Horn, and raised him to the same realm of mythic American hero that the Yankees, firemen, and policemen were lifted to in the wake of 9/11. Of the New York fans Horn said:

"They feel our heart, they feel our pain. We're supposed to be the new America's Team. That's fine because that's what America is all about, bonding together. . . . When Sept. 11th happened, my heart went out to everyone in New York." He continued, remembering that the Saints were the first visiting team at Meadowlands Stadium when the 2001 N.F.L. schedule resumed after 9/11. "I wanted to do everything I could to help them: the firemen, the policemen, the people who lost their families."[15]

In these columns, the Saints, like the Yankees after 9/11, were aligned with military might, servicemen, and national unity. However, Katrina would have been better situated by emphasizing the common black citizen as the focus of the tragedy. In fact, government officials, political- or service-oriented, were initially not considered the heroes of Katrina. Since 9/11 the service people lifted to heroic status by these columnists had been saturated with cultural meaning to refer to national strength and virility. In touting these identities as representative of the New Orleans region and/or the nation's patriotism, strength, and unity, however, these columnists avoided discussion of racial and class oppression that was so visible and prevalent in the story of the hurricane; oppression that was evidence of democracy and equality's lack in the nation.

This patriotic national identity was further reasserted as Silver used 9/11, the date of the Saints' first game, to suggest sport paid a service to the same sort of nation it obliged after 9/11. He recorded the Saints' victory over the Carolina Panthers first by emphasizing that the game took place on "the fourth anniversary of the Sept. 11 attacks."[16] He then quoted Horn as saying, "We're representing a region that's resilient as hell."[17] Silver continued to write that "many of the men [responsible for the Saints' win felt] that they had in some small way helped the healing process back home."[18] The Saints' return to and win on the football field thus served Silver's version of a New Orleans region that was resilient and in the process of healing. Such rhetoric resembled that of columnists' after 9/11, making it easy for columnists to suggest that New Orleans, like New York, was returning to normalcy or resiliency; without even a mention of the people that initially met under the Superdome roof after the storm.

The rhetoric reminiscent of columnists' reaction to 9/11 did not stop there. In the end-of-the-year *Sports Illustrated* issue, Silver again wrote of Horn. The final paragraph of his column consisted of an interior monologue reminiscent of the nationalistic phrase, "Let's roll." Silver wrote that Horn must be thinking to himself, "Y'all take care of each other. We gonna roll through this, no doubt."[19] In the aftermath of 9/11 the Bush administration adopted the phrase "Let's roll," which was to celebrate the heroes of 9/11. It was a phrase originally used by Todd Beamer, a passenger on Flight 93 who helped to down the plane in Shanksville, Pennsylvania, in order to prevent further terrorist attacks on American soil. Horn and sport in general served Silver's construction of a masculine and resilient New Orleans and nation. Overwhelmingly absent from this construction of New Orleans and America, however, was rhetoric of race and class. Hence, Silver constructed Katrina's tragedy to exist in damage to that which could be healed through a Saints' victory. Much like sports columns about King, Ali, Smith, and Carlos, these columns about Katrina allowed black citizens in their national identity so long as those black citizens were athletes and did not challenge white privilege.

Columnists further connected 9/11 to Katrina through sport and suggested football games served to lift the region's spirits. Skip Wood, a columnist for *USA Today*, wrote that the Panther fans on 9/11 cheered the Saints while also remembering "the terrorist attacks of exactly four years ago."[20] Bill Reiter of *The Kansas City Star* argued that "a storm can nearly rip the soul of a city. . . . and a sports team can help repair that."[21] Marc Narducci of the *Philadelphia Enquirer* wrote of the game in New York: "The spirit, camaraderie and patriotism were seen everywhere—from the Giants Stadium parking lot to the field in a football game disguised as a fund-raiser."[22] The resiliency and patriotism these columnists suggested sport permitted was yet another example of what Bill Nichols called disembodied knowledge: where rhetoric of the national ideal takes place in the absence of minority people.[23] Such columns made Katrina a story for "Sunday—a feel-good story to warm the hearts and wrap the flag around."[24] But a Saints game could not serve a region nearly void of citizens, a significant portion of which was without means to watch television because they were in other domed structures in Texas.[25] In a very real sense, then, these columnists were organizing their nation's memory of the storm to privilege those reading and watching its stories unfold; those people who were not the black and impoverished and who had found themselves in the Superdome only weeks earlier. They also reasserted white privilege, which was partially to blame for the systemic racial and economic neglect of New Orleans' black and poor in the first place. Such constructions of the storm and the nation through it continued for nearly a year, when columnists' wrote of the Saints' first game back in the Superdome.

WHEN THE SAINTS CAME HOME: THE NORMAL ECONOMICS OF IT ALL

When the Saints returned to the Superdome in 2006, columnists wrote of national officials and servicemen to suggest the region was returning to normalcy. Ian O'Connor of *USA Today* wrote of New Orleans police chief Eddie Compass standing next to Presidents Bill Clinton and George H.W. Bush at the coin toss for the opening of the Superdome. Compass said, "The Saints are God-sent to our city. . . . We're trying to get back to a normal life, and there's nothing more normal in New Orleans than watching the Saints."[26] Israel Gutierrez, a columnist for the *Miami Herald*, wrote of Presidents Bush and Clinton's attendance and argued that the return to the Superdome said something "inconceivably, can't-get-your-arms-around-it huge. But the fact that an event that significant can be back in New Orleans, that says normal."[27] Both of these columnists suggested the event, not the citizens' return, was indication that New Orleans was approaching normalcy. Hence, these columnists' nations were constructed as normal when males associated with the nation, none of whom experienced the intersection of race and class, appeared on the field of play—for ceremonies preceding the game. Sport served to return these columnists' nations to a patriotic national identity, what these columnists labeled the "normal" condition of their nations.

Moreover, columnists engaged in a tug-of-war for how the storm would be remembered in their versions of national identity. For instance, Brown wrote, "Some people said, '[the Superdome is] such a terrible memory, how can we rebuild it? I say, How can we not?"[28] Nancy Armour, national award winning writer for the Associated Press, suggested that the options for the Superdome were rebuilding and destroying it. Either option would "help heal the memories of the pain and suffering that occurred there."[29] Mary Foster, also of the Associated Press, wrote that the Saints' return to the Superdome would "erase some of the bitter memories that the Superdome had come to symbolize—the images of misery and suffering of a city plundered by the storm."[30] Despite Foster's work in helping find homes for pets Katrina left abandoned, she was ready for memories of the tragedy to be erased. These columnists advocated for an erasure of the memories of racial and economic inequality that manifested when black and impoverished people were left to suffer in the Superdome. As a result, they argued that the Superdome, rife with cultural memory regarding failure of American ideals, had to be refurbished or razed in order to allow a healing.

The desire to repress memories of past inequities, however, was one that equated to the avoidance of black impoverished citizens. That is, a repression would be a return to the same media aesthetics and political strategies that existed prior to the storm.[31] For instance, unlike his reaction to 9/11, President Bush, vilified for his slow and incompetent response to Katrina, dared not visit a sporting arena, even while some of the citizens he was elected to serve remained homeless in stadiums. His first address to the nation after Katrina took place on the lawn of the St. Louis Cathedral in Jackson Square, at night, with no reporters asking him questions, no victims of the storm around him. In his speech, he argued for a healing and used rhetoric quite similar to that used after 9/11. He said,

> Throughout the area hit by the hurricane, we will do what it takes we
> will stay as long as it takes to help citizens rebuild their communities
> and their lives. And all who question the future of the Crescent City
> need to know: There is no way to imagine America without New Or-
> leans, and this great city will rise again. [32]

The absence of New Orleans citizens was coupled with a look toward
rebuilding and, of course, resiliency. Bush's rhetoric worked to erase the
memory of national failure that occurred during Katrina, and his choice
in setting avoided the reality of black poverty. [33]

Likewise, columnists avoided representation of black poverty as they
suggested that with the return of the Saints and the Superdome, the city
returned. For instance, Armour, writing of the Saints first home game of
2006 and the subsequent celebration on Bourbon Street, proclaimed that:

> For anyone who questioned why the Saints would go back to a flood-
> ravaged city, or wondered if a football game could really make a differ-
> ence in the lives of people mired in misery, you have your answer.
> New Orleans was a rollicking, raucous sight to behold Monday night
> [sic]. [34]

Les Carpenter of the *Washington Post* wrote that the return of the Saints
was "the night New Orleans was reborn." [35] He cited NFL commissioner
Roger Goodell as saying that the game "means more to this community
and this nation and gives them an opportunity to show them the spirit
that is here." [36] These columnists suggested that New Orleans was on its
way to recovery as a result of the spirit that coupled the game. Armour
even suggested that the rebuilding of the Superdome was part of the
project of making the city "better than its pre-Katrina state," not once
questioning who would be included in that city. [37] Likewise, in an argument that suggested "New Orleans' greatest asset is its people," Michael
Wilbon of the *Washington Post* argued the city was on its way back. [38] This
he argued despite that only 46 percent of the city's population had returned and 190 murders had occurred there in 2007 as of July 20. [39] Esti-
mates at the time were that as many as 100,000 black and poor people had
yet to return. [40] Hence, the New Orleans that was in the process of healing
was one of the columnists' imaginations; one that privileged white and
middle-to-upper-class identities as citizens of New Orleans while delegit-
imating the black and impoverished; one that neglected the reality that
New Orleans was one of the most unsafe cities in the nation.

A few columnists paradoxically emphasized the region and nation's
structural oppression as problematic, but used the return of the Saints to
pay service to a white national identity. For instance, Paul Newberry of
the Associated Press wrote:

> Even before Katrina, this city was deeply divided by racial and social
> problems: rampant crime. Mediocre schools. A lack of good jobs for the
> underclass. But the Saints helped to break down some of those black-

and-white issues, a rallying point for an eclectic community even when
they struggled on the field.[41]

Here Newberry identified that racial oppression existed prior to the
storm. But he also suggested the Saints could heal that oppression.

Similarly, Wilbon suggested that sport paid a service to healing the
region from Katrina. He argued:

> You can be cynical if you want from 1,500 miles away and dismiss the
> notion that a . . . football team could somehow lift people in the worst
> times of their lives, ungodly times they never could have imagined. But
> the Saints are pretty much all they've got that is familiar.[42]

In the same column, Wilbon argued that the Saints functioned to keep
mainstream audiences aware of the damage in New Orleans. Wilbon
underscored that the area "looked like a bomb had hit it. All the gas
stations are closed."[43] He continued to write of other problems with the
region's infrastructure, thereby avoiding the use of the Superdome as a
trope for regional recovery. Wilbon, however, argued that the game provided a catharsis for the citizens. Yet, some of the people he used as proof
of this claim were those financially privileged enough to *choose* to rebuild
there or those who proved his thesis: Tulane basketball coach Perry
Clark, ESPN analyst Michael Smith, policemen and students at schools
gave voice to the citizens who whole-heartedly believed the return provided the region a service.

Hence, unlike many of his counterparts, Wilbon refused to close the
story of the tragedy with the Saints' return to the Superdome. But he
limited the tragedy to physical damage of the region, rather than the
racial and class oppression exposed there. As a result, Wilbon's column
was also underpinned by a racial frame similar in character to his
counterparts' columns, one that represented the region's normal state as
lacking the black impoverished.

Collectively, sports columnists who characterized New Orleans as re-
covering through the Saints' return to the Superdome privileged a particular sort of wound, the kind that can be healed by sports rhetoric. The
wounds being healed were not the sort initially revealed in the aftermath
of Katrina—those of racial and classed oppression. Rather, the wounds
being healed were those experienced by an audience that had not been
accustomed to having its class and race privilege challenged by stories of
structural racism, classism, and political neglect by the nation. Hence,
sports columnists' rhetoric of healing can be viewed as a return to a
socially constructed normalcy of mainstream media aesthetics that privileges middle class values. With the correct rhetoric, the oppressions once
revealed would be covered up again, and all would return to normalcy.
That return, moreover, was predicated on substituting the black impoverished with athletes or national politicians and servicemen to tell the
story of Katrina.

REMEMBERING NEW ORLEANS: A COUNTERNARRATIVE

Not all columnists privileged a white middle-class value system as they wrote of the Saints' service to national identity in the context of Katrina, though. Jon Saraceno of *USA Today* engaged in the rhetoric of tragedy as he argued that the NFL season should have postponed its season opener. He wrote that the games ought to have been postponed "out of respect" for those who died in Katrina.[44] He theorized that:

> If New York City—where the NFL has its offices on Park Avenue—had faced a disaster where an estimated 10,000 people perished, would it be business as usual this weekend? . . . What [would] the esteemed Mr. [Pete Rozelle] think—and do—if he were alive?[45]

Saraceno contrasted the landscapes of New York and New Orleans, suggesting that the former represented a more nationally significant identity than the latter because of its capital, wealth, and power. His implication was that New Orleans deaths did not register as significantly on the NFL's construction of national identity as deaths in New York, and this, he claimed, was a problem with a racial lens mainstream audiences took towards politics and humanity in America.

Stefan Fatsis of *The Wall Street Journal* contrasted New Orleans with New York as well. He wrote that the Saints could not heal the region because many of its fans did not have the ability to watch them play, thereby simultaneously resisting and relying on sport's service to a mythological national identity:

> But unlike the aftermath of the Sept. 11 terrorist attacks, when New York's baseball teams helped rally the city's spirits, the Saints—and the city's National Basketball Association franchise, the Hornets—don't have a city to rally.[46]

Here Fatsis took issue with his counterparts' use of 9/11 to write of Katrina and their suggestion that football could heal New Orleans. But he also accepted the notion that baseball served the nation after 9/11. Tim Dahlberg of the *New York Daily News* maintained the focus on New Orleans. He underscored that Saints fans watched the game in shelters and so could not have actually been served by football.[47]

Jason Whitlock of the *Kansas City Star* deconstructed the rhetoric of tragedy in which many of his counterparts engaged. He wrote that delaying the games would serve no purpose while also illustrating that rhetoric about football's healing qualities merely served to privilege wealthy identities:

> If I thought it would make a difference, I'd call for a stoppage of play, a respectful, patriotic, mournful pause of the games that entertain us. We did it after 9-11. But that was different. We paused in fear. We feared a World War, we feared a shadowy enemy, we feared another attack.

> Stopping was the absolute right thing to do. It served a purpose. This time, in the wake of Hurricane Katrina, the irrelevancy of sports has never been made more clear. It doesn't matter where or whether the New Orleans Saints play their games . . . You can't ease the pain of the men, women and children suffering, starving and, in some cases, dying in the streets of New Orleans. A strong performance by the Saints won't offer any relief to those who lost their material possessions to Katrina or to those who lost their faith in America's compassion to the nonstop neglect being broadcast on CNN, MSNBC and Fox News. You can argue that the people of the Gulf need the escape that sports, particularly football, provide. Do they really? . . . No. Katrina's victims are thirsting for a real escape. Those of us lucky enough and/or wealthy enough to be away from the front lines of the flooding, the disease, the anarchy and the hopelessness desire the entertaining escape.[48]

Rather than delivering significance to the Saints in the aftermath of Katrina, Whitlock exposed the consequences of doing so: it actually made the victims of the storm invisible and provided those "wealthy" enough to watch football with an escape from the reality of Katrina's story and the economic oppression it exposed.

Paul Attner of *The Sporting News* resisted the matrix of sport, nation, memory, and race privilege that underpinned columns suggesting the Saints healed the region or nation. He used the Superdome's "skin" as a metaphor for how the storm unveiled the historic race and class oppressions of New Orleans and the nation:

> And to have the Superdome fixed? The last we saw of the place, it was a symbol of so much that was wrong with the government's response to Katrina and about the desperation of humans in trouble. Winds tore apart its white roof, exposing a black skin.[49]

Attner's metaphor illustrated that the city's historic racial and classed oppression operated under a veil. Attner argued that sport could not close the story of Katrina. He also illustrated that the dome's refurbished state threatened to re-veil the raced and classed oppression of the area and memory of its existence in the nation. He cited that "the city has lost more than half of its pre-Katrina population of 450,000, and its economy remains hobbled."[50] In a sarcastic end to that paragraph, Attner wrote: "Now [the dome is] a symbol of a new beginning for the city, its roof shiny white again."[51] He continued by citing Horn who said that the opening game of the 2006 season would, ". . . [we will] exorcise the demons of what they endured inside the dome during Katrina.'"[52] He finally wrote, however, that "for New Orleanians and the Gulf Coast, the joy of the Saints is tempered by the reality of the enormous task ahead."[53]

Similarly, in writing of the dome's reopening, Ohm Youngmisuk of *The New York Daily News* chronicled the crime that occurred in the Superdome in fall 2005 as part of its history. He juxtaposed descriptions of the new dome with those of the lower Ninth Ward, which he characterized as a "ghost town littered by rubble and hundreds of abandoned and destroyed homes."[54] In that same column, he wrote of Dee Jabar, a black resident of the Ninth Ward in debt because of his decision to return. Jabar said, "While I'm struggling, they (the city) should be busy worrying about how to survive and rebuild rather than about a team that earns millions of dollars."[55] Giving voice to a black and financially worried citizen, Youngmisuk sat in opposition to his counterparts who argued that New Orleans was full of people who placed value on the Saints' healing power. Similarly, William Rhoden of the *New York Times* wrote that "what Katrina illustrated, quite graphically, [wa]s that the economic problems confronting communities from which many professional athletes come are too large for one foundation to solve."[56]

Whitlock continued on this theme arguing that television often hides impoverished faces behind white and wealthy faces. He wrote,

> Please let the games begin, bring on Herbstreit and Corso and Madden and Michaels and Brady and Manning. . . . We don't want to look at our poor and uneducated. We don't want to contemplate what their squalid suffering says about us. We build housing projects to isolate them, keep them out of view and away from anything we value—the Superdome, the French Quarter, the Convention Center. . . . Sports play virtually no role in bringing us together when it's time for us to muster the resolve and the compassion necessary to appropriately assist our underclass. For that, we still need lots of prayer and a collective integrity we've yet to acquire.[57]

Whitlock suggested that sport could not heal the economic inequities of New Orleans, or the nation, and that it even reinforced those inequities by hiding their reality. He also argued that the country, like the sporting industry, systematically deals with the inequity of the nation simply by making it invisible.

Seventeen months after Katrina, President Bush delivered a State of the Union Address in which not a single reference was made to Katrina, despite his promise, in the immediate aftermath of the tragedy, to be "fully involved with the" recovery of the region.[58] The extent to which Whitlock, Youngmisuk, and Rhoden, on the one hand, and Bush, on the other, focused on Katrina as a significant memory in their writing equated to a contest for establishing the impoverished and black, who became the face of Katrina, as part of the nation's story for 2006.

Ultimately, then, as some columnists used the Superdome's refurbished condition to suggest New Orleans had healed, they encouraged their mainstream audiences to consider that the problems of economic and racial oppressions had been fixed; to embrace cultural memories of the storm that matched the shared conventions of a unified, strong nation. Such representations of the dome not only repressed memory of the horrors inside of it, then, but also reinforced mythological definitions of national identity by hiding the structural oppressions and neglect that the tragedy initially exposed. In contrast, other columnists insisted on remembering oppression as a central element of Katrina's story, and the nation's problems. Representation of the Superdome and subsequent memory of the black impoverished as part of Katrina's story, as a result, was directly related to how columnists perceived race and poverty as part of their own individual nations.

A SUPER BOWL WIN

Years later, a glimpse of how the black and impoverished of New Orleans would be situated in the cultural memory of Hurricane Katrina was offered. In 2009--2010, the New Orleans Saints, America's team of only a few years ago, made a mythic run to the Super Bowl. In remembering Katrina and the devastation it exposed as they wrote of the Saints' Super Bowl run, many columnists implicitly engaged in a memory project working to include the black, impoverished, and tragedy-stricken in a political environment that was threatening to neglect their conditions again.

That is, many sports columnists regressed into rhetoric of the mythic that contrasted with Whilock, Youngmisuk, and Rhoden's in 2007. Mark Wiedmer of the *Times Free Press*, in a column that unabashedly tied sporting teams with the fates of the cities from which they came, wrote,

> Sports doesn't usually work this way, of course. Michigan's hard economic times weren't enough to deliver Michigan State a fairytale finish in last spring's NCAA title game against North Carolina. The national torment of 9/11 didn't lift the New York Yankees to victory in that year's World Series against Arizona. Sometimes the better team beats the better story. I believe this completed the exorcism of the Superdome. All the terrible things that happened inside that place just after Katrina may have finally been washed away. The Saints winning this is a cleansing for the whole city and bringing it together.[59]

Years after the tragedy, Wiedmer, through his sources, and the memories of other tragedies, worked to erase the memories of national failure through reference to victories in sport. Such rhetoric ultimately reasserted the very complacency toward racial and classed oppression that led to the Saints becoming "America's team" in the first place.[60] In short, when "America's team" wins, memory of national failure, and so potential for social justice, was erased through a return to what was called normalcy.

Bill Sasser of *The Christian Science Monitor* emphasized the emotion many sports fans had in watching their Saints win the Super Bowl as a reflection of the physical, economic, and social state of the region. "The Saints Super Bowl has come to symbolize New Orleans' post-Katrina revival."[61] In an ironic use of language, Sasser likened the emotion to the effects of the hurricane to express its power. "The wave of emotion that New Orleans is riding over its Super Bowl–bound team is evident everywhere. . . . Four and a half years after hurricane Katrina, the city, the football team, and its die-hard fans have more than hope."[62]

In contrast, Les Carptenter of the *Washington Post* saw great healing potential in a Super Bowl win. He wrote "around here, people feel like they need the Saints to win the Super Bowl."[63] Carpenter cited LaToya Cantrell, president of the Broadmoor Improvement Association, as saying of the Saints' trip to the Super Bowl:

> Football teams don't lift people to restore communities. Football teams are diversions. Football teams don't make cities right. Yet, somehow, this one has. And it is why no city has ever needed a team in the Super Bowl more than this one at this time.[64]

But Carpenter took an almost paradoxical stance in this section of his column. Not only did he illustrate that dilapidated state of the region, but he also suggested that football had the capacity to inspire great change and motivation for the citizens of New Orleans. He was careful to underscore that the physical state of New Orleans was not healed fully.

> The hurricane never leaves. It lives in the flood lines that have stained the city like a bathtub ring that 4 1/2 years of scrubbing cannot remove. It's found in the homes lovingly restored to a pre-storm splendor that abut crumpled structures untouched since the water rolled in. And it creeps into the worn voices that tell of years-long fights with insurance companies, waiting for the money to repair their houses so they might feel whole again. . . . The population, cut in half in the months after the storm, has recovered to about 300,000 by most estimates, which still puts it below the more than 400,000 who were here before the hurricane.[65]

Although Carpenter may have overemphasized the role football plays in everyday citizens' lives, he did acknowledge the physical damage of New Orleans, the significantly lowered population, and the structural oppressions that the storm's aftermath so clearly revealed were covered up. In fact, he underscored that New Orleans itself was characterized by a paradox. What was valuable about Carpenter's column was the precision with which he wrote about the physical landscape of New Orleans and its relationship to structural oppression:

> Racial tensions, laid bare to the world during Katrina, still linger, especially as the white neighborhoods have returned much faster than many of those that are black. The mistrust hasn't left. But people here say something strange has happened in the Saints' run to the Super Bowl. They are making connections that never would have come before. . . . It was everybody coming together regardless of race or age or anything. . . . It didn't matter the gender or the race, they just held tight

until the kick went through the goal posts and a celebration erupted like none they had ever seen. "In that dome it was a microcosm of the whole city, no one's race mattered," said Maggie Carroll of Broadmoor, who not only rebuilt her home along with her husband but also refurbished the one next door. "When that kick went through there were random hugs from total strangers."[66]

Claiming that racism, clearly visible in the landscape of New Orleans' recovery, could somehow be erased with the kick of a field goal denies that such racism is ingrained in the fabric of a region as a result of history. However, I would suggest, that this sort of suggestion is one of the most commonplace in cultural practices in America, and also is a major reason that those who are privileged by race do not realize it.

To elaborate, in *Why Are All the Black Kids Sitting Together in the Cafeteria*, Beverly Tatum views racism as a system of advantage based on race that is systemic in nature.[67] That system of advantage produces cultural and social power and advantages in educational, governmental, economic, and other structures. Tatum also distinguishes between racism and prejudice. Prejudice, according to her, is the dismissing or oppression of an individual as a result of that person's race. Too often mainstream media and individuals conflate these two related but separate definitions of oppression. The conflation, though, can be quite dangerous. For instance, it is admirable that during a celebration of the New Orleans' Saints win that a diverse group of people were able to unite. This was an example of a lack of prejudice among individuals. However in both mainstream media and culture in general, people claim that such unification is proof that racism does not exist. This is not the case. While there are many people who are not prejudiced, those recorded as celebrating in Carpenter's column included those same people who might benefit from and/or be oppressed by the structures of racism that exist. And these structures existed before, during, and after these celebrations.

Carpenter's column even acknowledges this. The hurricane-damaged areas yet to be fixed prior to the Saints' victory were still yet to be fixed after it, and those areas were, for the most part, inhabited by African Americans. The same structural racism that existed centuries prior to Katrina, that Katrina momentarily exposed, dictated the recovery program of the region. Whites and blacks hugging because of a football win does not equate to an erasure of structural racism, though. Carpenter, like much of mainstream media and culture, use single acts, such as a group of people without prejudice hugging as proof that structural racism no longer exists. I suggest this practice is one manner in which white privilege maintains its hold in America: single acts of goodness often are emphacized as proof of democracy and so focus on the structure of racism is lacking. However, they may not be the best cultural critics. Tatum actually suggests there are three degrees of racism within the white community: There is the actively racist, who, like the Ku Klux Klan member, uses these systems of advantage for her own benefit and to oppress; the passively racist, who gains advantage from the systems in place and does nothing to work against those systems—this person may be subconsciously racist; and there is the actively anti-racist person who realizes the injustice of the systems of advantage and works to change them.

It is the second group Tatum identifies that those of us in the third group ought to focus on. For instance, those in the second group view their treatment of individuals around them, many who happen to be of different races than themselves, and believe themselves not racist. Yet they argue against programs like Head Start, welfare, and affirmative action because they sincerely believe that their privileged experience is the same one that *all* Americans have; that because they are not prejudiced, the structural racism that continually oppresses is nonexistent. And this is the reason studying sport is so important. It allows those of us interested in racial studies access to those who are uninterested because they do not quite understand the conditions under which their privilege has been offered and thrived.

That is, while the memories of race and class oppression may be erased through the rhetoric of tragedy, the realities of such oppression are visible just beyond the walls of the stadium. Recent studies have shown that crime rates are high; the black population of New Orleans that was displaced because of Katrina is very slow to return; medical care services are shuttered. In short, while the New Orleans Saints provided the region momentary elation, and while much of the tourist industry has returned, the people, the citizens of the region, and the services meant to assist them have not. Specifically, at the end of 2009, New Orleans was ranked first in murder rate in the United States and Louisiana was rated worst in the nation in terms of health care. Data suggested that nearly half of the children attending public schools pre-Katrina had yet to return. In short, even with a Super Bowl championship on its resume, the New Orleans region had much work and many citizens to account for in order to reestablish its normal state.[68] Hence, while for some, the memory of horror in the Superdome may have been erased, the reality was that the same racist oppressions that existed pre-Katrina continued post-Katrina, albeit in a new form.

A MEMORY CONTEST

Again, the diverging standpoints regarding the Saints and the Superdome after Katrina equated to a contest for how race and poverty would be situated in sports columnists' national identities and cultural memories of it. Interestingly, for instance, *Kansas City Star*, the *New York Times*, *Sports Illustrated*, and the *New York Daily News* included columnists from camps that privileged and resisted mythological definitions of national identity as they wrote of Katrina. Within these publications there arose a healthy debate regarding the place of black poverty in sports columnists' national identity. The latter camp of columnists who confronted mythological definitions of nation potentially reached audiences embracing those definitions. As such, this camp potentially played a significant role in resituating the way many conservative people thought of the Bush administration and the way those embracing white privilege thought of black poverty. This camp's resistance of the traditional mythology of sport within the sports pages that have a readership consisting of those embracing mythological definitions of national identity is the very reason to study sport media through a racial lens: To illustrate that racial privilege exists and potentially change the way people think of race in the nation.

This chapter, consisting of columnists from a variety of races and both genders, complicates the notion that points of view that erase black poverty from their versions of national identity are limited only to whites.

Moreover, this chapter complicates any tendency among critics to label individual writers as adopting single standpoints regarding identity and nation. For instance, Rhoden, who was one of the columnists constructing a mythological national identity through the Yankees after 9/11, refused to do so through the Saints in the context of Katrina. Rhoden is a black writer who often exposes racism toward blacks in sport and the nation. Hence, one reason for his taking a role in producing mythologies after 9/11, but resisting it after Katrina, may be that Katrina exposed racism toward people with whom he, as a black man, has historically identified. That is, the intersectional nature of identity leads liberal columnists to support mythology in some contexts, and to resist it in others. To understand the extent of this mythology's power and the strategies of resisting it requires an examination of its elasticity and acknowledgement that we all may support it in different contexts without knowing it. Such examination allows people to understand hegemony and learn how to resist it in different contexts.

NOTES

1. Clyde Woods, *Development Arrested* (Chicago: Haymarket Books, 2000).
2. Michael Ignatieff, "The Broken Contract," *New York Times Magazine*, 25 September 2005, p. 6.
3. Stephan Fatsis, "Football's Saints Ponder Whether to Relocate," *The Wall Street Journal*, 8 September 2005.
4. David Weiss, "After the Storm," *New York Daily News*, 13 August 2006.
5. Michael Silver, "The Saints Come Through," *Sports Illustrated*, 19 September 2005: 94.
6. Gary Smith, "Dark Days," *Sports Illustrated*, 9 September 2006.
7. Michael Wilbon, "It's Not a Rivalry if the Other Team Never Wins," *Washington Post*, 19 September 2005, sec. E.

8. Dave Anderson, "The Saints Are Now America's Team," *New York Times*, 15 September 2005, sec. D.

9. *New York Times*, "Up from the Country, Patron Saints of the Road," 18 September 2005.

10. Anderson, "The Saints Are Now America's Team."

11. Silver, "The Saints Come Through." *Sports Illustrated*, 19 September 2005, 94.

12. Silver, "The Saints Come Through," 94

13. Silver, "The Saints Come Through," 95.

14. Lisa Olson, "A Story of Hope, But There's Much More to Do," *The New York Daily News*, 21 January 2007.

15. Anderson, "The Saints Are Now America's Team."

16. Silver, "The Saints Come Through," 94.

17. Silver, "The Saints Come Through," 98.

18. Silver, "The Saints Come Through," 94.

19. Michael Silver, "Athletes and Katrina," *Sports Illustrated*, 12 December 2005, p. 108.

20. Skip Wood, "Saints Win for Empty New Orleans," *USA Today*, 12 September 2005.

21. Bill Reiter, "Marching Home," *Kansas City Star*, August, 2006.

22. Marc Narducci, "For Saints 'Home' Opener, a Special Spirit Prevails," *The Philadelphia Enquirer*, 20 September 2005, sec. sports.

23. See Lauren Berlant, *The Queen of America Goes to Washington City* (Durham, NC: Duke University Press, 1997); Bill Nichols, "Getting to Know You," *Theorizing Documentary*, ed. Michael Renov (New York: Routledge, 1993), 176.

24. Tim Dahlberg, "Saints a Feel-Good Story for Now, but Future Not Bright for Their Fans," *The New York Daily News*, 21 September 2006, http://www.lexisnexis.com.

25. Sturken wrote that "debates about what counts as cultural memory are also debates about who gets to participate in creating national meaning, When people participate in the production of cultural memory . . . they do so both in opposition to and in concert with a concept of the nation." Marita Sturken, *Tangled Memories* (Los Angeles: University of California Press, 1997) 13.

26. Ian O'Connor, "Saints, Fans Made to Feel Like Giants in N.Y." *USA Today*, 20 September 2005, www.lexisnexis.com.

27. Israel Gutierrez, "For One Night, New Orleans Can Be 'Normal,'" *The Miami Herald*, 20 September 2006, http://lexis.com.

28. Clifton Brown, "With Bush Available, Saints Options Abound." *New York Times*, 29 April 2006, sec. D.

29. Nancy Armour, "As New Orleans Rebuilds, Saints' Return Another Step toward Normalcy," *Associated Press*, 11 August 2006.

30. Mary Foster, "Fans Celebrate Superdome Reopening," *Washington Post*, 26 September 2006, sec. E.

31. Herman Gray wrote that mainstream "representations of blackness operate squarely within the boundaries of middle-class patriarchal discourse about 'whiteness.'" Herman Gray, *Watching Race* (Minneapolis: University of Minnesota Press, 2001), 9.

32. George W. Bush, "Address to the Nation," 20 September 2005, http://www.whitehouse.gov/news/releases/2005/09/20050915-8.html, 21 September 2005.

33. It should also be noted that in his State of the Union Address of 2006, not a single mention of Katrina or the nation-state's responsibility to the region was made.

34. Bush, "Address to the Nation," 20 September 2005.

35. Les Carpenter, "A Roaring Return," *Washington Post*, 26 September 2006, sec. E.

36. Carpenter, "A Roaring Return."

37. Armour, "As New Orleans Rebuilds, Saints' Return Another Step toward Normalcy."

38. Michael Wilbon, "Hope Wears as Saint's Uniform," *Washington Post*, 26 September 2006, sec. E.

39. *360 with Anderson Cooper*, July 27, 2007. In 2004, the year prior to Katrina, the U.S. Department of Justice estimated that there were 56 murders per 100,000 people in New Orleans. *Time* magazine estimated New Orleans to be populated by 155,000 people as of March 2006. If there has not been an astronomical increase, the murder rate, in 2007, then, has increased greatly. See Charley Varley, "Crime Returns to the Big Easy," *Time*, 21 March 2007.

40. Steve Springer was careful to cite that the entirety of New Orleans citizens would not be present in the city for the game: "New Orleans is a city in need of cohesion, Hurricane Katrina left 1,293 people dead and today about 309,000 adults remain displaced. There were about 455,000 people living in New Orleans before Katrina. That number is now estimated at 190,000 to 220,000, according to the *Times-Picayune*." See Steve Springer, "The Parade Goes By," *Los Angeles Times*, 22 January 2007, www.lexisnexis.com.

41. Paul Newberry, "Amid the Rubble, a City Rallies Behind its Football Team," *Associated Press*, 24 September 2006, http://www.lexisnexis.com.

42. Wilbon, "Hope Wears as Saint's Uniform."

43. Wilbon, "Hope Wears as Saint's Uniform."

44. Jon Saraceno, "NFL Should Have Delayed Its Openers," *USA Today*, 6 September 2005, sec. C.

45. Saraceno, "NFL Should Have Delayed Its Openers."

46. Fatsis, "Football's Saints Ponder Whether to Relocate."

47. Tim Dahlberg, "Saints a Feel-Good Story for Now, but Future Not Bright for Their Fans."

48. Jason Whitlock, "The Games Just Wash over the Hopelessness of Katrina's Victims," *Kansas City Star*, 3 September 2005.

49. Paul Attner, "They're Home, There's Hope," *The Sporting News*, 29 September 2006, http://www.nexis.com.

50. Attner, "They're Home, There's Hope."

51. Attner, "They're Home, There's Hope."

52. Attner, "They're Home, There's Hope."

53. Attner, "They're Home, There's Hope."

54. Ohm Youngmisuk, "Rising after the Storm," *The New York Daily News*, 24 September 2006.

55. Youngmisuk, "Rising after the Storm."

56. William Rhoden, "Amid Ruins of Home, Sorrow and Solidarity," *New York Times*, 18 September, 2005. See also Tim Layden, "Marching In," *Sports Illustrated*, 22 January 2007; Rick Reilly, "Sports to the Rescue," *Sports Illustrated*, 6 September 2005.

57. Whitlock, "The Games Just Wash over the Hopelessness of Katrina's Victims."

58. See George W. Bush "State of the Union Address," 31 January 2007, http://www.whitehouse.gov/stateoftheunion/2007/; George W. Bush, "President Discusses Hurricane Relief to the Region," 9 September 2005, http://www.whitehouse.gov/news/releases/2005/09/20050915-8.html.

59. Sturken, *Tangled Memories*.

60. See Evan Barnes, "The 'Who Dat Nation' Is Super," *Los Angeles Sentinel*, 17 Feb 2010, A.1; Ben Walker, "Champs Become America's Team," *Journal–Gazette*, 8 February 2010, B. 8.

61. Bill Sasser, "Mardi Gras? Nah, It's New Orleans' Saints Super Bowl Warm-up," *The Christian Science Monitor*, 31 January 2010.

62. Sasser, "Mardi Gras? Nah, It's New Orleans' Saints Super Bowl Warm-up."

63. Les Carpenter, "Behind Its Team, the City Rallies," *Washington Post*, 7 February 2010, D.2.

64. Carpenter, "Behind Its Team, the City Rallies."

65. Carpenter, "Behind Its Team, the City Rallies."

66. Carpenter, "Behind Its Team, the City Rallies."

67. Beverly Tatum, "Why Are All The Black Kids Sitting Together in the Cafeteria?," (Basic Books, 2003).

68. See Bill Quigley, Davida Finger, "Katrina Pain Index, 2009," *The Louisiana Week-ly*, 30 August 2009, (83): 1–2, 49.

SIX

What's Sex Got to Do With It?

On March 11, 2011, the ground vibrated. Just hours later, the water came rushing forth. The enormity of the disaster was not yet fully understood. A tsunami, triggered by the quake, demolished towns and cities, ruined lives. A twenty-three foot wall of water pushed through city streets and found its way to a nuclear reactor, threatening, ultimately, a nuclear meltdown. Quickly, then, Japan's national disaster became a potential global catastrophe, and mainstream American media followed the story continuously.

As late as August, 2011, bodies were being unearthed from rubble and water-logged buildings were being razed. With over 20,000 dead or missing and more 130,000 buildings and homes demolished, Japan, even as this book goes to print, is devastated. In the immediate aftermath of the storm, the Obama administration deployed emergency response workers to the region in hopes of assisting the country's recovery. Also, President Obama, in the throes of debating solutions to a global economic crisis, addressed Americans:

> The United States stands ready to help the Japanese people in this time of great trial. . . . The friendship and alliance between our two nations is unshakeable, and only strengthens our resolve to stand with the people of Japan as they overcome this tragedy. . . . When you see what's happening in Japan, you are reminded that for all our differences in culture or language or religion, that ultimately humanity is one.[1]

Although certainly not the intent of Obama's speech, his rhetoric revealed and reflected a common practice among those in mainstream media when presenting points of view regarding geographically distant places experiencing tragedy: whether a famine in Africa, a mudslide in Central America, or a tsunami in Japan, presidential rhetoric often acknowledges cultural, racial, even religious differences in order to underscore a common humanity. But the language does not acknowledge gender or sexuality, and is also vague enough to identify tragic occurrences without familiarizing an American audience with the concrete, substantive examples of suffering with which they may identify. The result of such rhetoric is to shape American audiences' imaginations of foreign countries' experiences in a fashion that lacks specificity or understanding. Simultaneously, the lack of gendered language normalizes an assumption that all space—from the global environment to the fields of competition—is the domain of males. Michael Dear and Jonathan Flusty explained that the way we imagine space, based on how people generally talk about it, and cartography, is rife with power relations. Ultimately, too, they argued all public space has been constructed with a Eurocentric, male paradigm as its origin, and, as a result, to discuss locations in familiar rhetoric is to accept the male and Eurocentric patterns with which we already imagine these spaces.[2] Interestingly, when columnists wrote of the Japanese tragedy, even through women's soccer games featuring Japanese players, they often adopted a point of view characteristic of a male, European point of view.

In the weeks and months immediately following the tsunami, the story of Japan's hardships largely dissolved from American mainstream media's attention, thereby reinforcing the stereotype of the invisible and weak Asian.[3] By mid-June, rare was an update on cable news about the condition of Japan. Newspapers throughout America buried the stories deep in news sections if they covered the tragedy at all.[4] However, in late July of that year, the water-ravaged Japan found its way back into American mainstream audiences' consciousness through sport: the Japanese women's soccer team, an underdog since the beginning of the 2011 World Cup tournament, but characterized by grit and tenacity, earned its way to the World Cup final game against a formidable opponent, the American women's team.

In the final game of the World Cup, American sports columnists were placed in a new context in a variety of ways. The women's World Cup team of 2011, for instance, had garnered a huge following, one of the most robust for any women's team ever. Also, the team representing the tragedy-stricken area was not an American team, but a Japanese team. Hence, sports columnists were to tell the story of this tragedy through an American team that neither represented the area that was hit by tragedy, nor won its game.

This game was, in short, a new sort of one for those covering a tragedy in relation to a sporting event. American sports columnists generally manipulated the rhetoric of tragedy by using new forms of language, but with the same outcome of repressing tragic events from mainstream audiences' view or memory.

Specifically, two camps of columnists revealed themselves in writing of the 2011 World Cup games. The first camp of columnists wrote of the

World Cup games using traditional rhetoric of tragedy but used different strategies of engaging it in order to create stories of the Japanese country's redemption. They did this in many ways. For instance, some associated the Japanese win in the World Cup with that country's potential to heal or catalyze national recovery. They also found ways to make their columns palatable to mainstream audiences by privileging the American and male audience in their writing, rather than the female and/or Japanese. They did this by removing almost all discussion of the Japanese tragedy from the mouths of Japanese citizens or athletes and placing it in the mouths of American sports critics and columnists. In this way, these columnists' rhetoric resembled the traditional Western rhetoric of the globe: it placed the American, white, male point of view front and center in the stories about the Japanese female/male. Finally, many columnists in this camp reached to find a reason to excuse the American loss in the final game. Not only did this strategy privilege the Western point of view, but it also treated women athletics differently than male athletics.

The second camp repositioned the story of tragedy to be about the history of American gender relations in sports. Within this camp, one set of columnists confused the huge audience of the final game of the World Cup with an achieved gender equity in the United States. Another set, however, looked at mainstream culture's tendency to sexualize women athletes and suggested little progress regarding gender equity had been made since the last World Cup. Rather, this camp argued, the space of the field of play was yet masculine and the women were placed there to please the males in that audience. Although this camp was much more conscious and critical of the masculine assumptions upon which the sports sphere rested, it too reframed the story of tragedy to discuss American problems rather than Japanese.

A TRAGEDY ONLY IN NAME

One of the ways in which the first camp of columnists engaged in the traditional rhetoric of tragedy was by claiming that the Japanese women's team, representing the Japanese nation, had the capability to provide a distraction or catharsis for the entire nation. Much like the columnists of past tragedies, these columnists made such claims in the absence of actual citizens or officials of Japan. For instance, Bruce Dowbiggin of the *Boston Globe* emphasized empathy for the Japanese, but his column focused on American responses to the Japanese tragedy.

> The back story of Japan's victory was, of course, the tragic tsunami and earthquake last March that devastated the world's third largest economy, killing 23,000 and leaving its very future in doubt. Even a mother of one of the American players conceded that a piece of her heart went out to the Japanese team.[5]

Similarly, Gavin Blair of *The Christian Science Monitor* wrote, "the [American] players dedicated their performances to the victims of the devastating March 11 earthquake and subsequent tsunami, and said they drew inspiration from the hardships faced in disaster-hit areas."[6] Although these two columns provided good evidence about the Japanese state, they also narrated the Japanese tragedy from the American point of view.

Yoree Koh argued that the Japanese win "was more than a sports win. Coming four months after the devastating March 11 earthquake and tsunami, and weeks of bungling by the nation's leaders in response, the title gives the struggling, weary country a tenacious national symbol to rally around."[7] Matthew Futterman quoted former U.S. Coach Tony Dicco as saying, "Japan was playing for something more than just a win, they were playing to heal a nation."[8] John Fiensten wrote that Japan's win in the World Cup provided many in Japan with an escape and diversion from the realities of horror that visited the country as a result of the natural disaster. He then wrote that "Japan's victory in the Women's World Cup final wasn't about redemption for one man but about finding a moment of joy and escape for a country still in mourning."[9] Much like columns written in the context of other tragedies, these columnists argued that the Japanese team had the capacity to heal the wounds that Japan experienced. Jenkins's column, on the surface, seemed to resist the rhetoric of tragedy. She wrote:

> Let's get this straight: The World Cup has not magical powers that can make a tsunami and a nuclear meltdown un-happen. But it can console, and uplift and send a message home about fighting back, and you'd be one ugly American to begrudge them this victory.[10]

It seemed here that Jenkins understood the tenuous connection between sport and the ability of a nation to heal. Jenkins's column argued sport played a role in offering an emotional uplift that would allow the country to preservere. While Jenkins's language seemed initially to resist the rhetoric of tragedy, I would suggest her column actually utilized that rhetoric because it suggested a team's performance could lift a country's spirits.

Although these columnists were far from malicious in their writing, they all used a traditional, generic mode of writing about tragedies. In claiming that the Japanese team provided the Japanese nation with a diversion, potential to heal, or redemptive story, they also neglected to interview or cite any sources from Japan. The Japanese nation benefitting from a soccer win was, in these columns at least, one imagined solely by the columnists writing about the victory. Likewise, their tendency not to interview Asians or even the Japanese women on the team indicates the same paradigm regarding mainstream media's approach to Asians: treating them as an invisible other and subsequently prohibiting the Japanese woman a voice in the white, male-dominated American mainstream.[11]

Columnists of this camp also grappled with fitting their stories of tragedy and redemption into a narrative frame that would be palatable for an American audience. Specifically, they worked to underscore the importance of a Japanese win while minimizing the reasons behind or meaning of the American loss. For instance, Dowbiggin congratulated the Japanese women, but refused to apologize for the American loss.

> The sporting world's cynics would say close only counts in horseshoes. And they would be oh so wrong in the case of the U.S. women's soccer team's razor-thin loss to Japan on Sunday, which dashed hopes for an unprecedented third Women's World Cup championship for the Americans. From start to dramatic finish in the global tournament, the American women shone, in both skill and sportsmanship—as well as, well, sheer joy. They captivated American fans with dramatic play and clutch performances. We offer both condolences on their loss in the final match and congratulations for their superb overall performance.

Fienstein continued, suggesting "there was much more at stake for the Japanese" team.[12] He argued the Japanese women's win was not only a result of the team's playing for an entire nation, but also provided a story germane to sports' role in humanity. Dave Anderson of the *New York Times* summed up the year's promising moments in sports indicating the women's World Cup team from Japan was "inspired by their nation's devastation from the March earthquake and tsunami" and the American team's loss was secondary to the story.[13] Sally Jenkins argued that the women played with "honor" and that "the only people who [we]re entitled to feel bad about the United States' loss . . . [we]re the handful of American players who thought the trophy was in their grasp so many times . . . "[14] But she also noted that the women had the game and trophy "within their grasp so many times" that they may well be disappointed.[15]

Claiming that the American loss was excusable, however, was, in consequence, different than arguing the Japanese win permitted the Japanese nation to heal. To elaborate, the tendency among these columnists to forgive the American loss was a way in which to fit the story of the World Cup into a narrative frame that catered to long-standing audience expectations in sport. Although she wrote specifically of women's role in baseball history, Anne R. Roshcelle's argument is appropriate to apply here. She wrote that women's baseball history extends back as far as 1859 and that there are two reasons that this history has traditionally been denied: "One, baseball was defined culturally as a male domain, and two, major league baseball was controlled by men, who barred women from playing. Women, therefore, could only become marginal players, not major leaguers.[16] In the case of the 2011 American women's World Cup team, the women were already assumed to play on a secondary tier to those male athletes who dominated the landscape of mainstream sports. The columnists who argued the outcome of the game was not important given the context in which it was played—whether that context was the tragedy in Japan or the overwhelming support of the women—fell into arguments that did indeed treat women's athletics as if they were not professional or focused on winning. Hence, the narrative frame adopted by these columnists was one that was familiar to the American sports audience: one that dismissed the notion that female athletics was primarily interested in competition. These columnists' rhetoric of tragedy solidified the American sports sphere as the domain of males, the females as simply invading that space.

There was one final way in which even well-intentioned columnists found new ways to close the tragedy's story. Many columnists indicated the need for donation to assist in the recovery from tragedy. However, it is important to frame this call for donation as a means to repress memories of the tragedy's residual effects. After 9/11, Katrina, and now in the context of the 2011 tsunami, many columnists used sport to emphasize the necessity and import of donating to relief efforts.[17] Of course, columnists' advocacy of donating money was part of the positive social role they played after these tragedies. Likewise, donating money was, in no uncertain terms, admirable. However, calls for donation and donating itself were also means through which the aesthetics that privileged white, male, American audiences reasserted themselves as normal after tragedy. Specifically, donation, it could be argued, substituted for memory of the nation-state's failures, global responsibilities, or for attempts to correct long-standing structural problems. Often, donation requests appeared on screen during competitions or in sports columns about those competitions, and audience members, through online transactions donated money to a cause—Hurricane Katrina, 9/11, the 2011 Japanese tsunami. In all of these cases, the ease of payment most likely increased participation. However, a swipe of a credit card does not substitute for activism or a memory of structural inequality. Offering a credit card number also allows a receipt, which is the feeling that that one contributed to, even worked to solve the problems underpinning the tragedy at hand. This feeling, however, exists only because one may not feel obligated to remember the long-standing problems that caused or were caused by the tragedy itself. In short, payment is another way of forgetting and renouncing further responsibility. In the case of Japan's tragedy, a transaction on a credit card literally could end the story of the tragedy as donation could equate to ending the story completely for the payee. This is especially true given that sports columnists, following traditional modes of writing, for the most part, concluded their stories about tragedy with the end of the World Cup. A swipe of the credit card coupled with reading a few columns about redemption that also reestablish sport as an American and male space, and all could seem to have returned to normal—normal being the male, American point of view.[18]

Unlike columns written in the context of other tragedies, however, these columns were overwhelmingly devoid of any sources that experienced the tragedy firsthand. This overwhelming absence of firsthand Japanese sources was a result of the columnists' understanding that American mainstream audiences traditionally take an American-centered point of view on stories, and would be happy to accept the tsunami story's closure. That closure, as a result of the lack of Japanese trauma narrated through firsthand resources, coupled with rhetoric of healing, redemption, or donation was possible. Hence, these columnists limited mainstream audiences' knowledge and imagination about the current state of Japan through omission of the Japanese.

Patricia Zimmerman argued that news outlets often use traditional narrative modes to garner interest rather than provide news. She wrote that as major news conglomerates are owned by fewer and fewer people, the sort of acceptable stories those who work for them may write are limited, and so is the information for and imagination of those reading them. Hence, fitting these columns about a foreign country's tragedy into a narrative that closes, was a result of writers' understanding what stories the public most desires—redemption after tragedy, and a focus on the American, male point of view. Moreover, the lack of a Japanese point of view in these columns leads to an exacerbation of the differences between the West and Orient that Edward Said wrote of where "the Oriental becomes more Oriental, the Westerner more Western—and limit the human encounter between different cultures, traditions, and societies."[19] In short, the perceived geographical and cultural distance between America and the Orient was on display in these columns about the Japanese tragedy. There seemed to be a vacuous hole in representing the actual Japan in these stories that were, ironically, about Japan's geographical and humanistic state.

GENDER POLITICS DISCUSSED

The next camp of sports columnists writing of the World Cup also altogether eschewed the Japanese point of view in favor of the American. The consequences of this have already been elaborated upon. But they favored the American point of view by framing the World Cup to reveal the condition of gender politics in America. Specifically, these columnists theorized the place of women's sports in the American mainstream. The American sports sphere, these columnists openly admitted, was heretofore the domain of the male.

Many columnists wrote about the American women in the World Cup as if the number of people following the team and their fandom was a referendum on women's sports. For instance, Dowbiggin cited that 13.5 million Americans viewed the World Cup match on ESPN. Jason Gay of

The Wall Street Journal wrote that the women's team "went from footnote to America's Team."[20] (Interestingly, then, Gay utilized the rhetoric of tragedy, but in this case, the American team, the team not associated with tragedy, came to represent a nation). His notion that the women's team became America's team led to an argument that "an excited country— accused so often of being ambivalent to women's sports—charged on board. Now all of us know Abby Wambach. Now we know Hope Solo. Now we know Megan Rapinoe."[21] He also underscored that sports stores throughout the country received complaints that jerseys with women's American World Cup team names on the back were not made in men's sizes. Likewise, Meghan Rose, through her sources, suggested that the American women's team's success illustrated that there was equity between the genders, at least in terms of how the mainstream public consumed sports. "'I think it's great that they've proven that women can play this sport as well as men," said Canton's Sarah Berry, who was in attendance at Saturday's game to see her favorite player, Rapinoe.[22] To these columnists, the outcome of the game was secondary to the support that the women experienced in a sports sphere generally reserved for male fandom and athletes. Underpinning these columns, however, was an implicit understanding that the gender dynamic in the sports sphere previously privileged the male. Yet, there was a hope that the 2011 team's popularity was a harbinger of further progress regarding gender equity in America. This equity, it was theorized, would manifest because women athletes were welcomed into the imagined space generally reserved for males: The mainstream sports sphere.

To be sure, the surge in support the general American public offered to the American women's World Cup team was remarkable and worthy of note. But many columnists confused the number of fans with gender equity. More important to gender equity would be understanding of why this team garnered such support in a sphere that traditionally catered to males.

Although it is fair to argue that the women of the 2011 World Cup team did indeed benefit from a much larger and warm reception, to claim that this reception was indicative of a more progressive America is a bit problematic. Jere Longman began a critique of the team's reception, stating, "At this World Cup, the United States took a step backward in terms of diversity. All its players were white."[23] White women represented the country, indicating a reestablishment of the long-storied paradigm where women of color are placed on the fringes of consciousness and social movements regarding gender equity for all women. That is, to claim that the reception of this woman's team represented a progress in gender relations was to reify a problematic argument regarding feminism: white women's progress equates to gender equity. Such arguments, when coupled with the columns that dismissed the Japanese points of view, illustrate that the American sports sphere generally accepted white women in the domain of sports and fandom, but no others. The imagined space of sports, like the imagined public spaces of America and the globe, were Westernized, and a woman's team could be "America's team" so long as it reflected that point of view.

Longman also offered a history of how the American women's World Cup team had been received in the past. He indicated a distinction between the 2011 and 1999 USA women's World Cup teams' experiences regarding reactions to gender. He wrote that 2007:

> was a sports-bra-baring celebration of possibility, a confirmation of the heights that women could scale if given the full opportunity to participate as promised by the gender-equity legislation known as Title IX . . . "In '99, there was a clear consciousness that it was important for women's soccer and all girls and women in sports," said Brandi Chastain, who scored the winning penalty kick in the final and led the jersey-waving celebration in that tournament. "This team I think now is being seen as more mainstream."[24]

Citing Chastain, Longman implied that the 2011 team was mainstreamed. However, Longman also showed that many women athletes have resorted to sexualizing their bodies for the sake of marketing. "Players from Germany and France posed nude in desperate attempts to draw attention for the World Cup."[25] Likewise, it cannot be overlooked that American female athletes have, for over a decade, made such sexualization the norm. Christine Brennan of *USA Today* wrote a column about these practices in 2000 and specifically highlighted American soccer's icon, Brandi Chastain, and her decision to pose for *Goal* magazine. She wrote,

> What's troubling about [women athletes taking their clothes off is that it is a] trend [and] that there seems to be a warped attitude among some female athletes that it's not only proper to take off your clothes for a picture, it's actually liberating. To them, it has become a kind of hyper-feminist act: Now that they've made it, they can take it all off.[26]

Here Brennan argued that part of the popularity of women athletes is bound up with a paradoxical approach to feminism. The liberated women, because she has been liberated through sports, sexualizes her body. Yet, sexualizing one's body potentially reinforces a patriarchal foundation: pleasing the male sexually. Coupled with the racial make-up of the team, it seems that the American public's reception of the team is hardly progressive at all. In short, the sports sphere was still reserved for males and white females working to please them. Marketing experts merely figured out a way to allow women a space in that male dominated sphere: Sexualize them so that they become desirable to the male fan. This sexualization, moreover, explained why many columnists did not criticize the women for their play, given that they were viewed not as athletes, but female objects. In short, the reception of the women's team was predicated on a long-standing, oppressive tradition where "women . . . [we]re expected to look right, and to look right for a gaze who is masculine."[27]

However, two male sports columnists resisted the tendency to minimize the women's team held in the male-dominated sports sphere. In fact, one overtly criticized his counterparts for the position they took regarding the women's loss. Bryant Gumbel openly criticized the play of the American women and also the media covering it. In the process, he attempted to open the space of the field of play to women.

> "Had a men's team turned in a similar performance," he said on the season premiere of Real Sports with Bryant Gumbel, "papers and pundits nationwide would have had a field day assailing the players, criticizing the coach, and demanding widespread changes to a men's national team that flat-out choked. Yet the common reactions to this ladies' loss were simply expressions of empathy for the defeat of the unfortunate darlings and pride in their oh-so-heroic effort."[28]

According to Gumbel the American women's play lacked luster, and so did coverage of the game itself. He argued that one of the major reasons there was little criticism of the women's team was not that Japan had experienced a tragedy, but that gender roles were so solidified in America that men were loath to criticize women athletes for their performance. In fact, the outcome of the game seemed secondary to fans, according to Gumbel. Gumbel's argument implied an acceptance of women's athletics as being as serious about competition as male athletics.

Interestingly, Mitch Albom disagreed about the lack luster play of the women, yet managed to address gender in a fashion that maintained an equitable approach to women's athletics. He argued the women's team was great to watch "because they play[ed] with joy. They celebrate[d] with passion. They d[id] interviews as if they're thrilled to be asked a question. The essence of any sports story is still the story—not the gender—and this is a terrific story."[29] Where Albom differed from his counterparts, however, was that he saw the story not to be about the gender of the athletes involved in the World Cup final. Rather, he believed the passion of the athletes to be the most significant and exciting element of the World Cup. Hence, Albom found a universal trait—passion—by which to judge the women's play, and subsequently, avoided approaching his analysis with a clouded lens. In this way, Longman and Albom welcomed women into the space of American sports and worked to widen the "nation" that sports served to include women and men who watched women for their love of competition.

The phenomena of popularizing women's sport through the sexualization of the female athlete indicates the stronghold heterosexuality has over the sporting sphere in general, and that the male perspective dominates that sphere. The very act of sexualizing a female athlete illustrates the perceived futility of making a case for gender equity in sport. Many women athletes, in fact, have, for all intents and purpose, made a significant portion of their career the sexualization of their bodies. Take, for instance, Anna Kournikova, professional tennis player turned model who has yet to win a championship; or Danica Patrick of car racing who also has not won a title. Even Lindsey Vonn, champion Olympic Skier turned sexualized object, has gained a mainstream following despite that skiing is far out of the mainstream's eye. All of these women have bared their bodies to the male gaze in return for being welcomed into the mainstream sports sphere. In short, the female athlete, in return for transforming her body from athletic to object, has been welcomed into the sports sphere. That condition, however, places her on a tier below male athletes welcomed in based on their physical talent. To ignore that the rise in women's sports' popularity coincided with this new marketing ploy is to ignore a powerful ideology that yet exists in sports and that yet plays a significant role in shaping the lives of people who watch sport.

A FINAL THOUGHT ABOUT THE MASCULINE SPORT SPHERE

The 2011 World Cup was marked by controversy regarding sexuality reflective of a heterosexual approach mainstream audiences take to sport. Leading up to the World Cup, many sports columnists noted the major controversy of the competition to be Eucharia Uche, the Nigerian coach's remarks regarding lesbianism and her team. Jere Longman wrote that Uche "tarnished her team's appearance with homophobic remarks, saying that she had attempted to rid the squad of lesbian behavior, calling homosexuality 'a dirty issue' and 'spiritually, morally very wrong.'"[30] Many cultural critics would indicate that either America or American sport has come a long way in terms of its reception of gay people, in this case, lesbians. However, this notion mistakes silence about homosexuality for socially just approaches to it. For instance, American sport's first openly gay athlete who was not retired at the time of her coming out was Cheryl Swoops in 2005. Her coming out splashed news stories on television, but there was a general dearth of writing on her sexuality in the sports pages and columns. On a sports talk show on November 22, 2005, ESPN ombudsman George Solomon suggested that the lack of coverage stemmed from an unfortunate stereotype prevalent in 2005, that all women athletes were lesbians.[31] Solomon's commentary was supported by the fact that the New York Liberty team that Swoops played on was the consistent site for many lesbian groups to perform protests, even against the team. The lesbian activist group said it was "tired of the W.N.B.A. and the New York Liberty denying that lesbians are packing Madison Square Garden week after week for women's basketball games."[32] Hence, Swoops's announcement may not have been a surprise, but there still was little robust discussion of it in the sports pages. The lack of coverage, even if the stereotype is prevalent, was problematic.

Hence, I would argue that the sporting sphere has not actually progressed much at all in terms of its privileging of the male heterosexual. In fact, one of the last, untapped oppressive dynamics in sport is the notion mainstream audiences approach sport with, which is that all of the athletes they are watching are heterosexual. Although there have been male athletes like Esera Tuaolo and Billie Bean, who, after retirement came out as gay, there have been no male athletes in our major sports to follow the example of Swoops and come out during their career. No doubt a major reason for the general absence of gay male athletes to come out of the closet is a result of fear. Tuaolo, for instance, in an interview for the *Advocate* said, "I've seen fans throw batteries at players just because they're from the other team. So you can imagine what they would do if they knew a player was gay."[33] The same year that Tuaolo and Bean both came out, New York Mets Manager Bobby Valentine suggested that Major League Baseball was ready for its first gay player. Upon this rumor, the *New York Post* ran a back cover story claiming that Mets catcher Mike Piazza was gay. In response to the article, Piazza, who has since married a woman, held a press conference in order to clarify his sexuality. There are two manners in which to examine Piazza's reaction. First, coupled with Tuaolo and Bean's assertions above, it is important to conceptualize Piazza's choice to hold a press conference as illustrative of the powerful ideology of the audience of sport. The relationship between the athletes and the fans themselves is what scares some players from coming out as gay and/or, in Piazza's case, ensuring that fans know of their heterosexuality. This indicates that for fans to enjoy a contest that consists of only male athletes interacting with one another requires fans to deny any form of sexuality on the field: What theorists call homosociality. Homosociality is the presence of same-sexed people in a single space who all are assumed to be heterosexual so that no sexual desire is perceived to be present. The audience of sport is invested in being the gazers of an athlete, one that is male, but assumed to be heterosexual and also desexualized. The average heterosexual sports fan desires to witness sports in a sexual vacuum, unless of course, women are the objects of the gaze. Second, Piazza's press conference can be viewed in the frames of the old Don't Ask Don't Tell policy. Of the press conference, *Post* columnist Harvey Araton wrote that "in this world, the sexuality of the athlete is no more my business than that of the men and women who share the press box with me. What athletes do with their bodies is not my story, as opposed to how they manufacture those becoming more muscular by the minute."[34] However, this is not the case. The column itself is about the potential that Piazza is gay, and the fact that mainstream culture attended to this rumor indicates the importance that sporting audiences place on not looking at an athlete they know to be homosexual. In short, the lack of discussion about homosexuality in American sports columns has generally been a product of the unwritten contract between sports fan and athlete that all are heterosexual.

The implications of sport media's sexualizing its women athletes for the male and desexualizing its male athletes for the heterosexual male has grand implications on people outside of professional sport, though. In a July 1, 2003, column Lipsyte wrote, "If pro players feel threatened, what chance does a kid have to stand up for gays or even reject homophobic remarks . . . shame and humiliation [about sexuality] have always been cheap-shot coaching aids."[35] Lipsyte noted that pro sports and the sports media reporting on it plays a material role in shaping lives of gay athletes in locker rooms and throughout the nation. Columnists, in short, play a significant role in forming the world athletes and young people live in. Any media that accepts the assumption that all male athletes are heterosexual implicitly if not overtly supports homophobia.

Ultimately, then, the 2011 World Cup and the Japanese tsunami illustrated the conditions under which a team—American or otherwise—is capable of representing *the* nation. So long as the male heterosexual, American point of view is privileged, a team of any gender can come to represent *the* American nation. And as long as this is the paradigm in sport, sport itself will be one element of culture that is complicit in the silencing of young homosexual people, and their being made to feel inferior.

NOTES

1. Barack Obama, Address to the Nation, March 11, 2011, obama-speech.org/transcript.php?obama_speech_id=4685, 1 December 2011.
2. Michael Dear and Jonathan Flusty, *The Spaces of Postmoderity* (Boston: Blackwell Publishers, 2002).
3. See Neil Gotanda, "A Tale of Two Judges," in Wahneema Lubiano, ed. *The House that Race Built* (New York: Random House, 1997), 66–87.
4. A review of the same mainstream newspapers upon which this book relies shows this to be true.
5. Bruce Dowbiggin, *The Globe*, 23 July 2011, S. 4.
6. Gavin Blair, "Crisis-weary Japan Lifted by World Cup Victory," *The Christian Science Monitor*, 18 July 2011.
7. Yoree Koh, "Soccer Win Brings Joy to Nation," *The Wall Street Journal*, 18 July, 2011, A. 7.
8. Japan Outlasts U.S. to Win World Cup," *The Wall Street Journal*, 17 July 2011.
9. John Fienstien, "For Sunday's Champions, a Moment of Redemption," *Washington Post*, 17 July 2011.
10. Sally Jenkins, "This Cup Runneth Over," *Washington Post*, 18 July 2011, D. 1.
11. See Kandice Chuh, *Imagine Otherwise* (Durham, NC: Duke University Press, 2003).
12. Fienstien, "For Sunday's Champions, a Moment of Redemption."
13. Dave Anderson. *The New York Times*, 21 November 2011, B. 11.
14. Jenkins, "This Cup Runneth Over."
15. Jenkins, "This Cup Runneth Over."

16. Ann Roschelle, "Dream or Nightmare? Baseball and the Gender Order," in Robert Elias, ed., *Baseball and the American Dream*, Armonk, NY: M. E. Sharpe, 2001, 237.

17. See Ohm Youngmisuk, "Rising after the Storm"; Michael Wilbon, "Hope Wears as Saint's Uniform"; Dave Anderson, "The Saints Are Now America's Team."

18. These sports related choices to donate are often bound up with particular moments, such as the World Cup, or athletes, such as Lance Armstrong, to such an extent that memory becomes tangled as to what one is paying for. A yellow bracelet, a promise to pay ten dollars toward a relief effort: Is one paying for a bracelet? To represent one's own strength, in the face of cancer or simply one's own strength? Hero worship of an athlete? One's love for a friend? The point is that the bracelet or the donation, once meant to raise consciousness about the dearth of funding for cancer or poverty, is simply now muddied to the point that the bracelet has become but one of many other colored bracelets indicating support for something. Hence, while donation is most certainly important and admirable, I would suggest that it is also a way in which to shirk responsibility for remembering the tragedies that underpinned the funding in the first place.

19. Edward Said, *Orientalism* (New York: Vintage, 1979), 46.

20. Jason Gay, "A Year's Worth of Nerves in a Day," *Wall Street Journal*, 18 July 2011.

21. Gay, "A Year's Worth of Nerves in a Day."

22. Meghan Rose, "'I'm Really Just Proud': Fans Pay Tribute to World Cup Players. Sellout Crowd Shows up at KSU Soccer Stadium," *Atlanta Journal Constitution*, 24 July 2011 http://www.proquest.com/, 18 December 2011.

23. Rose, "'I'm Really Just Proud': Fans Pay Tribute to World Cup Players. Sellout Crowd Shows up at KSU Soccer Stadium."

24. Jere Longman, "Advancing Slowly on a Daunting Road," *New York Times*, 18 July 2011.

25. Longman, "Advancing Slowly on a Daunting Road."

26. Christine Brennan, "Women Athletes Need to Keep Their Clothes on," *USA Today*, 24 August 2000, C. 15.

27. Gillian Rose, *Feminism and Geography: The Limits of Geographical Knowledge* (Oxford: Blackwell Publishers, 1993).

28. Bruce Dowbiggin, *The Globe*, 23 July 2011, S. 4.

29. Mitch Albom, "U.S. Women's Soccer Team Converting Men, Too," *Detriot Free Press*, 17 July 2011.

30. Longman, "Advancing Slowly on a Daunting Road."

31. Kojo Nnamdi.

32. Ira Berkow.

33. Bruce C. Steele, "Tackling Football's Closet, *Advocate*, 26 November 2003.

34. Harvey Araton. "Baseball Focuses on the Trivial," *New York Times*, 23 May 2002, p. D 1.

35. Robert Lipsyte, *New York Times*, 1 July 2003.

Conclusion

Running Full Court: Ice Cube to Gin Blossoms

I am the patriarch.

I am privilege.

I am white.

I write this facetiously, but much of my work stems from an understanding that I was born with a significant amount of privilege. I come from an upper-middle-class, suburban family, and am white, heterosexual, and male. I even was the president of a fraternity at a liberal arts school.

That privilege, too, was coupled with a love of sports. I believe that I would be much more involved in them today if when I was young, I did not see something of perfection, grace, or beauty in Ryne Sandberg's pop-up slide when he stole a base. But I did. And so in my pursuit of his grace on the field, I attempted to steal third base while playing pony league during my high school years. But this time, no dust plumed the way it had when I watched Sandberg, the way it had when I stole previous bases; no cheers from the stands boomed (but then again, they rarely did for our team). Rather, Basil Alwatar, the third baseman, who had been my opponent in multiple leagues, loomed over me frantically waving and calling for help. In the ambulance, somebody told me I would have been safe if I hadn't rolled into the grass. I broke both bones in my lower leg, each of them in two places and returning to any organized sport after that, in many ways, was futile. But the lessons I learned by playing in these leagues never escaped me.

In fact, I don't remember much about my younger years that does not involve sport. What I remember most distinctly about grade school Saturdays is leaving two hours before game time so my mother and I could zoom through Evanston's Seventh Ward—code word for rich, white streets—to pick up my friends Todd Doyle and Dan Floyd for football practice. Then we trolled through Fifth Ward streets—code word for black and lower class streets—to pick up a number of my friends, almost all of whom would later be jailed for misdemeanor offenses. This, despite the Doyle, Gavin, and Floyd parents' best efforts to hold them back from the pull of crime and violence that Fifth Ward streets wielded; despite the effort to offer them home, solace, and finances for education.

Those pulls were especially strong because, after fifth grade, institutional racism was visible even to our naïve eyes. We saw our black and poor friends, if at all, only on the fields or courts of sport. In short, Evanston's educational system was divided along the same lines housing was and so the presence of covert racism was hardly a secret to any of us. The second element of high school that I remember is that despite this de facto segregation which stemmed from a matrix of oppressions, sport was the one place that, on school grounds, I met with my other friends of color after middle school.

I cannot overemphasize the important social role sport played for my friends and me as a result of social institutions' failures to deliver on America's democratic promises of equality. By the time I reached my senior year in high school, the role of sport in my life was fully solidified. My senior year in high school was athletically and socially as active as any other year of my life. On the blacktops of Evanston my buddies and I, all the stereotypical high school athletes of a racially diverse and big high school, met on Hinman Avenue and ran full-court. Because of the educational and housing segregations, these courts and the athletic practices we came from would be the only times we would see each other, save the parties we attended later on those same evenings. All of us saw this, and often conversation revolved around the fundamental problems with the way Evanston's power structures were set up. As Ice Cube boomed from the windows of a car, followed by the Gin Blossoms, institutional racism was the topic of conversation of my younger years. We were a generation that grew up idolizing Spike Lee and Martin Scorsese's different yet eloquent versions of New York life. The crossovers were on the court, in our racial make-up, and in our tastes. Always, we were grateful for our full-court games, where the joy of competition and being young was unrestricted by those structures that often prohibit such interaction: educational tracking and class-based housing, which equates to racially isolated neighborhoods. Little did we know that even this seemingly safe space, the blacktop, would suffer from a similar sort of covert racism only a few years later.

Eventually Evanston's city council demanded that Hinman Avenue's full-courts be dismantled—that a single hoop on one side of every court in the white and affluent Ward 3 be taken down. Though the rhetoric was about protecting grade school children from being trampled by us menacing teenagers, even then we knew that it really amounted to another form of structural racism defining rigid boundaries between black/white, low/high class. The problem, in short, was the many black teenagers who infiltrated this ward as a result of the integrated friendships established. The space of the basketball court, in short, mirrored the racial make-up of the educational system and housing in Evanston.

At the time, I wrote news articles about this basketball issue, which sparked immediate interest from the more level-headed city council members. Quickly, however, the issue dissolved into the same place most racial issues did: rhetoric that championed Evanston for being racially diverse, and tolerant, which, when these individuals interacted with each other, it was. But these catchphrases about diversity and progress that our town's political players have, for a long while, hung their proverbial hats upon, allowed them to deny that any structural racism was existent in Evanston.

Eventually, I left Evanston to attend Dickinson College. The halls I lived in, like the classes I attended, were overwhelmingly white. The major difference between Dickinson and Evanston, however, was that many of the students I encountered were overt about their thinking that racism did not exist in America. (In contrast, the faculty, overwhelmingly white as well, was quite liberal.) I still remember a conversation among my peers in the cafeteria in which I was the lone voice resisting the notion that African Americans were by nature intellectually inferior. I was shocked and surprised that at this place, a liberal arts college with a history of producing elite lawyers, politicians, and thinkers, beliefs that were overtly protective of white privilege that were held by the students. But then again, I had never been somewhere so white, and I began to realize that not all whites are liberal; that there are places where, feeling safe, some white people—who have not met with many other races— overtly express beliefs about other races that they might not express in other contexts. Looking around, as well, I noticed that almost every person of color at Dickinson in 1994 was an athlete, again illustrating that sport has a social role to resist the racist structures of institutions. For a long while I challenged these peers of mine who expressed what I held as problematic beliefs. And after a half a semester there, I was ready to transfer.

However, my father—a man after whom I model myself, who fought for equal housing in Chicago and now Evanston, whose actions about educational policy are directed at offering all members of the community equal access and also improving minority achievement, maintaining integrated schools, and who, with my mother, set up a soup kitchen nearly thirty years ago that is still running strong—demanded that I not transfer. When I told my parents of how bothered I was by the overwhelmingly white college I was attending, they said something I keep in mind still today: "You can learn just as much from the problems at Dickinson as you did from those at your high school." They were right. It was there that I realized there are ideologies that differ among people of the same race, and that hearing what one considers to be the "wrong" side of an argument and engaging with it may be more important than making one's own argument heard. In fact, I think that some of the best training I received in creating logical, sound arguments about social issues came from the late nights I spent arguing with people at Dickinson. It was there also that I realized that I was just as sheltered as those I called "'sheltered.'" I grew up understanding, but not being able to articulate the privilege my whiteness and upper-middle classness offered, and I expected the same of my peers. However, because many of them grew up in towns that were rural, white, and privileged, then went to a school full of similar people, and finally entered professions that led to financial and racial privilege—because of all these steps, the realities of privilege and poverty remain, for many of them, unknown. Still, I know we were all sheltered, just in different ways.

Now I teach and work in administration at Prince George's Community College, an institution that is more than 70 percent minority. Here I have realized the significant and important role those in education can play, especially in this era of cable news, iPods, and streaming media. But this did not come about simply because of an interest in sports. I began thinking seriously about this book in 2004, a few weeks after the nation had concluded a bitter presidential election. In December of that year, I had dinner with some old friends, friends with whom I shared opposing political views, but with whom I was able to begin discussing the Iraq War by first bringing up President Bush's opening pitch of game five of the 2001 World Series. Their memories of that event provided us with a safe space to engage in political debate, even though that year's venomous campaign made political discussions difficult to hold. It was then that I solidified my own belief that narratives about sport and national identity not only become bridges between and among people with different political viewpoints. They also shape how we think about ourselves in relation to the mythological nation.

At the most basic and important of levels, then, this book's underlying premise is that what storytellers represent and remember (whether they tell stories in newspapers, books, or in bars) is bound up with power and reflective of their values and of their concepts of identity. The same is true of us as we consider and discuss national identity after tragedies. I will never forget how, after Hurricane Katrina, and the devastation and destruction, one of my acquaintances, a self-admitted George W. Bush apologist, noted all the cars he saw on television that were left in New Orleans. The implication was that the people on rooftops, in the Superdome, washed away by water, should have evacuated with those cars. This implication, in my mind, removed any blame regarding the tragedy from the politicians in leadership positions and the historic structural inequities that characterized the region. It also removed any need to acknowledge his own privilege. For the underlying assumption in his comment was that everybody has enough money to own a car. Such assumptions deny the existence of poverty and subsequently the notion of civic responsibility a common citizen may otherwise have.

On a more national level, as columnists write stories about tragedy and sport, they hold up certain kinds of people and not others as representative of America and its history. The same is true of how we talk about and remember these events. In an era in which controversy characterizes news media, and sport media has proliferated by relying on controversy, there would seem, on the surface, to be more obvious topics of study for a sports-media scholar. And for those not involved with education, deep study of sport may seem unnecessary and extravagant. But the era we are in demands identifying places where those who are sheltered in one way may speak with those who are sheltered in another, in order to create understanding between and among us; in order to better the nation itself.

Let me show how sport is one of those places. Any avid fan of baseball has, at one time or another, been invested in its mythology. In 2006, the year I began actually writing this book, some of that mythology was being corrected with the election of fourteen Negro League players and officials to the Baseball Hall of Fame. But there is ample reason to see that election, which somehow neglected to allow Buck O'Neill into those hallowed grounds, as symptomatic of a culture that resists embracing black players as part of the mythology of baseball in the first place. Why, for instance, is Josh Gibson, who hit a homerun every 15.9 at bats, not considered in the common culture as a home run king? This says as much about what the common American perceives as legitimate baseball leagues as it does anything else. Much about my passion for sport, social justice, education, and the nation sees this marginalization of black players from the Negro Leagues and from national memory as revealing the way in which America in general has been trained to consider legitimate identities when viewing professional sports.

Similarly, after 9/11, I was one of the millions of Americans who, watching the Yankees' improbable run to the World Series, attached national significance to the sporting events. But the sadness when New York lost the Series could not match the sadness of those who lost loved ones in the terrorist attacks. Nor could the story of 9/11 really be told through the Yankees, even though the efforts were made over and again. Caught up in the emotion of those Towers falling, the images of President Bush throwing out the first pitch of game three, the Air Force flyovers, and the players wearing NYPD/NYFD hats, I did not question the role these games and the narratives of them played in constructing a specific form of national identity.

But upon reflection, and with a certain sense of disappointment, I see the spectacle of 9/11, and other moments in which sport was narrated to have significance after national tragedy as playing a part in national mythology that resembles that which left Negro League players out of the Hall of Fame. It is a nostalgia that works emotively and privileges the same people who have always been privileged in America: white males. The emotion, that is, is predicated on a misremembering of actual events, actual oppressions, both in the distant and near past. There is not any reason to believe that the narrators of sporting events after national tragedy are misled or motivated toward bad ends. Rather, it is more helpful to think of them as part of a complex that has a history in sport media, and part of a culture that seeks meaning after these events. But in the immediate aftermath of tragedy, and sometimes decades following, there may be no meaning to find, except one that may be found for those already historically privileged. In the absence of obvious meaning, a storyteller of sports has only the past to rely on, the national mourning to attend to, both of which have been constructed in problematic ways as a result of misremembering systematic oppression.

Hence, it is not helpful to consider the narrators of sporting events as wrong, but constructing a concept of national identity that offers meaning, even if that meaning is misdirected. My purpose in this book, then, was not to vilify, but examine what sort of stories these writers tell and subsequently examine what stories audiences desired. In the process, I wanted to illustrate that these stories often denied the reality of oppressions and subsequently risked perpetuating it.

Nor is this an attack on sport. Too often, news media, sociologists, and those of us in the local taverns and Super Bowl parties pretend that sport is an entity separate from other activities, like politics. Sport and the reporting on it, though, does play a role in the way national identity is perceived, and this project was intended to identify that role while also eschewing the mythology often underpinning sport. This book was meant only to illustrate that sport media is a place that is rife with potential for those of us interested in social justice. Those of us in academia, if we are to reach out to audiences beyond our classrooms, need to consider sport and cultural phenomena like it as legitimate for study, for these are the places where those we may consider "sheltered" already are.

OCCUPY HIGHER EDUCATION

American Studies in a Moment of Danger by George Lipsitz was concerned with redefining academia's place in the greater culture.[1] Common sense, he argued, is a product of who controls what is defined or constructed as "normal," and is often rife with powerful notions of identity. According to Gramsci and later Lipsitz, whoever controls the institutions that produce knowledge—educational, media, legal, political, and cultural institutions, to name a few—also has great power in controlling what is considered common sense and so understanding of what is normal. In short, these philosophers identify why educational institutions play such a significant role in defining identities. They illustrate that there is great power and so motivation in controlling the kinds of knowledge produced in educational institutions: Not only do high schools and colleges produce knowledge, but also people who run other cultural institutions that produce knowledge come from these educational institutions.

The moment for understanding the role education plays in today's changing media environment, however, is urgent. For example, those of us in education are currently facing a political and social environment in which the kinds of students allowed within our doors and the kinds of knowledge being taught in the classroom are being scrutinized. Both of these threats potentially make education, and subsequently our ability to shape the status of commons sense, look exactly like our mainstream media, where one only has to interact with ideas and aesthetics with which one is comfortable.

In *From Walden Pond to Jurassic Park*, Paul Lauter suggested that there is a developing tendency to view students as consumers and educational knowledge as something to be owned and manipulated by non-expert political leaders.[2] New state and federal policies throughout the country are limiting educational access for poor and minority students through coded language—such as banning "remedial classes" from four-year institutions. Given that students of color and lower economic classes are much more likely to test into such courses, these kinds of policies create the same sort of structural racism I saw in Evanston's educational system. Specifically, banning remedial courses is a policy with implications that may seem benign, but potentially create educational institutions that are heavily white, middle and upper class. This is despite politicians' and many citizens' common claim that education is the great equalizer. Decisions to cut remedial courses, moreover, are often not being made by faculty and administrators in the educational sector, but by politicians who know that condemning remediation plays well in the national media. However, the reality of these decisions is that by limiting access to higher education for those who have historically been oppressed, these colleges increase the labor population and the perpetuation of the structural inequalities outside of the college campus.

Access is not the only limitation that is being placed on institutions of higher learning. Both Lauter and Lipsitz argued that new spaces and ways of making academic scholarship politically relevant need to be developed by scholars to resist the way in which conservative politicians and media pundits attempt to reach into college classrooms to restrict the sort of knowledge being taught in them. In both the national media and in policy generation higher education is losing a culture war. Not only is there a tendency to question the fiscal efficacy of having a college education in mainstream America, but also higher education is increasingly having its funding cut by the same conservatives banning remedial education. Part of this cutting in funding, especially in disciplines that are cultural in nature, however, is a result of scholars having astute and acidic criticisms of the government. But they often lack the political savvy to garner wide audiences who may read their work outside of academic halls. That is, there is a tension between the conservative politicians who seek to limit funding, access, and the kind of knowledge being taught in

colleges on the one hand, and academics who use extreme language regarding conservatives and thereby potentially alienate such conservatives. And the cycle is created and perpetuated. To clarify, in tracking
American studies as a discipline in terms of both the funding it received
and the sort of work coming out of the discipline, it is easy to see a slow
decay of financial support from the federal government that coincided
with the sort of content within the field at the time. Immediately after
WWII, American studies focused on the nation's mythological state and
privileged white males in both its methods and conclusions. The nation's
politicians were left unchallenged by the scholarship coming out of cultural studies on college campuses, and monies were offered to the discipline at a higher rate than they are today. Today, however, American
studies and fields of studies like it are languishing as a result of very little
funding. Likewise, the Right belittles our work and has a bigger pulpit
from which to make its broad claims about the danger of teaching points
of view that do not align with the white point of view. There is no doubt
that this belittling and cutting of funding is a result of the focus much of
our work places on race, sexuality, gender, and the like. The more these
themes and points of view are central to scholars' work, the more federal
and state policies are legitimately criticized for past and current short-
comings. It is no coincidence, I would argue, that these disciplines are
among the first on the educational chopping block when finances are
tightened, then.

But the effect of this three-decade-long assault on these educational
fields through governmental limits of funding should also be examined
for how it intertwines with cultural conceptions of identity and legitimate
political stances. As I was putting the final edits on this book, Rick Santorum was a leading candidate for the Republican nomination in the 2012
presidential race. He was running on a campaign of moral values while
vilifying homosexual identities and also the notion that women are equal
to men. That Santorum was such a popular candidate and that his stance
regarding feminism was so well-received only further illustrates the way
white and patriarchal approaches to politics and knowledge intersect. To
be clear, as points of view that would challenge patriarchy and whiteness
are limited in educational institutions, the politicians who also limit such
points of view have every reason to believe their electorate will buy into
their conceptions of "moral values," or what morality is.

Hence, politicians have begun actively reaching into college classrooms, using techniques that extend beyond funding and rhetoric. As
this book goes to print, the conservative Tea Party is assaulting different
kinds of multicultural education throughout the country, with the most
effective campaigns located in Arizona. In writing of this assault, *Forbes*
writer Melik Kaylan argued:

Arizona Superintendent of Education Tom Horne authored the legislation to "ban ethnic studies," in the shorthand phrase of those against the initiative, and Gov. Jan Brewer signed it into law this Tuesday, May 11. . . . A little background first: Horne is quoted as saying that he opposes courses that "promote the overthrow of the U.S. government," teach that "Republicans hate Latinos," and generally incite ethnic division through books with titles like Occupied America: A History of Chicanos.[3]

Kaylan's summary revealed that the Right has, in many states, sought to find a political means by which to limit the sort of knowledge students are exposed to at many levels of education. In schools, towns, and states where institutional racism exists, these kinds of political infiltrations into curricula are the Right's "war of position." Not only does limiting multicultural education further solidify the oppressive standpoints that have led to white privilege, but it also works to ensure learners will not challenge this point of view, and those points of view become common sense. Couple this with the fact that the media is overtly attacking higher education's superstar scholars with a goal of protecting conservatives: David Horowitz, a regular on *The O'Reilly Factor*, has a relatively new book, *The Professors: The 101 Most Dangerous Academics in America,* which makes no pretense about the fact that he wants parents to forbid students to enter our classes; he chronicles the work of Angela Davis, bell hooks, Gayatri Spivak, Fredric Jameson, and many others in short summaries to give parents "information" on which professors, and thus, which knowledge they should keep from their children. The potential result, eventually, is that our classrooms become void of any people who come from the families of privilege. Lipsitz claimed that in an era where media moguls like Rupert Murdoch "have extraordinary influence . . . we neglect them at our peril."[4] He is completely right. Given that those like Santorum and Horowitz find their base on Fox News, Murdoch's empire, and that conservatives watch this station, it is not a far leap to suggest that in the current mediated, economic, and political environment, the college classroom that challenges the mythologies of America will be full of those who already do not buy into them. Likewise, the college campuses, under current conditions, are more and more moving toward a return to the same kinds of people and thinking that problematically justified those same mythologies. The college classroom, in short, is the next great battle ground in the culture war.

But those of us in the academy are at times guilty of similar limitations. The language that academics have traditionally used in writing about the Right has been potentially off-putting to those students in our classrooms who may be conservative. The result is that our work ensures that it preaches only to the choir. What we often miss, though, is that by engaging in the same kind of rhetoric the Right uses, we feed into the

Right's power-grabbing by alienating the Right and its followers rather than engaging with them.

Let me illustrate by way example. Just as Fox News often preaches to the choir and uses inflammatory rhetoric about the Left to ensure the choir is its audience, so do our classes entitled "White Privilege and the Media." Students who sign up for such courses are often already interested in the subject and those turned off by the title, conservatives, would most likely take another class. One has to wonder how much mind changing is possible in such classes. Even how we speak about national identity while in classes may alienate those we need to reach out to. For instance, C. R. King cited Mary Karenga, who defined national identities that privilege whiteness or even middle-classness as "white supremacist." She argued that white supremacy "[i]s a social problem, a problem of thought and practice," not necessarily an ideology found in Ku Klux Klanners or the like.[5] In short, Karenga would call my peers in college or the politicians in Evanston white supremacists. This sort of language does not engage those causing the problems and potentially allows those embracing such ideologies off the hook with an excuse that we alienated them. Moreover, Karenga's use of "white supremacy" potentially blurs the distinct kinds of violence in which "white supremacy" and "white privilege" engage.

Those who benefit from white privilege and buy into mythological versions of national identity are often good people without understanding of the hegemony they buy into and the privilege from which they benefit. This is how hegemony and privilege work. To make that clear to audiences outside of academic halls, I suggest that scholars in identity studies and disciplines to which it is related adopt terminology that can clearly and quickly delineate between (white) privilege and white supremacy, as the latter is often associated with terrorism.[6]

Ultimately, the distinction between white privilege and white supremacy, which King and Karenga conflate, is imperative to maintain for two reasons. First, it allows a clear identification of audiences to and for whom scholarship is written. One of the many audiences for our studies, I argue, is that which is privileged by whiteness. This is one of our audiences because one of our goals is to reach out to those embracing white privilege to educate them and to encourage them to renounce that power. In contrast, white supremacists and terrorists do not comprise one of our audiences. The distinction in terms "white privilege" and "white supremacy," as a result, allows the clear distinction in scholars' audiences and goals while acknowledging that different viewpoints exist in whites—among them are those who work against white privilege, those who embrace white privilege, and white supremacists. This distinction is an example of the kind of tactical strategy we ought to consider. To reach any audience requires that one not turn its members off immediately. Hence, I have avoided use of "white supremacy" throughout this book, except when referring to organized groups related to white terror. This is merely one strategy in reaching out to audiences beyond academic halls in order to confront hegemony. That being said, we also need to consider retheorizing the language we use and the themes for study in order to entice those of a variety of tastes into our classrooms.

If we academics are to make our work politically relevant by changing students' minds, we need to consider a strategy reciprocal to the Right. Rather than using media and politics to reach into the classroom, we need to teach media and politics in the classroom with the hope our students bring what we teach them to their media consuming experiences. One way of doing this is to consider working with themes like sports that would attract conservatives into our leftist classrooms. To do this, though, requires a seeking out of themes that conservatives would consider embracing, such as sports and the like.

All of the above arguments suggest that scholars need to acknowledge the necessity of working with new paradigms in the courses we teach, examine where struggles for controversial debate can take place, and think of ways to alter knowledge beyond the walls of our classrooms. I am, in short, suggesting we adopt Lipsitz's framework of the spider who "attempts to work from within to transform the very structures of oppression into mechanisms for liberation."[7] That is, part of the advantage of sport media as a site for study is that we can, through it, strategically address the discriminators with the hope of changing them. For if the goal is to challenge privilege, then the audience must consist of those privileged by that identity and the institutions catering to it.

I admit that expecting those adopting privileged standpoints to renounce privilege because of media, education, or scholarship is an idealistic endeavor. But so is most of our work in education. Moreover, I see this as the necessary next step in conceiving of new ways to engage with the globalizing world that is changing the kinds of obstacles educators face. Finding new spaces to widen the knowledge of the national identity, is a maneuver that may be helpful, even necessary, for those who have faith in the struggles for hegemony.

Finally, I see coalitions being built between and among both sport media and sports scholars as potentially leading to projects that reach beyond our classrooms, and educating audiences consisting of those embracing problematic stances about race and privilege. Although advocating for coalitions between scholars and sport media seems a utopian end to this project, I was struck by Bill Rhoden's comment on *Outside the Lines* as he pondered whether or not the allergic reaction to Barry Bonds's home run chase was racist. He proclaimed, "We need a sociologist here."[8] In that same vein, in writing this book, I have been lucky enough to have the guidance of wonderful scholars at the University of Maryland as well as the expertise of Steve Gietschier, senior managing editor of research at *The Sporting News*. His expertise as a historian and in sport media has helped me immensely. Beyond his attention to historical detail, his questions regarding my reading of columnists' work have helped me to articulate arguments about race and identity in ways I hope are clearer to audiences outside of academia. Perhaps most important, he guided me to tone down my language so that it would be embraced by a wider public. I hope my work to tone down the language was successful. Coalitions between experts in fields seem only to help projects, and, more importantly, knowledge and communication. I would hope that sport media and sociologists of identity, national identity, and media could find each other in future projects as well. For it is through talking to each other that we learn, progress, and include. It is through the talking that we understand rather than simply disagree. It is through new ways of seeing that we can perhaps begin to move past the borders of the neighborhoods we were born in; the races we are comfortable with; the stigmas we believe are common sense, but are simply bigoted. It is through the remembering that we begin to reperceive the past and understand what has been covered up. It is through the engaging of opposing standpoints that we widen who we engage with and increase the potential for social justice rather than protecting our own powerful place.

NOTES

1. George Lipsitz, *American Studies in a Moment of Danger*. Minneapolis: University of Minnesota Press, 2001.
2. Paul Lauter, *From Walden Pond to Jurassic Park*. Duhram, NC: Duke University Press, 2001.
3. Malik Kaylan, "Defending Arizona's Education Law," *Forbes*, 5 May 2010.
4. George Lipsitz, *American Studies in a Moment of Danger*, 321.
5. C. R. King. "Cautionary Notes on Whiteness and Sport Studies," *Sociology of Sport Journal* 22, no. 3 (2005): 397–408; 401.
6. Hegemony is the normalization of a particular identity and/or power. Many groups can engage in such practices: some black nationalists in the 1970s, for instance, it can be argued, engaged in black hegemony. White hegemony is the normalization of whiteness, as defined in chapter 1.
7. Lipsitz, 163.
8. Outside the Lines, ESPN, 23 February 2005.

Appendix

The following is a brief biography of the columnists who are cited often in the dissertation. It is not an exhaustive list of columnists read in forming ideas for the dissertation.

Bob Addie, a columnist for the *Washington Post, The Washington Times Herald,* and *The Sporting News,* he covered the Senators for over twenty years. In 1981, he was given the J. G. Tyler Spink Award for his contributions to baseball writing, an award voted upon by his peers.

J. A. Adande wrote a column for the *Los Angeles Times* from 1997 to May 2007. Prior to this, Adande was a writer for the *Washington Post* and the *Chicago Sun Times.* Since 2005, he has been a regular on the ESPN show *Around the Horn.* His work has appeared in *The Best American Sports Writing.*

Mitch Albom is a columnist for *The Detroit Free Press,* hosts a nationally-syndicated radio show, and frequently appears on ESPN's *Sports Reporters.* He also is the author of seven books including *Tuesdays with Morrie,* which was on top of the *New York Times* best seller list for four straight years.

Dave Anderson, since 1971, has been a columnist for the *New York Times.* He won the 1981 Pulitzer Prize and the 1994 Associated Red Smith Award for his column. In 1990, he was inducted to the National Sportswriters Hall of Fame. His columns appear nationwide in syndicated format.

Paul Attner has been a writer for *The Sporting News* since 1984. His work received awards from the Professional Basketball Writers of America, Professional College Basketball Writers of America, and Professional Football Writers of America.

Thomas Boswell a nationally-syndicated *Washington Post* columnist since 1984, has written many best-selling books about baseball, not the least of which is his collection of columns. A mentee of Shirley Povich, Boswell is a student of baseball and has appeared in many films about baseball, including *Baseball* by Ken Burns and memory projects for ESPN.

Christine Brennan has been a columnist for *USA Today* since 1997. She has covered the Olympics since 1984. She has served as a sports commentator for NPR, ESPN, and ABC News.

Arthur Daley was a nationally syndicated columnist for the *New York Times* from 1942–1973. In 1956, he became the second sports columnist ever to win the Pulitzer Prize for excellence in sports writing.

Tony Kornheiser a *Washington Post* columnist since 1984, was an analyst for *Monday Night Football* and host of ESPN's *Pardon the Interruption*. In 1997, Kornheiser was a finalist for the Pulitzer Prize in commentary. He also hosts a nationally syndicated radio show.

Robert Lipsyte, an internationally syndicated columnist for the *New York Times* since 1965, is considered by many an authority on Muhammed Ali. In 1992, Lipsyte was runner-up for the Pulitzer Prize in commentary. In 1996 he won the Meyer Berger Award for distinguished reporting from Columbia University. He is a prolific and award-winning young adult author. Finally, he works for ESPN as an authority on boxing and baseball.

Mike Lupica is a nationally syndicated columnist with the *New York Daily News*. He currently hosts ESPN's *The Sports Reporters*. He served as editor of the 2004 edition of *The Best American Sports Writing*.

Jack Mann, a writer of horse racing and baseball, was a columnist for the *New York Times*. He twice won the Walter Haight Award for excellence in turf writing. He also wrote a biography on Ty Cobb.

Jim Murray, columnist with the *Los Angeles Times* from 1972–1998, won a Pulitzer Prize for his commentary. He was selected National Sports Writer of the Year fourteen times.

Bill Plaschke, a columnist for the *Los Angeles Times* since 1996, won the Associated Press' award for National Sports Columnists of the Year in 2005. He is a regular on ESPN's *Around the Horn* and is consistently featured in *The Best American Sports Writing*.

Shirley Povich, a nationally syndicated columnists of the *Washington Post* from 1926–1974, was one of the nation's most-read columnists during this time.

Rick Reilly, *Sports Illustrated* columnist since 1985, has been voted Sportswriter of the Year eight times. His latest book, *Hate Mail from Cheerleaders*, is a compilation of his columns and was at the top of the *New York Times* best-seller list.

William Rhoden, a columnist for the *New York Times* since 1981, appears regularly on ESPN's *The Sports Reporters*. His latest book, *Forty Million Dollar Slaves*, examines the black athlete in sport and challenges the notion of equality resulting from integration.

Red Smith, *New York Herald Tribune* and later the *New York Times* columnist won a Pulitzer Prize in 1976 for sports writing. From 1947–1982, Red Smith was considered the nation's most widely read sports columnist, as his work was syndicated in more than 200 papers.

George Vecsey has been a columnist for the *New York Times* since 1982. He has authored multiple books on baseball.

Jason Whitlock, a columnist for the *Kansas City Star*, has written for ESPN2 and AOL Sports. He has appeared on ESPN's *Sports Reporters* and *Pardon the Interruption*.

Michael Wilbon, columnist for the *Washington Post* since 1987, is cohost of ESPN's *Pardon the Interruption*.

Dave Zirin, a columnist for the *Los Angeles Times* and the *Nation* magazine, was Press Actions' 2005-2006 Sports Writer of the Year. Besides authoring many books about sports, race, and nation, Zirin appears on ESPN's *Outside the Lines* frequently.

Bibliography

Aaraton, Harvey. "Just Sports Business as Usual If the Saints Go Marching Out." *New York Times*, 20 September 2005, sec. D.

Abbott, W. W. "The Papers of George Washington, Preface," 1999 http://gwpapers.virginia.edu/articles/abbot_3.html (11 February 1999).

Abramson, Jesse. "Army, Navy Squads Drill; For Nothing." *New York Herald Tribune*, 24 November 1963, sec. 4.

———. "Sports Silent Tribute to President Kennedy—Most College Football Games Are Called Off." *New York Herald Tribune*, 23 November 1963, sec. 4.

Adande, J.A. and Jennifer Frey. "Security Tightens in Village, but Athletes Still Come Out to Play." *Washington Post*, 28 July 1996, sec. A.

Addie, Bob. "Golden Arms Abound." *Washington Post*, 7 April 1968 sec. E.

———. "Muted Ceremonies Likely on Tuesday." *Washington Post*, 6 April 1968, sec. E.

———. "Opening-Day Memories." *TheWashington Post*, 10 April 1968, sec. D.

———. "HHH Ignores Protest." *Washington Post*, 11 April 1968, sec. E.

———. "Killebrew Reflections." *Washington Post*, 12 April 1968, sec. D.

———. "Senatorial Possibility." *Washington Post*, 9 June 1968, sec. C.

———. "An Affair of State?" *Washington Post*, 19 October 1968, sec. C.

Adler, Jerry. "Terror and Triumph." *Newsweek*, 5 August 1996: 24–33.

Albright, Robert C. "March Leaders Press Civil Rights Case." *Los Angeles Times*, 29 August 1963.

Albom, Mitch. "Road to Recovery Takes Unlikely Turn." *Detroit Free Press*, 23 September 2001.

———. "U.S. Women's Soccer Team Converting Men, Too," *Detriot Free Press*, 17 July 2011.

American Psychiatric Association. *DSM-IV*, Washington, DC: 2000.

Amdur, Neil. "Negro Hopes to Pin Down Medal." *New York Times*, 12 October 1968, sec. L.

Anderson, Benedict. "Imagined Communities" 90–91 in *Nationalism*, edited by John Hutchinson and Anthony D. Smith. New York: Oxford University Press, 1994.

Anderson, Dave. "Olympics Not Games Anymore." *New York Times*, 28 July 1996, sec. D.

———. "The Saints Are Now America's Team." *New York Times*, 15 September 2005, sec. D.

———. "Sorry, But Magic Isn't a Hero." *New York Times*, 14 November 1991, sec. B.

Angell, Roger. "Can You Believe It?" *New Yorker*, 26 November 2001.

Applebome, Peter. "Grim Reality Doesn't Scare Most Fans from Games." *New York Times*, 28 July 1996.

Armour, Nancy. "As New Orleans Rebuilds, Saints' Return Another Step Toward Normalcy." *Associated Press*, 11 August 2006.

Associated Press. "Dr, King to Press Anti-War Stand." *New York Times*, 24 March 1967, sec. A.

———. "A Friend and Champion Is Missing From Sports." *New York Herald Tribune*, 24 November 1963, sec. 4.

Attner, Paul. "They're Home, There's Hope." *The Sporting News*, 29 September 2006. (Lexis)

———. "The League Will Go On, but so Will Its Grief," *The Sporting News*, 24 September 2001.

Baldwin, James. "White Man's Guilt," in *Black on White*, edited by David Roediger, New York: Shocken, 1998, pp. 177–80.

Barry, Dan. "New York Carries On, but Test of Its Grit Has Just Begun." *New York Times*, 11 October 2001, sec. B.

Bass, Amy. "Whose Broad Stripe and Bright Stars," 184–207 in *Sports Matters*, editors John Bloom and Michael Willard, New York: New York University Press, 2002.

Battista, Judy. "Evening of Good Will Turns Giants' Way." *New York Times*, 20 September 2005.

Bederman, Gail. *Manliness and Civilization*. Chicago: University of Chicago Press, 1996.

Beegan, Daniel. "Studds Says Reagan Has Shown Little Concern over AIDS." Associated Press, 19 September 1985.

Berlant, Lauren. *The Queen of America Goes to Washington City*. Durham, NC: Duke University Press, 1997.

Birrell, Susan and Mary G. McDonald. *Reading Sport: Critical Essays on Power and Representation*. Northeastern University Press: Boston, 2000.

Black, Joel. *Reality Effect*. New York: Routledge, 2002.

Blair, Gavin. "Crisis-weary Japan Lifted by World Cup Victory," *The Christian Science Monitor*, 18 July 2011.

Bodley, Hal. "Selig Facing Difficult Decision on Resuming Games." *USA Today*, 13 September 2001, sec. C.

Booth, William. "Blast Hit Heart of Party." *Washington Post*, 28 July 1996, sec. A.

Boswell, Thomas. "Magic Opens the Doors." *Washington Post*, 15 November 1992, sec. C.

———. "A Bond Linking Us All." *Washington Post*, 29 July 1996, sec. C.

———. "Terror Leaves Games in Somber Mood." *Washington Post*, 28 July 1996, sec. C.

———."Beyond the Quest for Gold, Games Have a Silver Lining." *Washington Post*, 5 August 1996, sec. D.

———. "Reassuring Our Convictions." *Washington Post*, 28 January 1998, sec. D.

Brady, Dave. "Sport Figures Surrounded RFK." *New York Times*, 6 June 1968, sec. C.

Brennan, Christine. "Women Athletes Need to Keep Their Clothes On," *USA Today*, 24 August 2000, C. 15.

Brinson, Susan J. "Gender, Terrorism, and War," *Signs*, 1, August 2002, 437.

Brown, Clifton. "With Bush Available, Saints Options Abound." *New York Times*, 29 April 2006, sec. D.

Buckley, Steve. "Thankfully, Games Go On." *The Boston Herald*, 22 November 2001, p. 92.

Burd, Laurence. "March to Aid Negro Cause, Kennedy Said." *Chicago Tribune*, 29 August 1963.

Burns, Ken. *Unforgivable Blackness*. WETA.

Bush, George W. "Address to the Nation," 20 September 2005, last modified 17 July 2007, http://www.whitehouse.gov/news/releases/2005/09/20050915-8.html

———. "President Bush's Address to the Nation 11 September 2001." September 11, 2001, last modified 6 July 2007, http://www.whitehouse.gov/news/releases/2001/09/20010911-16.html

———. "President Discusses Hurricane Relief to the Region," 9 September 2005, last modified 17, July 2007, http://www.whitehouse.gov/news/releases/2005/09/20050915-8.html

———. "State of the Union Address." 31 January 2007, last modified 5 September 2007, http://www.whitehouse.gov/stateoftheunion/2007/

Cady, Steve. "Owens Recalls 1936 Sprinter's Ordeal." *New York Times*, 17 October 1968, sec. C.

Cameron, Ardis. *Looking for America*. Boston: Blackwell Publishing, 2005.

Carpenter, Les. "A Roaring Return." *Washington Post*, 26 September 2006, sec. E.

Carsley, William. "Athletes Who Care and Those Who Don't." *Chicago Tribune*, 25 October 1968.

Chase, Marilyn. "Johnson Disclosure Underscores Facts of AIDS in Heterosexual Population." *Wall Street Journal*, 11 November 1991, sec. B.

Chuh, Kandice. *Imagine Otherwise*. Durham, NC: Duke University Press, 2003.

Clinton, William Jefferson. "First Inaugural Address," last modified 7 July 2007, http://www.bartleby.com/124/pres64.html

CNN, "Who Planted the Bomb?" CNN, 27 July 1996.

Coll, Steve. "Barrage of Bullets Drowned Our Cries of Comrades." *Washington Post*, 1 May 2005, sec. A.

Collins, Patrica Hill. *Black Feminist Thought*. New York: Routledge, 2000.

Conklin, Mike. "Magic Lesson: Disease Doesn't Play Favorites." *Chicago Tribune*, 8 November 1991, sec. S.

Cowley, Jason. "Sport." *New Statesman*, 24 May 2004. (Proquest).

Daley, Arthur. "A Strange Afternoon." *New York Times*, 25 November 1963, sec. L.

———. "A Day of Mourning." *New York Times*, 26 November 1963, sec. L.

———. "Philadelphia Thriller." *New York Times*, 8 December 1963, sec. L.

———. "Sunk Without a Trace." *New York Times*, January 1964, sec. L.

———. "The Long Season Begins." *New York Times*, 6 April 1968, sec. 5.

———. "Day of Decision." *New York Times*, 24 April 1967.

———. "The Trail Blazer." *New York Times*, 9 April 1968, sec. 5.

———. "The Incident." *New York Times*, 10 October 1968, sec. S.

Dahlberg, Tim. "Saints a Feel-Good Story for Now, but Future Not Bright for Their Fans." *Daily News*, 21 September 2005. (Lexis)

Danzig, Alison. "Service Game Fitting Climax to Surprising Year." *New York Times*, 9 December 1963, 50.

Dear, Michael and Flusty, Jonathan, eds. *The Spaces of Postmoderity*, Boston: Blackwell Publishers, 2002.

Deford, Frank, *Picture Perfect: The Stories Behind the Greatest Photos in Sports*, 2002.

Denton, Karen "The Olympics, Homelessness, and Civil Rights," *The ACLU Reporter*, Fall 1999.

Dodd, Mike. "The World of Sports Is on Hold." *USA Today*, 12 September 2001, sec. C.

Dowbiggin, Bruce. *The Globe*, 23 July 2011, S. 4.

Downey, Mike. "Bittersweet End." *Los Angeles Times*, 5 August 1996, special section.

———. "It Was Clear Case of Rush to Judgment." *Los Angeles Times*, 28 October 1996, sec. C.

———. "Putting a New Georgia on Their Minds." *Los Angeles Times*, 28 July 1996, special section S.

Dubow, Josh. "Booing New York Means Baseball's Back to Normal," 15 March 2002. (Lexis)

Duffy, Brian. "Terror at the Olympics." *U.S. News & World Report*, 121, no. 5 (August 1996).

Dwarkin, Shari Lee and Faye Linda Wachs. "Disciplining the Body." 258–270 in *Reading Sport: Critical Essays on Power and Representation*, Editors Susan Birrell and Mary G. McDonald. Boston: Northeastern University Press, 2000.

Dyreson, Mark. *Making the American Team*. Chicago: University of Illinois Press, 1998.

Early, Gerald. *Body Language*. Saint Paul, MN: Gray Wolf Press, 1998.

Farber, David. *The Age of Great Dreams*. New York: Farrar, Straus & Giroux, 1994.

Fatsis, Stephan. "Football's Saints Ponder Whether to Relocate." *The Wall Street Journal*, 8 September 2005.

Fienstien, John. "For Sunday's Champions, a Moment of Redemption," *Washington Post*, 17 July 2011.

Folliard, Edward T. "Kennedy Says March Advanced Negro Cause," *Washington Post*, 29 August 1963, sec. A.

Foster, Mary. "Fans Celebrate Superdome Reopening." *Washington Post*, 26 September 2006, sec. E.

Foucault, Michel. *History of Sexuality*. New York: Penguin, 1996.

Fountain, Charles. *Life and Times of Grantland Rice.* New York: Oxford University Press, 1993.

Frankel, Max. *High Noon in the Cold War.* New York: Random House, 2004.

Freud, Sigmund. *Beyond the Pleasure Principle.* Translated by James Strachey, New York: W. W. Norton, 1989.

Fusco, Caroline. "Lesbians and Locker Rooms," 87–116, in *Sport and Postmodern Times,* edited by Genevive Rail. New York, NY: State University of New York Press, 1998.

Gay, Jason. "A Year's Worth of Nerves in a Day," *Wall Street Journal,* 18 July 2011.

Gerstle, Gary. *American Crucible.* Princeton, NJ: Princeton University Press, 2001.

Gramsci, Antonio. "Hegemony, Relations of Force, Historical Bloc." *Prison Writings,* last modified 6 June 2005, http://www.marxists.org/archive/gramsci/editions/reader/index.htm.

Gellner, Ernest. "Nationalism and Modernization," 55–63 in *Nationalism,* edited by John Hutchinson and Anthony D, Smith. New York: Oxford University Press, 1994.

Goldberg, Bernard. *Do You Believe in Miracles,* HBO Films, 2005.

Gotanda, Neil, "A Tale of Two Judges," 66–87 in Wahneema Lubiano, ed. *The House That Race Built,* New York: Random House, 1997.

Gutierrez, Israel. "For One Night, New Orleans Can Be 'Normal.'" *The Miami Herald,* 20 September 2006.

Gray, Herman. *Cultural Moves.* Los Angeles: University of California Press, 2005.

———. *Watching Race.* Minneapolis: University of Minnesota Press, 2001.

Grunwald, Michael. "FBI Charges Fugitive in Atlanta, Olympic Bombings." *Washington Post,* 15 October 1996, sec. A.

Hall, Stuart. "Cultural Studies and Its Theoretical Legacies," 277-94 in *Cultural Studies,* edited by L. Grossberg et al. London: Routledge, 1992.

Harper, Philip Brian Harper. "Eloquence and Epitaph: Black Nationalism and the Homophobic Impulse in Responses to the Death of Max Robinson," 239–263 in *Fear of a Queer Planet,* edited by Michael Warner, Minneapolis: University of Minnesota, 1993.

Head, Bessie. *A Question of Power,* Oxford: Heinemann, 1987.

Hirsch, Marrianne and Valerie Smith. "Feminism and Cultural Memory: An Introduction," 1-19 in *Signs,* 28: (2002).

Hilton, Bruce. "AIDS Week: Better Late Than Never?" *San Francisco Chronicle,* 4 February 1990, sec. A.

Hooper, Barbara and Edward Soja, "The Spaces That Difference Makes," 183–205 in *Place and the Politics of Identity,* edited by M. Keith and S. Pile. London: Routledge, 1993.

Ignatieff, Michael. "The Broken Contract." *New York Times Magazine,* 25 September 2005, 6–15.

Jenkins, Sally. "This Cup Runneth Over," *Washington Post,* 18 July 2011, D. 1.

Johnson, James Weldon. *The Autobiography of an Ex-Colored Man.* New York: Penguin Books, 1990.

Johnson, Lyndon. "Address to the Nation Upon Proclaiming a Day of Mourning." 5 April 5, 1968, *American Experience,* last modified 29 August 1997, http://www.pbs.org/wgbh/amex/presidents/36_l_johnson/psources/ps_mourning.html

Kaylan, Malik. "Defending Arizona's Education Law," *Forbes,* 5 May 2010.

Kellner, Douglas. *Media Culture.* New York: Routledge, 1995.

Kepner, Tyler. "Patriotism Does Not Erase the Trepidation." *New York Times,* 18 September 2001, sec. C.

———. "Emotional Return Home for the Mets." *New York Times,* 21 September 2001, sec. C.

———. "At Yankee Stadium, Tributes and a Monument to Heroism." *New York Times,* 12 September 2002, sec. D.

Kindred, Dave. "Muhmmad Ali Will Always Be the Greatest." *The Sporting News,* 28 July 1996.

———. "Georgia Will Always Be on Our Mind?" *The Sporting News,* 12 August 1996.

————. What Is It with These Fools?" *The Sporting News*, 5 August 1996.

King, C. R. "Cautionary Notes on Whiteness and Sport Studies," 397–408 in *Sociology of Sport Journal* 22, no. 3, 2005.

King, Martin Luther Jr. "Black Soldiers in Vietnam," last modified 23 August 2007, http://www.socialistworker.org/2003-2/464/464_08_BlackAthletes.shtml

Koh, Yoree. "Soccer Win Brings Joy to Nation," *The Wall Street Journal*, 18 July 2011, A. 7.

Koppett, Leonard. "Pro Football Attendance Unaffected." *New York Times*, 25 November 1963, sec. 4.

————. "Decision Is Made by the Pentagon." *New York Times*, 27 November 1963, sec. L.

Kornheiser, Tony. "The End Is Such a Deflating Experience." *Washington Post*, 5 August 1996, sec. C.

————. "A Hero's Message of Hope." *Washington Post*, 8 November 1991, sec. C.

Lapointe, Joe. "Baseball: Fans Wear Their Emotions." *New York Times*, 12 September 2002, sec. D.

Lauter, Paul. *From Walden Pond to Jurassic Park*. Durham, NC: Duke University Press, 2001.

Layden, Tim. "Marching In." *Sports Illustrated*, 22 January 2007.

Lipsitz, George. *Possessive Investment in Whiteness*. Minneapolis: Temple University Press, 1999.

————. *American Studies in a Moment of Danger*. Minneapolis: University of Minnesota Press, 2001.

Lipsyte, Robert. "Fighter Charges Board with Bias." *New York Times*, 18 February 1966.

————. "I'm Free to Be Who I Want." *New York Times*, 29 May 1967.

————. "Striking Nerves." *New York Times*, 16 December 1967.

————. "One Who Got Away." *New York Times*, 8 April 1968.

————. "Here We Go Again." *New York Times*, 17 October 1968.

————. "Case Closed." *New York Times*, 1 July 1978.

————. "Magic as Hero: It's Not the Most Comfortable Fit," *New York Times*, 15 November 1991, sec. D.

Longman, Jere. "Advancing Slowly on a Daunting Road," *New York Times*, 18 July 2011.

Low, Seth M., "The Anthropology of Cities," 383–409 in *Annual Review of Anthropology* (25): 1996.

McCarthy, Coleman. "Residue from Rockets' Red Glare." *Washington Post*, 20 August 1996, sec. D.

McDonald, Mary G. "Mapping Whiteness," 245–55 in *Sociology of Sport Journal*, no. 3 (2005).

McDonnell, Terry. "Brothers." *Sports Illustrated*, 5 September 2006.

Mann, Jack. "Big D." "Reaction at Aqueduct—Tears, Shock, Disbelief." *New York Herald Tribune*, 24 November 1963, sec. 4.

————. *New York Herald Tribune*, 2 December 1963, sec. 4.

————. "D-Day Plus 11." *New York Herald Tribune*, 25 November 1963, sec. 4.

Markus, Don. "Spirited Ceremony Brings Games to a Close." *Baltimore Sun*, 5 August 1996, sec. C.

Markus, Robert. "Middies Are Favorite by 14 Points." *Chicago Tribune*, 7 December 1963, sec. E.

Marsh, Irving T. "Weekend of Mourning—Most Sports Blacked Out." *New York Herald Tribune*, 23 November 1963, sec. 4.

Milbank, Dana. "At Yankee Stadium, President Makes a Pitch for Normalcy; Bush Calls for Americans to Find 'Balance' of Caution and Defiance." *Washington Post*, 31 October 2001, sec. A.

Minot, George E. "Nats Plant Drives on Gridiron." *New York Times*, 9 April 1968, sec. B.

————. "Senators Open Baseball Season Today." *New York Times*, 10 April 1968, sec. D.

Morrison, Toni. "Home," 3–10, in *The House That Race Built*, edited by Wahneema Lubiano, New York: Random House, 1997.

Morrissey, Rick. "Well-known Soldier a Hero, Plain and Simple." *Chicago Tribune*, 31 May 2004, sec. S.

Morrow, Lance. "An Equal and Opposite Darkness," 72 in *Time*, 5 August 1996, 148: (7).

Murray, Jim. "Warning HIV: No Hiding Now." *Los Angeles Times*, 10 November 1991, sec. C.

Muscatine, Alison. "Magic's Revelation Transcends Sports; Athletes' Tragedies Have Greater Impact." *Washington Post*, 10 November 1991, sec. D.

Nadell, Martha Jane. *Enter the New Negroes.* Cambridge, MA: Harvard University Press, 2004.

Narducci, Marc. "For Saints 'Home' Opener, a Special Spirit Prevails." *Philadelphia Enquirer*, 20 September 2005, sec. sports.

Negri, Antonio and Michael Hardt. *Empire.* Cambridge: Harvard University Press, 2000.

New York Times. "The Draft: Cassius versus the Army." 30 April 1967.

———. "Up From the Country, Patron Saints of the Road." 18 September 2005.

Newberry, Paul. "Amid the Rubble, a City Rallies Behind Its Football Team." *Associated Press*, 24 September 2006. (Lexis)

Newhan, Ross. "Kennedy Recalled as a Man for All Seasons." *Los Angeles Times*, 7 June 1968, sec. F.

Nichols, Bill. "'Getting to Know You . . .': Knowledge, Power, and the Body," 164–70 in *Theorizing Documentary*, edited by Michael Renov, London: Routledge, 2005.

O'Connor, Ian. "Saints, Fans Made to Feel Like Giants in N.Y." *USA Today*, 20 September 2005. (Lexis)

Obama, Barack, Address to the Nation, 11 March 2011, obama-speech.org/transcript.php?*obama*_speech_id=4685, 1 December 2011.

Olson, Lisa. "A Story of Hope, but There's Much More to Do." *New York Daily Herald*, 12 January 2007.

Omi, Michael and Howard Winant. *Racial Formation in the United States.* New York: Routledge, 2002.

Ostler, Scott. "The Question Is How, Not When to Play." *San Francisco Chronicle*, 13 September 2001, sec. E.

Outside the Lines. ESPN, 23 February 2005.

Pope, S. W. *Patriotic Games.* New York: Oxford University Press, 1997.

Pope, S. W., Mark Dyerson, and Steven Geitscher. "Virtual Games: The Media Coverage of the 1996 Olympics," 63–73, in *Journal of Sports History* (27):1, Summer 1997.

Parry-Giles. *The Rhetorical Presidency, Propaganda, and the Cold War, 1945–1955.* Westport, CT: Greenwood, 2001.

Parry-Giles, Shawn and Trevor, "Political Scopophilia, Presidential Campaigning, and The Intimacy Of American Politics," 191–205 in *Communication Studies*, 47(3).

Peirce, Charles P. "Black Sunday: Forty Years Ago This Weekend, as America Grieved for President John F. Kennedy, Stunned NFL Players Were Told to Take the Field." *Sports Illustrated*, 24 November 2003.

Plaschke, Bill. "Looking for Right Spirit? Being List with Ghaffari." *Los Angeles Times*, 5 August 1996, sec. S.

———. The True Meaning of Sacrifice." *Los Angeles Times*, 24 April 2004, sec. D.

Povich, Shirley. "Clay defended as Boxer, not American Patriot." *Los Angeles Times*, 4 February 1967, sec. B.

———. "This Morning." *Washington Post*, 7 April 1968, sec. C.

———. "This Morning." *Washington Post*, 10 April 1968.

———. "This Morning." *Washington Post*, 11 April 1968, sec. C.

———. "This Morning." *Washington Post*, 14 April 1968, sec. C.

———. "This Morning." *Washington Post*, 19 October 1968, sec. C.

———. "This Morning." *Washington Post*, 24 October 1968, sec. K.

Price, S. L. "Stained Games," 22–28 in *Sports Illustrated*, 5 August 1996 (85): 6.

Pucin, Daine. "Terrorism Can't Defeat Heroism." *Los Angeles Times*, 16 September 2001, sec. D.

Reagan, Reagan. "Proclamation 5709: AIDS Awareness Month." 29 September 1987, http://www.reagan.utexas.edu/archives/speeches/1987/092987e.htm

Reed, Ralph. "Divided America? Don't Mind the Gap." *The American Enterprise*, October–November, 2004.

Reilly, Rick. "Sports to the Rescue." *Sports Illustrated*, 6 September 2005.

———. "War Games." *Hate Mail from Cheerleaders*, New York: Sports Illustrated Books, 2007, 313–15.

Reiter, Bill. "Marching Home." *Kansas City Star*, August, 2006.

Rhoden, William. "This Time, a Deeper Appreciation." *New York Times*, 24 October 2001, sec. S.

———. "Amid Ruins of Home, Sorrow and Solidarity." *New York Times*, 18 September 2005.

———. "A Saints' Superdome Title Isn't a Giant Leap of Faith." *New York Times*, 25 December 2006.

Rich, Frank. "It's All Newsweek's Fault." *New York Times*, 22 May 2005.

Roschelle, Ann. "Dream or Nightmare? Baseball and the Gender Order," in Robert Elias, ed. *Baseball and the American Dream*, Armonk, NY: M. E. Sharpe, 2001, 232–52.

Rose, Gillian. *Feminism and Geography: The Limits of Geographical Knowledge*, Oxford: Blackwell Publishers, 1993.

Rose, Meghan. "'I'm Really Just Proud': Fans Pay Tribute to World Cup Players. Sellout Crowd Shows up at KSU Soccer Stadium," *Atlanta Journal-Constitution*, 24 July 2011.

Rosenthal, Ken. "Glitz, Hype Overshadow Real Tragedy." *Baltimore Sun*, 31 July 1996, sec. D.

Sacks, Peter M. *The English Elegy: Studies in the Genre from Spenser to Yeats*. Baltimore: Johns Hopkins University Press, 1996.

Said, Edward. *Orientalism*, New York: Vintage, 1979.

Saraceno, Jon. "NFL Should Have Delayed Its Openers." *USA Today*, 9 September 2005, sec. C.

Schmid, A. P. and Longman, A. J. *Political Terrorism, A New Guide to Actors, Authors, Concepts, Data bases, Theories, and Literature*. Amsterdam: Transaction Books, 1988.

Shapiro, Walter. "Baseball Strike Talk Cheapens Post-Sept, 11 Patriotism." *USA Today*, 28 August 2002, sec. A.

Shohat, Ella and Robert Stam, *Unthinking Eurocentrism*. New York: Routledge, 1994.

Silver, Michael. "The Saints Come Through." *Sports Illustrated*, 19 September 2005, 94–98.

———. "Athletes and Katrina." *Sports Illustrated*, 12 December 2005, p. 106–8.

Smith, Barbara. "Across the Kitchen Dialogue." *This Bridge Called My Back*, edited by Cherrie Moraga and Gloria Anzaldua. New York: Kitchen Table: Women of Color Press, 1983.

Smith, Gary. "Dark Days." *Sports Illustrated*, 9 September 2006.

———. "Remember His Name." *Sports Illustrated*, 5 September 2006, 88–101.

Smith, Gavin. "The Ending Is Up to You," 21–26 in *Film Comment*, July–August 2004.

Smith, Henry Nash. *Virgin Land: The American West as Symbol and Myth*. Cambridge: Harvard University Press, 1950.

Smith, Red. "One Drunk, Unarmed." *New York Herald Tribune*, 23 November 1963, sec. 4.

———. "Carnival." *New York Herald*, 25 November 1963, sec. 4.

———. "De Gustibus." *New York Herald Tribune*, 28 November 1963, sec. 4.

———. "Five for Navy." *New York Herald Tribune*, 8 December 1963, sec. 4.

———. "Olympic Emotions Reach All Levels." *Washington Post*, 18 October 1968, sec. D.

Soja, Edward. *Postmodern Geographies. The Reassertion of Space in Critical Social Theory,* London: Verso Press, 1989.

Spaid, Elizabeth Levitan. "Churches Still Stuggling to Cross Racial Divide." *Christian Science Monitor,* 10 April 1993, p. 6.

———. "Atlanta's Freaknik a Symbol of Atlanta's Racial Divide, or Just a Party?" *Christian Science Monitor,* 18 April 1997, p. 4

———. "Blast Quiets but Can't Quiet Olympic Spirit." *Christian Science Monitor,* 29 July 1996, sec. D.

———. "Georgia Contests Test What Pulls Votes: Race or Party?" *Christian Science Monitor,* 1 October 1996, p. 1.

Sports Illustrated 50. New York: Sports Illustrated, 2004.

Springer, Steve. "The Parade Goes By." *Los Angeles Times,* 22 January 2007. (Lexis)

Steele, Bruce C. "Tackling Football's Closet, *Advocate,* 26 November 2003.

Steinhauer, Jennifer. "In Uncharted Territory, Guiliani Campaigns against Fear." *New York Times,* 18 October 2001, sec. B.

Stuckey, Mary. *Defining Americans.* Lawrence: KS: University Press of Kansas, 2004.

Sturken, Marita. "Masculinity, Courage, and Sacrifice." *Signs,* Autumn 2002, 444–45.

———. *Tangled Memories.* Los Angeles: University of California Press, 1997.

Tatum, Beverly. *Why Are All the Black Kids Sitting Together in the Cafeteria?,* New York: Basic Books, 2003.

Tierney, Mike. "Another Day off as Nation Mourns." *Atlanta Journal Constitution,* 13 September 2001, sec. F.

Tompkins, Jane. *Sensational Designs.* New York: Oxford University Press, 1985.

Toomer, Jean, *Cane.* Penguin Books: New York, 1993.

Varley, Charley, "Crime Returns to the Big Easy." *Time,* 21 March 2007.

Vecsey, George. "Sydney 2000: A Symbol More Than a Gesture." *New York Times,* 16 September 2000.

———. "Can American Sports Ever Get Back to Normal?" *New York Times,* 16 September 2001, sec. 1.

Verdi, Tom. "A Collective Smile Turns to Sorrow." *Chicago Tribune,* 9 November 1992, sec. S.

Voight, David. *America through Baseball.* Chicago: Burnham Publishing, 1976.

The Wall Street Journal. Japan Outlasts U.S. to Win World Cup," 17 July 2011.

Washington Post Local Segmentation Study, 2004, washingtonpost.com

Weiss, David. "After the Storm." *Daily News,* 13 August 2006.

Werden, Lincoln A. "Cahill's Plans for Army Eleven Include Its First Negro Regular." *New York Times,* 4 June 1966.

West, Cornell. *Race Matters.* New York: Vintage, 1994.

Wexler, Laura. "Techniques of the Imaginary Nation: Engendering Family Photography," 63–78 in *Looking for America,* edited by Cameron Ardis. Boston: Blackwell Publishing, 2005.

Whannel, Garry. *Media Sport Stars.* New York: Routledge, 2002.

Wharton, David. "War Isn't Their Kind of Game." *Los Angeles Times,* 24 April 2004, sec. A.

Whitlock, Jason. "The Games Just Wash over the Hopelessness of Katrina's Victims." *Kansas City Star,* 3 September 2005.

———. "We Can't Be Afraid to Watch and Enjoy Sports." *Kansas City Star,* 8 October 2001.

Wiedmer, Mark, "Saints Heavenly Win Bigger than Football," *Chatanooga Times Press,* 8 February 2010, p. C.1.

Wilbon, Michael. "Available at Your Peril," *Washington Post,* 10 November 1991, sec. D

———."It's Not a Rivalry if the Other Team Never Wins." *Washington Post,* 19 September 2001, sec. D.

———. "Hope Wears as Saint's Uniform." *Washington Post,* 26 September 2006, sec. E.

Wilstein, Steve. "Patriotism and Protest at Yankee Stadium." Associated Press, 22 July 2004. (Lexis)

Wilheim, Gene. "'Paradigm Dramas in American Studies: A Cultural and Institutional History of the Movement," *Locating American Studies, The Evolution of a Discipline*, edited by Lucy Maddox. Baltimore: Johns Hopkins University Press, 1999.

Wong, Edward. "Runs, Hits, and Healing at Stadium." *New York Times*, 26 September 2001, sec. 1.

Wood, Skip. "Saints Win for Empty New Orleans." *USA Today*, 12 September 2005.

Woods, Clyde. *Development Arrested*. Haymarket Books, 2000.

Wright, Richard. "Big Black Good Man," 187–89 in *Portable Literature*, edited by Kirszner, Mandell, Fort Worth, TX: Harcourt, 2000.

Youngmisuk, Ohm. "Rising after the Storm." *Daily News*, 24 September 2006.

Ziff, Sid. "And They Came Out." *Los Angeles Times*, 24 November 1963, sec. D

———. "Big Sports Stories," *Los Angeles Times*, 29 May 1967, sec. C.

———. "Floyd Is New Man." *Los Angeles Times*, 4 June 1967, sec. H.

Zimmerman, Patricia. *States of Emergency: Documentaries, Wars, Democracies*. Minneapolis: University of Minnesota Press, 2004.

Zirin, Dave. "Pat Tillman, Our Hero." *U.S. News & World Report*, 10 May 2004.

Zuckerman, Mortimer. "A Hero's Parting Message." *U.S. News & World Report*, 10 May 2004: 72.

Zukin, Sharon. *Landscapes of Power: From Detroit to Disney World*, Berkeley: University of California Press, 1991.

Index

About the Author

Michael Gavin lives in Baltimore, Maryland, with his wife and two daughters. He is the senior academic administrator at Prince George's Community College, where he also is a professor of English. Although the Cubs have not won a World Series, he finds hope in each baseball season and knows that Chicago's north side deserves happiness in the future. He wants to dedicate this book to his wife, Alycia, whose love is everything to him; to his daughter, Isabelle, who laid on his shoulder as he wrote the first draft of this book; his daughter Maya, whose laughter brings the sun; his father, whose values are this book; his mother, whose passion for justice inspires him; his sister, who is a rock; to his E-town crew, who taught him all there is to know about friendship; his Dickinson boys, who showed him everything there is about loyalty; and his peeps in DC/Baltimore, you know who you are, you are my lattice.